5th Workshop on Balto-Slavic Natural Language Processing (BSNLP 2015)

International Conference on Recent Advances in Natural Language Processing 2015

Hissar, Bulgaria
10 – 11 September 2015

ISBN: 978-1-5108-1785-2

Printed from e-media with permission by:

Curran Associates, Inc.
57 Morehouse Lane
Red Hook, NY 12571

Some format issues inherent in the e-media version may also appear in this print version.

Printed by Curran Associates, Inc. (2016)

For permission requests, please contact the Association for Computational Linguistics at the address below.

Association for Computational Linguistics
209 N. Eighth Street
Stroudsburg, Pennsylvania 18360

Phone: 1-570-476-8006
Fax: 1-570-476-0860

acl@aclweb.org

Additional copies of this publication are available from:

Curran Associates, Inc.
57 Morehouse Lane
Red Hook, NY 12571 USA
Phone: 845-758-0400
Fax: 845-758-2634
Email: curran@proceedings.com
Web: www.proceedings.com

Preface

This volume contains the papers presented at BSNLP 2015: the fifth in a series of Workshops on Balto-Slavic Natural Language Processing. This BSNLP Workshop is the first endorsed by SIGSLAV—the newly established ACL Special Interest Group on Natural Language Processing in Slavic Languages.[1]

The driving motivation behind convening the BSNLP Workshops is twofold. On one hand, the languages from the Balto-Slavic group are important for NLP due to their widespread use and diverse cultural heritage. They are spoken by over 400 million speakers worldwide. Due to the recent political and economic developments in Central and Eastern Europe, the countries where Balto-Slavic languages are spoken were brought into new focus in terms of rapid technological advancement and rapidly expanding consumer markets. In the context of the European Union, the Balto-Slavic group today covers about one third of all speakers of EU's official languages.

On the other hand, research on theoretical and applied NLP in many of the Balto-Slavic languages is still in its early stages, although it is continually progressing. The advent of the Internet over twenty years ago established the dominant role of English in a broad range of on-line activities, which further weakened the position of other languages, including the Balto-Slavic group. Consequently, as compared to English, there is still a lack of resources, processing tools and applications for most of these languages, especially ones with smaller speaker bases.

Despite this "minority" status, the Balto-Slavic languages offer a wealth of fascinating scientific and technical challenges for researchers and practitioners to work on. The linguistic phenomena specific to Balto-Slavic languages—such as rich morphological inflection and relatively free word order—present highly intriguing and non-trivial challenges to building NLP tools, and require richer morphological and syntactic resources. Related to this theme, the invited talk by Tanja Samardžic, titled "A computational cross-linguistic approach to Slavic verb aspect" discusses challenges encountered in the computational treatment of the complex phenomena related to verbal aspect in Slavic languages. The talk presents how fine-grained aspectual classes can be automatically extracted using parallel corpora, and then used in temporal classification of events across languages. In the second invited talk, titled "Challenges in launching an NLP start-up company: Research meets the Real World," Josef Steinberger discusses his experience in transferring research results related to Slavic languages into commercial products.

The main goal of the BSNLP 2015 Workshop is to bring together all related stakeholders, including academic researchers and industry practitioners who are involved in work on NLP for Balto-Slavic languages. The Workshop aims to further stimulate research on NLP for these languages and to foster the creation and dissemination of relevant tools and resources. The Workshop serves as an interactive platform for researchers to exchange ideas and experiences, discuss difficult and shared problems, and to facilitate making new resources more widely-known.

This Workshop continues the proud tradition established by the previous BSNLP Workshops:

1. the First BSNLP Workshop, held in conjunction with ACL 2007 Conference in Prague, Czech Republic;
2. the Second BSNLP Workshop, held in conjunction with IIS 2009: Intelligent Information Systems, in Kraków, Poland;
3. the Third BSNLP Workshop, held in conjunction with TSD 2011, 14th International Conference on Text, Speech and Dialogue in Plzeň, Czech Republic;

[1] `http://sigslav.cs.helsinki.fi/`

4. the Fourth BSNLP Workshop, held in conjunction with ACL 2007 Conference in Sofia, Bulgaria.

This year we received 29 submissions, out of which 16 were accepted for presentation: 13 as regular papers and three as interactive presentations (resulting in an overall acceptance rate of 55%). Compared to previous BSNLP workshops, this year we have a mixed balance of papers on enabling technologies and higher-level tasks, such as information extraction, sentiment analysis and text classification. This shows the ongoing trend towards building user-oriented applications for Balto-Slavic languages, in addition to working on lower-level NLP tools.

The papers directly deal with at least seven Balto-Slavic languages: Bulgarian, Croatian, Czech, Lithuanian, Polish, Russian, and Serbian. Three of the papers discuss approaches to syntactic and semantic analysis. Three papers are about information extraction. Three papers cover sentiment analysis and text classification. Other papers address a broad range of topics, including word-sense disambiguation, corpus analysis, text and author modeling, and linguistic resources.

It is our sincere hope that this work will help to further strengthen the community and stimulate the growth of research in this rich and exciting field.

BSNLP Organizers:
Jakub Piskorski (Polish Academy of Sciences)
Lidia Pivovarova (University of Helsinki)
Jan Šnajder (University of Zagreb)
Hristo Tanev (Joint Research Centre)
Roman Yangarber (University of Helsinki)

Organizers:

Jakub Piskorski, Polish Academy of Sciences, Poland
Lidia Pivovarova, University of Helsinki, Finland
Jan Šnajder, University of Zagreb, Croatia
Hristo Tanev, Joint Research Centre of the European Commission, Ispra, Italy
Roman Yangarber, University of Helsinki, Finland

Program Committee:

Željko Agić, University of Copenhagen, Denmark
Tomaž Erjavec, Jožef Stefan Institute, Slovenia
Darja Fišer, University of Ljubljana, Slovenia
Radovan Garabik, Comenius University in Bratislava, Slovakia
Maxim Gubin, Facebook Inc., Menlo Park CA, USA
Tomas Krilavičius, Vytautas Magnus University, Kaunas, Lithuania
Vladislav Kuboň, Charles University, Prague, Czech Republic
Natalia Loukachevitch, Moscow State University, Russia
Preslav Nakov, Qatar Computing Research Institute, Qatar
Petya Osenova, Bulgarian Academy of Sciences, Bulgaria
Karel Pala, Masaryk University, Brno, Czech Republic
Maciej Piasecki, Wrocław University of Technology, Poland
Jakub Piskorski, Polish Academy of Sciences, Warsaw, Poland
Lidia Pivovarova, University of Helsinki, Finland
Tanja Samardžić, University of Zurich, Switzerland
Agata Savary, University of Tours, France
Kiril Simov, Bulgarian Academy of Sciences, Bulgaria
Inguna Skadina, University of Latvia, Latvia
Jan Šnajder, University of Zagreb, Croatia
Josef Steinberger, University of West Bohemia, Czech Republic
Stan Szpakowicz, University of Ottawa, Canada
Marko Tadić, University of Zagreb, Croatia
Hristo Tanev, Joint Research Centre, Italy
Irina Temnikova, Qatar Computing Research Institute, Qatar
Marcin Woliński, Polish Academy of Sciences, Warsaw, Poland
Roman Yangarber, University of Helsinki, Finland

Invited Speakers:

Tanja Samardžić, University of Zurich, Switzerland
Josef Steinberger, University of West Bohemia, Czech Republic

Table of Contents

Workshop Program

Thursday, September 10, 2015

09:00–09:10 Welcoming Remarks: BSNLP Organizers

09:10–10:00 Invited Talk

A Computational Cross-Linguistic Approach to Slavic Verb Aspect
Tanja Samardžić

10:10–11:00 Session I: Syntax

11:00–11:30 Coffee Break

11:30–12:35 Session II: Information Extraction

Thursday, September 10, 2015 (continued)

12:35–14:00 Lunch

14:00–14:50 Invited Talk

Challenges in Launching an NLP Start-up Company: Research Meets the Real World
Josef Steinberger

15:00–15:30 Interactive Session

15:00–15:10 *Regional Linguistic Data Initiative (ReLDI)*
Tanja Samardžić, Nikola Ljubešić and Maja Miličević

15:10–15:20 *Online Extraction of Russian Multiword Expressions*
Mikhail Kopotev, Llorenç Escoter, Daria Kormacheva, Matthew Pierce, Lidia Pivovarova and Roman Yangarber

15:20–15:30 *E-law Module Supporting Lawyers in the Process of Knowledge Discovery from Legal Documents*
Marek Kozłowski, Maciej Kowalski and Maciej Kazula

15:30–16:00 Coffee Break

16:00–17:00 Discussion on BSNLP/SIGSLAV Activities: Shared NLP Task

Friday, September 11, 2015

09:00–09:45 Session III: Semantics

09:00–09:25 *Experiments on Active Learning for Croatian Word Sense Disambiguation*
Domagoj Alagić and Jan Šnajder

09:25–09:45 *Automatic Classification of WordNet Morphosemantic Relations*
Svetlozara Leseva, Ivelina Stoyanova, Maria Todorova, Tsvetana Dimitrova, Borislav Rizov and Svetla Koeva

09:55–11:00 Session IV: Corpus Analysis and Resources

09:55–10:20 *Applying Multi-Dimensional Analysis to a Russian Webcorpus: Searching for Evidence of Genres*
Anisya Katinskaya and Serge Sharoff

10:20–10:40 *Distinctive Similarity of Clausal Coordinate Ellipsis in Russian Compared to Dutch, Estonian, German, and Hungarian*
Karin Harbusch and Denis Krusko

10:40–11:00 *Universalizing BulTreeBank: a Linguistic Tale about Glocalization*
Petya Osenova and Kiril Simov

11:00–11:30 Coffee Break

Friday, September 11, 2015 (continued)

11:30–12:35 Session V: Sentiment Analysis and Text Classification

12:35–12:40 Closing Remarks

12:40–14:00 Lunch

Universal Dependencies for Croatian (that Work for Serbian, too)

Željko Agić
University of Copenhagen, Denmark
zeljko.agic@hum.ku.dk

Nikola Ljubešić
University of Zagreb, Croatia
nljubesi@ffzg.hr

Abstract

We introduce a new dependency treebank for Croatian within the Universal Dependencies framework. We construct it on top of the SETIMES.HR corpus, augmenting the resource by additional part-of-speech and dependency-syntactic annotation layers adherent to the framework guidelines. In this contribution, we outline the treebank design choices, and we use the resource to benchmark dependency parsing of Croatian and Serbian. We also experiment with cross-lingual transfer parsing into the two languages, and we make all resources freely available.

1 Introduction

In dependency parsing, the top-performing approaches require supervision in the form of manually annotated corpora. Dependency treebanks are costly to develop, and they typically implement different annotation schemes across languages, i.e., they are not homogenous with respect to the underlying syntactic theories (Abeillé, 2003). Today we know this hinders research in cross-lingual parsing (McDonald et al., 2011), and subsequently the enablement of language technology for under-resourced languages.

The Universal Dependencies (UD) (Nivre et al., 2015) project[1] aims at addressing the issue by providing homogenous dependency treebanks. The treebanks feature uniform representations of parts of speech (POS), morphological features, and syntactic annotations across 18 languages in the current release (Agić et al., 2015).[2] The POS tagset is a superset of Petrov et al. (2012), while the dependency trees draw from the universal Stanford dependencies of de Marneffe et al. (2014). The intricacies of UD are well beyond the scope of our contribution. Instead, we spotlight the parsing and cross-lingual processing of two South East European (SEE) under-resourced languages (Uszkoreit and Rehm, 2012).

In their pivotal contribution to cross-lingual parsing, McDonald et al. (2013) reveal the twofold benefits of uniform representations, as they i) enable more exact evaluation of dependency parsers, and ii) facilitate typologically motivated transfer of dependency parsers to under-resourced languages with improved accuracies. In short, their research indicates that enabling POS tagging and dependency parsing for, e.g., Macedonian would largely benefit should a treebank for a similar language—say, Croatian—exist within an uniform representations framework such as UD.

This work opened up a cross-lingual parsing research avenue that addresses issues such as multi-source transfer, in which multiple source treebanks are combined to improve target language parsing (McDonald et al., 2011), or annotation projection, in which the trees are transferred via parallel corpora and parsers trained on the projections (Tiedemann, 2014). Apart from dependency parsing, this line of work also includes the developments in cross-lingual POS tagging, mainly drawing from the work of Das and Petrov (2011), even if seeded much earlier through the seminal work of Yarowsky et al. (2001). Most of this work, however, does not include the under-resourced SEE languages, and thus we stress that topic in particular in our paper.

Contributions. We focus on dependency parsing of two under-resourced South Slavic languages, Croatian and Serbian, and its implications on cross-lingual parsing of related languages. We list the following contributions: i) a novel, UD-conformant dependency treebank for Croatian, ac-

[1] http://universaldependencies.github.io/docs/
[2] http://hdl.handle.net/11234/LRT-1478

Proceedings of the 5th Workshop on Balto-Slavic Natural Language Processing, pages 1–8,
Hissar, Bulgaria, 10–11 September 2015.

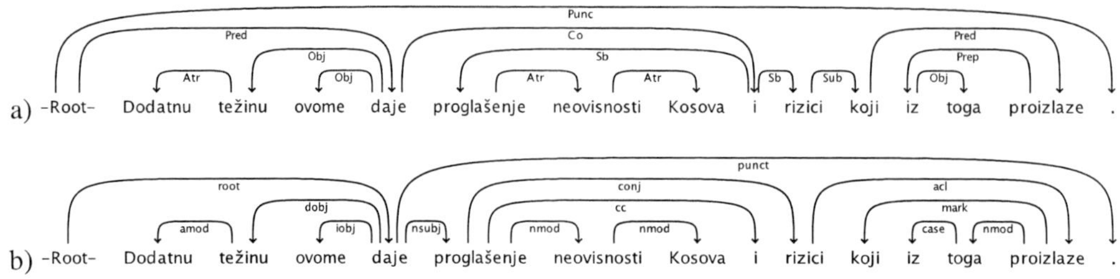

Figure 1: An example sentence from the treebank (training set, #143), with a) SETIMES.HR, and b) UD annotations. Gloss: *Added weight to-this gives the-proclamation of-independence of-Kosovo and the-risks that from it arise.*

companied by cross-domain test sets for Croatian and Serbian, ii) a set of experiments with parsing the two languages within the UD framework, and iii) cross-lingual parsing experiments targeting Croatian and Serbian by source models from two sets of 10 treebanks. We make our datasets available under free-culture licensing.[3]

2 Treebank

UD requires adherence to POS tagset, dependency attachment, and edge labeling guidelines, as well as to the universal morphological feature specifications, the inclusion of which is at this point not mandatory. We provide an UD treebank for Croatian, implementing all the annotation layers.

2.1 Text

Our treebank is built on top of an existing Croatian corpus, the SETIMES.HR dependency treebank (Agić and Ljubešić, 2014). We apply the UD annotation layers on top of its training and testing sets. The sample amounts to 3,557 training sentences of newspaper text, and another 200 development sentences from the same source, which sums up to the 3,757 sentences of the original SETIMES.HR corpus. The training sets are available for Croatian and Serbian, from newswire and Wikipedia, equaling $4 \times 100 = 400$ sentences.

In summary, we take the Croatian text from the SETIMES.HR treebank as a basis for building the Croatian UD treebank, and we include its training, development and test sets in the process. SETIMES.HR also provides Serbian test sets, so we include those as well. As a result, we provide a multi-layered linguistic resource for Croatian and Serbian, offerring two layers of morphological and syntactic annotations on top of the same text. While the usefulness of this particular approach in contrast to opting for an entirely different text sample could be argued, our decision was motivated by i) facilitating empirical comparability across different annotation schemes, and by ii) the line of work by Johansson (2013) with combining diverse treebanks for improved dependency parsing, which we wish to explore in future work focusing on sharing parsers between closely related languages.

2.2 Morphology

SETIMES.HR implements the Multext East version 4 morphosyntactic tagset (MTE4) (Erjavec, 2012). We manually convert it to UD's universal POS tags (UPOS) and universal morphological features, and we make the mapping available with the treebank. Out of the 17 UPOS tags, 14 are used in our treebank, leaving out determiners (DET), interjections (INTJ), and symbols (SYM) as no respective tokens of these types were instantiated in the treebank text. We cast all MTE4 abbreviations into the appropriate UPOS tags—predominantly as nouns, but sometimes also as adverbs such as the Croatian equivalent of "e.g." ("npr.")—by observing the sentence contexts. We also map all the MTE4 morphology into the universal feature set, which accounts for a total of 540 morphosyntactic tags, compared to the 662 in the original dataset, as certain MTE4 features are currently not present in the UD specification. We closely adhere to UD, i.e., we do not introduce any language-specific features at this point.

2.3 Syntax

The annotation for syntactic dependencies was conducted manually by four expert annotators. We decided in favor of manual annotation over implementing an automatic conversion from SE-

[3] `https://github.com/ffnlp/sethr`

Syntactic tag	%	Gloss	Syntactic tag	%	Gloss
acl	1.89	adjectival clause	expl	0.00	expletive
advcl	0.70	adverbial clause modifier	foreign	0.01	foreign words
advmod	2.12	adverbial modifier	goeswith	0.08	goes with
amod	8.34	adjectival modifier	iobj	0.22	indirect object
appos	1.69	appositional modifier	list	0.00	list
aux	4.35	auxiliary	mark	3.59	marker
auxpass	0.71	passive auxiliary	mwe	0.32	multi-word expression
case	9.80	case marking	name	1.56	name
cc	3.09	coordinating conjunction	neg	0.30	negation modifier
ccomp	1.03	clausal complement	nmod	17.05	nominal modifier
compound	3.02	compound	nsubj	5.97	nominal subject
conj	3.80	conjunct	nsubjpass	0.65	passive nominal subject
cop	1.41	copula	nummod	2.05	numeric modifier
csubj	0.12	clausal subject	parataxis	1.47	parataxis
csubjpass	0.03	clausal passive subject	punct	12.86	punctuation
dep	0.01	unspecified dependency	remnant	0.14	remnant in ellipsis
det	0.98	determiner	root	4.51	root
discourse	0.71	discourse element	vocative	0.00	vocative
dislocated	0.01	dislocated elements	xcomp	1.50	open clausal complement
dobj	3.92	direct object			

Table 1: Syntactic tags in Croatian UD, sorted alphabetically, and listed together with their relative frequencies and short glosses. The frequencies are calculated for Croatian only, and for the entire collection (train, dev, test). The syntactic tags are further explained in the UD documentation: `http://universaldependencies.github.io/docs/u/dep/all.html`.

TIMES.HR to provide Croatian UD with a clean, unbiased start, contrasting the manual creation experience of McDonald et al. (2013) to the one of automatic conversions within the HamleDT project of Zeman et al. (2014).

As with morphology, we use only the universal dependency relations, without introducing language-specific dependency relations. We apply 39 out of 40 universal relations, leaving out only a single speech-specific function (reparandum). We list all the relations with their relative frequencies in Table 1. The annotators strictly adhered to the UD attachment rules, which focus on the primacy of content words in governing dependency relations, which is different from all the existing annotations of Croatian syntax (Agić and Merkler, 2013). Once again, as a general discussion on UD is well beyond the scope of our contribution, we refer the reader to the official UD documentation for all matters relating to the formalism itself. Instead, we focus on a brief comparison of Croatian UD and SETIMES.HR regarding their dependency annotations.

The two schemes apparently differ both in the sets of dependency relations, and in the attachment rules. For the most part, the 15 syntactic tags of SETIMES.HR are generalizations of the 39 Croatian UD concepts. As for the attachment rules, we exemplify some of the differences in Figure 1. First and foremost, there are apparent differences in the treatment of coordination and subordination. In SETIMES.HR, coordinated subjects ("proglašenje" and "rizici") are governed by the coordinator ("i"), while in UD, the first encountered subject ("proglašenje") is assigned the subject role, and the remaining two coordination members are attached to it as siblings with distinct labels. Subordinate clauses are governed by subordinating conjunctions in SETIMES.HR, and in UD, the conjunction ("koji") is attached to the clause predicate ("proizlaze"). A similar rule applies to prepositional phrases ("iz toga"). There are also minor differences in the treatment of genitive complements.

We also look into the non-projectivity of the two syntactic annotation layers. We note from the work by Agić et al. (2013b) that approximately 20% of sentences are non-projective in a Prague-

		Croatian				Serbian					
		NEWS		WIKI		NEWS		WIKI		OVERALL	
Treebank	Features	*UAS*	*LAS*	*UAS*	*LAS*	*UAS*	*LAS*	*UAS*	*LAS*	*UAS*	*LAS*
SETIMES.HR	MTE4 POS	82.2	76.3	77.1	67.9	80.8	74.0	79.8	71.1	80.0	72.3
	+ MTE4 FEATS	84.3	79.2	80.7	73.7	83.0	77.8	82.6	74.7	82.7	76.4
Croatian UD	UPOS	84.8	77.9	80.8	72.4	82.4	75.8	82.1	75.2	82.5	75.3
	+ UPOS FEATS	86.9	81.5	84.5	77.3	86.0	81.5	83.7	77.9	85.3	79.6

Table 2: Parsing accuracy on Croatian and Serbian test sets for the lexicalized models trained on the two Croatian treebanks. Overall scores are highlighted.

style treebank of Croatian (HOBS) (Tadić, 2007). We observe that 10.1% of all sentences are non-projective in SETIMES.HR, while the UD syntax further lowers this figure to only 7.6%. This bears relevance in dependency parsing, as long-distance non-projective relations are more difficult to retrieve by dependency parsers. To some extent, it also reflects the scheme-dependent properties of languages, as it is hard to argue about the exact amount of non-projectivity in Croatian beyond simply confirming its existence given these three distinct figures.

3 Experiments

We conduct two sets of experiments. The first one features monolingual parsing of Croatian and the transfer, albeit trivial, of Croatian parsers to Serbian as a target language, while in the second one, we transfer delexicalized parsers from a number of well-resourced languages to Croatian and Serbian as targets in a cross-lingual parsing scenario.

3.1 Setup

Parser. In all our test runs, we use the graph-based parser of Bohnet (2010).[4] It trains and parses very fast, and it records top-level performance across a number of morphologically rich languages (Seddah et al., 2013). Other than that, it natively handles non-projective structures, which is an important feature for languages such as Croatian and Serbian, and treebanks exhibiting non-projectivity in general. We evaluate using standard metrics, i.e., labeled (LAS) and unlabeled (UAS) attachment scores.

Features. Given the specific experiments, we run either lexicalized or delexicalized parsers. We train lexicalized parsers using the following features, which relate to CoNLL-X specifications: word forms (FORM), coarse-grained POS tags (CPOS), morphological features (FEATS), and the dependencies (HEAD, DEPREL). In delexicalized parsing, we drop the lexical features (FORM), and the morphological features (FEATS), to arrive at the single-source delexicalized transfer parsing baseline of McDonald et al. (2013). As the focus of our assessments lies exclusively in dependency parsing, we do not experiment with POS tagging, and we use gold POS tags in all experiments, as well as gold morphological features. For a detailed account on the predicted tag impact in parsing Croatian and Serbian, see (Agić et al., 2013b), and note here that the decrease is easily quantifiable at 2-3 points LAS on average.

Data. In the first batch of experiments, we train the parsers on the 3,557 sentences from SETIMES.HR and Croatian UD, i.e., we omit the development set from all runs. In the second batch, we use the source treebanks from the CoNLL 2006-2007 datasets (Buchholz and Marsi, 2006; Nivre et al., 2007), and the UD version 1.0 release.[5] The test sets always remain the same, albeit they do appear in their lexicalized or delexicalized forms: they are the 4 x 100 Croatian and Serbian newswire (NEWS) and Wikipedia (WIKI) samples.

Next, we provide a more detailed insight into the experiments as we discuss the results of the two batches.

3.2 Croatian as Source

Here, we train parsers on Croatian training data, and evaluate them on Croatian and Serbian test sets. We parse with the SETIMES.HR data and

[4] https://code.google.com/p/mate-tools/

[5] http://hdl.handle.net/11234/1-1464

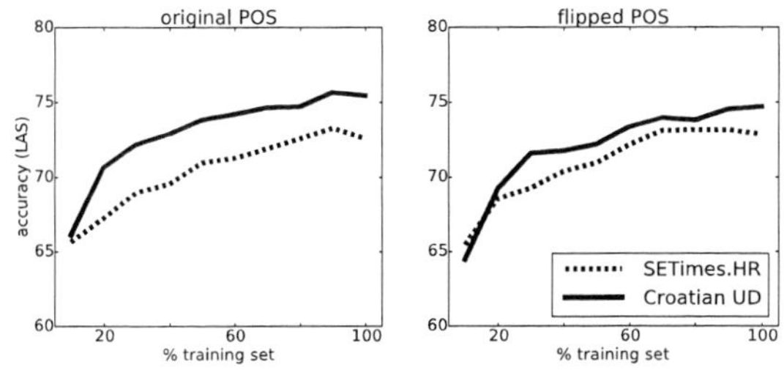

Figure 2: Learning curves (LAS) for the two treebanks with original and exchanged POS annotations. Tested on the merged test sets.

	CoNLL		UD			
	hrv	srp	hrv		srp	
Source	*UAS*	*UAS*	*UAS*	*LAS*	*UAS*	*LAS*
Bulgarian	49.8	49.2	64.1	50.6	66.6	53.8
Czech	36.3	36.1	69.9	54.8	71.9	57.3
Danish	42.1	42.2	56.7	44.2	56.9	45.6
German	40.6	41.5	58.1	41.8	60.0	45.1
Greek	61.7	63.4	52.0	32.8	53.8	35.1
English	46.3	46.5	54.6	41.3	57.1	44.1
Spanish	30.4	33.5	60.8	43.7	64.1	47.5
French	40.3	42.7	56.6	41.4	56.3	42.3
Italian	43.2	45.0	61.3	45.5	62.5	47.6
Swedish	40.2	41.2	55.9	42.7	56.4	44.4
AVERAGE	43.1	44.1	59.0	43.9	60.6	46.3

Table 3: Cross-lingual parsing accuracy for the delexicalized parsers on Croatian (hrv) and Serbian (srp) as targets. We highlight the best CoNLL and UD scores separately.

MTE4 features, as well as with the UD data and UPOS features. As for the features, we compare the POS-only setups to the setups using POS and full morphological features. The results are presented in Table 2. Note that we should not (and do not) directly compare SETIMES.HR and UD accuracies, as they are not directly comparable due to different annotation schemes.

Overall—on the merged Croatian + Serbian test sets—the parser scores at 76.4 points LAS with the best SETIMES.HR model, the one using full MTE4 morphology. Around 4 points are lost when dropping the morphology and using only POS. The system performs the best on in-domain newswire data, and records drops when moving out to Wikipedia text. Accuracies on Croatian and Serbian data are virtually identical on average, with slight preference to Croatian in-domain and Serbian out-of-domain text. Identical patterns hold for the UD experiments as well, but the scores surpass the previous ones by 2-4 points LAS, reaching the average accuracy of 79.6 points LAS for parsing Croatian and Serbian with UD. This is the highest reported score for parsing Croatian and Serbian so far, cf. Agić et al. (2014b). The average gain from adding full UD morphology on top of UPOS amounts to 4.3 points LAS. All UAS scores reported in Table 2 correspond to their respective LAS patterns.

To actually compare UD to SETIMES.HR, we perform another experiment. Since the same text is annotated twofold in our treebank—with two sets of morphological and syntactic annotation layers—we control for the morphological annotation to observe its effects on parsing. Namely, in the Table 2 report, we used each syntactic layer with its native morphological layer: SETIMES.HR with MTE4, and UD with UPOS. Now, we flip the morphology, and report the scores: we parse for SETIMES.HR syntax by using UPOS features, and for UD syntax by using MTE4 features. This way, we get to see whether the difference in LAS scores is accounted for by the morphological features, or facilitated by the annotation schemes themselves. We report this experiment in the form of learning curves in Figure 2. We notice that SETIMES.HR parsing does not benefit at all from using the UPOS features, as the scores remain virtually identical. In contrast, the UD parsing accuracy slightly decreases when using MTE4 instead of UPOS, while still maintaining the edge over SETIMES.HR. From this we conclude that 1) the decrease in the UD scores reflects the better parsing support provided by UPOS in comparison to MTE4, and that 2) the SETIMES.HR scheme is inherently harder to parse, since it plateaus for both POS feature sets, while UD benefits from the change (back) to UPOS. The first observation is unsurprising given that UPOS differentiates, e.g., between main and auxiliary verbs, or common and proper nouns, while MTE4 POS does not. The second observation is much more interesting, especially given the syntactic tagset differences, as there are only 15 tags in SETIMES.HR, and 39 in Croatian UD. The result seems to indicate that UD outperforms SETIMES.HR without sacrificing the expressivity. However, we do note—following Elming et al. (2013)—that our evaluation is intrinsic, and that the two treebanks should be compared on downstream tasks that require parses as input.

3.3 Croatian and Serbian as Targets

In this experiment, we basically replicate the single-source delexicalized transfer setups of (McDonald et al., 2011; McDonald et al., 2013), but with Croatian and Serbian as target languages. We select ten languages with treebanks in both the CoNLL 2006-2007 datasets and the UD version 1.0 release, making for 2 x 10 = 20 different treebanks. We delexicalize the treebanks, keeping CPOS the only observable feature, and train the delexicalized parsers. Finally, we apply the parsers on the Croatian and Serbian test sets, evaluating for attachment scores.

Before discussing the scores, we record a few relevant details about our setup. First, we only parse the SETIMES.HR test sets using the CoNLL models, and the UD test sets using the UD models. This is to illustrate the difference between evaluating cross-lingual parsers in heterogenous and homogenous environments regarding the treebank annotations, but now with an outlook on Croatian and Serbian. Second, building on that setup, we only evaluate the CoNLL parsers for UAS, while the UD parsers are inspected for both UAS and LAS, as the syntactic tagsets do not overlap between the CoNLL datasets or with the SETIMES.HR tagset. In contrast, the core UD tag collection is uniform across the languages. Third, the CoNLL datasets we use are the POS tags of Petrov et al. (2012), so we map the UPOS tags to those in all our CoNLL experiments. The mapping itself is trivial, as UPOS is a simple extension of the (Petrov et al., 2012) tagset. Fourth and final, all ten source languages are European by virtue of overlapping CoNLL and UD, and not by deliberately excluding other datasets. The group does have typological subsets of interest for cross-lingual parsing of Croatian and Serbian.

Our observations for transferring the CoNLL parsers are consistent with those of McDonald et al. (2011): the accuracies do not seem to bear any typological significance, and the scores are relatively low, signalling underestimation. The best cross-lingual parser seems to be the one induced from the Greek treebank, while those of more closely related Slavic languages—Bulgarian and Czech—fall far behind in scores. Actually, in this scenario, Czech is the second worst choice for parsing Croatian and Serbian, in spite of having a very large and consistently annotated treebank. This is apparently due to the treebank heterogeneity, as we know from a large body of related work from McDonald et al. (2011) on.

In contrast to the CoNLL scores, the UD parsers perform much better, and in much more accordance with our typological intuitions. The best two parsers are trained on Bulgarian and Czech data, the latter one scoring a notable 69.9 and 71.9 points UAS on Croatian and Serbian. The LAS scores are expectedly much lower, and the accuracies are consistent with related work (McDonald et al., 2013; Agić et al., 2014b). On average, the UD treebanks score 15 or more points UAS above the CoNLL treebanks. This figure in itself only instantiates the concerns with evaluating parsers on heterogenous resources, and the alleviation of these concerns via resource uniformity. On top of that, we establish a typological ordering of ten languages as sources in parsing Croatian and Serbian.

4 Related Work

Tadić (2007) marks the beginning of Croatian treebanking by discussing the applicability of the Prague Dependency Treebank (PDT) syntactic annotation scheme (Böhmová et al., 2003) for Croatian, supporting the discussion with a small sample of 50 manually annotated Croatian sentences dubbed the Croatian Dependency Treebank (HOBS). By the time parsing experiments of Berović et al. (2012) and Agić (2012) were conducted, HOBS already consisted of more than 3,000 sentences. Its latest instance—complete with Croatian-specific annotations of subordinate clauses, but otherwise fully PDT-compliant—encompasses 4,626 sentences of Croatian newspaper text (Agić et al., 2014a). A version of HOBS is available under a non-commercial license.[6]

SETIMES.HR is a treebank of Croatian built on top of the newspaper text stemming from the SETIMES parallel corpus of SEE languages.[7] It was built to facilitate accurate parsing of Croatian through a simple dependency scheme, and also to encourage further development of Croatian resources via very permissive free-culture licensing. The treebank currently contains approximately 9,000 sentences, and it is freely available for all purposes. Agić and Ljubešić (2014) observe state-of-the-art scores in Croatian lemmatization, tagging, named entity classification, and dependency parsing using SETIMES.HR with stan-

[6] http://meta-share.ffzg.hr/

[7] http://opus.lingfil.uu.se/SETIMES.php

dard tools. Furthermore, this line of research explores the usage of Croatian resources as sources for processing Serbian text (Agić et al., 2013a; Agić et al., 2013b), and also the possibility of sharing models between SEE languages (Agić et al., 2014b). These experiments result in promising findings regarding model transfer between related languages, and they bring forth state-of-the-art scores in processing Croatian, Serbian, and Slovene, offerring freely available resources.

Given the extensive lines of work in Croatian treebanking—with three different reasonably-sized dependency treebanks, cross-domain test sets, and practicable accuracies—it is safe to argue that Croatian is departing the company of severely under-resourced languages when it comes to dependency parsing. In contrast, Serbian treebanking is at this point virtually non-existent. To the best of our knowledge, its only reference point seems to be a study in preparing the morphological annotations for a future—possibly also PDT-compliant—dependency treebank of Serbian (Djordjević, 2014). In absence of such a treebank, Agić et al. (2014b) provide state-of-the-art scores in Serbian parsing using the PDT and SETIMES.HR schemes, while our work presented in this paper offers a very competitive UD parser for Serbian via direct transfer from Croatian.

5 Conclusions

We have presented a new linguistic resource for Croatian: a syntactic dependency treebank within the Universal Dependencies framework. It consists of approximately four thousand sentences, and comes bundled with two-domain test sets for Croatian and Serbian. It is built on top of an existing treebank of Croatian, the SETIMES.HR corpus. We have intrinsically evaluated the resources in a monolingual parsing scenario, as well as through cross-lingual delexicalized transfer parsing into Croatian and Serbian using twenty different source parsers. We recorded state-of-the-art performance in parsing the two languages, at approximately 80 points LAS. All the resources used in the experiment are made publicly available: `https://github.com/ffnlp/sethr`.

Future work. We have described the first instance of Croatian UD. We seek to improve the resource in many ways, and to utilize it in experiments featuring dependency parsing. The treebank is currently not documented, and we aim at providing proper documentation via the UD platform for the next release. Moreover, we currently do not make use of any language-specific features in morphology and syntax. Following the experience of other Slavic languages in the UD project, we might augment the Croatian annotations with language specifics as well. Finally, albeit not exclusively, the research in Croatian parsing and sharing resources between the SEE languages requires extensive downstream evaluation, which we hope to provide in future experiments, together with resources facilitating future downstream evaluations for these languages.

Acknowledgements. We thank the anonymous reviewers for their comments. We also acknowledge the efforts of our annotators in producing the first version of the syntactic annotations, and in facilitating the process of UD adoption for Croatian.

References

Anne Abeillé. 2003. *Treebanks: Building and Using Parsed Corpora*. Springer.

Željko Agić and Nikola Ljubešić. 2014. The SETimes.HR linguistically annotated corpus of Croatian. In *LREC*, pages 1724–1727.

Željko Agić and Danijela Merkler. 2013. Three syntactic formalisms for data-driven dependency parsing of Croatian. *LNCS*, 8082:560–567.

Željko Agić, Nikola Ljubešić, and Danijela Merkler. 2013a. Lemmatization and morphosyntactic tagging of Croatian and Serbian. In *BSNLP*, pages 48–57.

Željko Agić, Danijela Merkler, and Daša Berović. 2013b. Parsing Croatian and Serbian by using Croatian dependency treebanks. In *SPMRL*, pages 22–33.

Željko Agić, Daša Berović, Danijela Merkler, and Marko Tadić. 2014a. Croatian dependency treebank 2.0: New annotation guidelines for improved parsing. In *LREC*, pages 2313–2319.

Željko Agić, Jörg Tiedemann, Kaja Dobrovoljc, Simon Krek, Danijela Merkler, and Sara Može. 2014b. Cross-lingual dependency parsing of related languages with rich morphosyntactic tagsets. In *LT4CloseLang*, pages 13–24.

Željko Agić, Maria Jesus Aranzabe, Aitziber Atutxa, Cristina Bosco, Jinho Choi, Marie-Catherine de Marneffe, Timothy Dozat, Richárd Farkas, Jennifer Foster, Filip Ginter, Iakes Goenaga, Koldo Gojenola, Yoav Goldberg, Jan Hajič, Anders Trærup Johannsen, Jenna Kanerva, Juha Kuokkala, Veronika Laippala, Alessandro Lenci,

Krister Lindén, Nikola Ljubešić, Teresa Lynn, Christopher Manning, Héctor Alonso Martínez, Ryan McDonald, Anna Missilä, Simonetta Montemagni, Joakim Nivre, Hanna Nurmi, Petya Osenova, Slav Petrov, Jussi Piitulainen, Barbara Plank, Prokopis Prokopidis, Sampo Pyysalo, Wolfgang Seeker, Mojgan Seraji, Natalia Silveira, Maria Simi, Kiril Simov, Aaron Smith, Reut Tsarfaty, Veronika Vincze, and Daniel Zeman. 2015. Universal dependencies 1.1.

Željko Agić. 2012. K-best spanning tree dependency parsing with verb valency lexicon reranking. In *COLING*, pages 1–12.

Daša Berović, Željko Agić, and Marko Tadić. 2012. Croatian dependency treebank: Recent developments and initial experiments. In *LREC*, pages 1902–1906.

Alena Böhmová, Jan Hajič, Eva Hajičová, and Barbora Hladká. 2003. The Prague dependency treebank. In *Treebanks: Building and Using Parsed Corpora*, pages 103–127. Springer.

Bernd Bohnet. 2010. Top accuracy and fast dependency parsing is not a contradiction. In *COLING*, pages 89–97.

Sabine Buchholz and Erwin Marsi. 2006. CoNLL-X shared task on multilingual dependency parsing. In *CoNLL*, pages 149–164.

Dipanjan Das and Slav Petrov. 2011. Unsupervised part-of-speech tagging with bilingual graph-based projections. In *ACL*, pages 600–609.

Marie-Catherine de Marneffe, Timothy Dozat, Natalia Silveira, Katri Haverinen, Filip Ginter, Joakim Nivre, and Christopher D. Manning. 2014. Universal stanford dependencies: A cross-linguistic typology. In *LREC*, pages 4585–4592.

Bojana Djordjević. 2014. Initial steps in building Serbian treebank: Morphological annotation. In *Natural Language Processing for Serbian: Resources and Applications*, pages 41–53.

Jakob Elming, Anders Johannsen, Sigrid Klerke, Emanuele Lapponi, Hector Martinez Alonso, and Anders Søgaard. 2013. Downstream effects of tree-to-dependency conversions. In *NAACL*, pages 617–626.

Tomaž Erjavec. 2012. Multext-East: Morphosyntactic resources for central and eastern European languages. *Language Resources and Evaluation*, 46(1):131–142.

Richard Johansson. 2013. Training parsers on incompatible treebanks. In *NAACL*, pages 127–137.

Ryan McDonald, Slav Petrov, and Keith Hall. 2011. Multi-source transfer of delexicalized dependency parsers. In *EMNLP*, pages 62–72.

Ryan McDonald, Joakim Nivre, Yvonne Quirmbach-Brundage, Yoav Goldberg, Dipanjan Das, Kuzman Ganchev, Keith Hall, Slav Petrov, Hao Zhang, Oscar Täckström, Claudia Bedini, Núria Bertomeu Castelló, and Jungmee Lee. 2013. Universal dependency annotation for multilingual parsing. In *ACL*, pages 92–97.

Joakim Nivre, Johan Hall, Sandra Kübler, Ryan McDonald, Jens Nilsson, Sebastian Riedel, and Deniz Yuret. 2007. The CoNLL 2007 shared task on dependency parsing. In *EMNLP-CoNLL*, pages 915–932.

Joakim Nivre, Cristina Bosco, Jinho Choi, Marie-Catherine de Marneffe, Timothy Dozat, Richárd Farkas, Jennifer Foster, Filip Ginter, Yoav Goldberg, Jan Hajič, Jenna Kanerva, Veronika Laippala, Alessandro Lenci, Teresa Lynn, Christopher Manning, Ryan McDonald, Anna Missilä, Simonetta Montemagni, Slav Petrov, Sampo Pyysalo, Natalia Silveira, Maria Simi, Aaron Smith, Reut Tsarfaty, Veronika Vincze, and Daniel Zeman. 2015. Universal dependencies 1.0.

Slav Petrov, Dipanjan Das, and Ryan McDonald. 2012. A universal part-of-speech tagset. In *LREC*, pages 2089–2096.

Djamé Seddah, Reut Tsarfaty, Sandra Kübler, Marie Candito, Jinho D. Choi, Richárd Farkas, Jennifer Foster, Iakes Goenaga, Koldo Gojenola Galletebeitia, Yoav Goldberg, Spence Green, Nizar Habash, Marco Kuhlmann, Wolfgang Maier, Joakim Nivre, Adam Przepiórkowski, Ryan Roth, Wolfgang Seeker, Yannick Versley, Veronika Vincze, Marcin Woliński, Alina Wróblewska, and Eric Villemonte de la Clergerie. 2013. Overview of the SPMRL 2013 shared task: A cross-framework evaluation of parsing morphologically rich languages. In *SPMRL*, pages 146–182.

Marko Tadić. 2007. Building the Croatian dependency treebank: The initial stages. *Suvremena lingvistika*, 63:85–92.

Jörg Tiedemann. 2014. Rediscovering annotation projection for cross-lingual parser induction. In *COLING*, pages 1854–1864.

Hans Uszkoreit and Georg Rehm. 2012. *Language White Paper Series*. Springer.

David Yarowsky, Grace Ngai, and Richard Wicentowski. 2001. Inducing multilingual text analysis tools via robust projection across aligned corpora. In *HLT*, pages 1–8.

Daniel Zeman, Ondřej Dušek, David Mareček, Martin Popel, Loganathan Ramasamy, Jan Štěpánek, Zdeněk Žabokrtský, and Jan Hajič. 2014. HamleDT: Harmonized multi-language dependency treebank. *Language Resources and Evaluation*, 48(4):601–637.

Analytic Morphology – Merging the Paradigmatic and Syntagmatic Perspective in a Treebank

Vladimír Petkevič Alexandr Rosen Hana Skoumalová Přemysl Vítovec
Charles University in Prague, Faculty of Arts
first_name.surname@ff.cuni.cz premysl.vitovec@gmail.com

Abstract

We present an account of analytic verb forms in a treebank of Czech texts. According to the Czech linguistic tradition, description of periphrastic constructions is a task for morphology. On the other hand, their components cannot be analyzed separately from syntax. We show how the paradigmatic and syntagmatic views can be represented within a single framework.

1 Introduction

Analytic verb forms (henceforth AVFs) consist of one or more auxiliaries and a content verb. The auxiliaries can be seen either as marking the content verb with morphological categories or as being part of a multi-word expression, to which the categories are assigned. This is the perspective taken by all standard grammar books of Czech, which treat AVFs as a morphological rather than a syntactic phenomenon. AVFs are listed in conjugation paradigms quite like synthetic forms for a good reason: from a meaning-based view, whether a certain category in a certain language happens to be expressed by a single word or a string of words is an epiphenomenon.

From a different perspective, each of the components has its role in satisfying a syntactic grammaticality constraint and in making a contribution to the lexical, grammatical or semantic meaning of the whole. This approach is common in both corpus and generative linguistics (including theories such as LFG or HPSG),[1] where each form is treated as a syntactic word and AVFs belong to the domain of syntax. As a result, morphological categories are not assigned to units spanning word boundaries. This is for several reasons: (i) an AVF does not emerge as a single orthographical word (often even phonological word); (ii) AVFs may be expressed by a potentially discontinuous string of a content verb and multiple auxiliaries, sometimes in an order determined by information structure rather than by rules of morphology or syntax proper; (iii) some auxiliary forms share properties with some content words – like weak pronouns, the past tense auxiliary is a 2nd position clitic.

Our claim is that the two views are compatible, complementary and amenable to formalization within a single framework, combining the traditional paradigmatic view with a syntagmatic view. This reconciliatory effort is part of a more general goal: a choice of different interpretations of annotated corpus data, depending on the preferences of a user or an application.

AVFs are assigned a syntactic structure: the (finite) auxiliary is treated as the surface head, governing the rest of the form – the deep head.[2]

In Czech, AVFs are used to express the verbal categories of mood, tense and voice in periphrastic passive (all moods and tenses), in periphrastic future, in 1st and 2nd person past tense, in pluperfect and in present and past conditional. In all these forms the auxiliary is *být* 'to be'. Here we focus on past tense and conditional forms, including pluperfect and past conditional, but the solution works for all the above AVFs, and covers also negation of some components of the AVFs by the prefix *ne-* and can be extended to some other kinds of function words, such as prepositions and conjunctions. In (1)–(4) below we show some properties of the past and conditional forms. The finite auxiliary is marked for person, number and mood, while the *l*-participle[3] is marked for gender and number. Past tense (1) consists of the auxiliary in the present tense and the *l*-participle of

[1] See, e.g., Webelhuth (1995), Dalrymple (1999), Pollard and Sag (1994).

[2] We use the term *government* in the sense of "subcategorization" or "imposition of valency requirements."

[3] We avoid the frequently used term *past participle* because the same form is also used in *present* conditional.

Proceedings of the 5th Workshop on Balto-Slavic Natural Language Processing, pages 9–16,
Hissar, Bulgaria, 10–11 September 2015.

the content verb. Present conditional (2) consists of the conditional auxiliary and the content verb's *l*-participle. Past conditional (3) includes an additional *l*-participle of the auxiliary. In (4) we show that other words can be inserted, the auxiliary *l*-participle can be repeated, and any *l*-participle can be negated.

(1) *Já jsem přišel*
I be.PRS.1SG come.PTCP.M.SG
'I have come.'

(2) *Já bych přišel*
I be.COND.1SG come.PTCP.M.SG
'I would come.'

(3) *Já bych byl přišel*
I be.COND.1SG be.PTCP.M.SG come.PTCP.M.SG
'I would have come.'

(4) ***Kdybys*** *tenkrát* ***nebyl***
If-be.COND.2SG back then be.PTCP.M.SG.NEG
býval *tak duchapřítomně*
be.PTCP.M.SG.ITER so readily
***zasáhl**...*
intervene.PTCP.M.SG
'If you haven't intervened so readily back then...'

We exemplify the solution using a treebank of Czech. The framework is based on the HPSG.[4] The annotation, originally produced by a stochastic dependency parser, is checked by a formal grammar, using a valency lexicon and implemented in Trale.[5] Trees complying with grammatical and lexical constraints are augmented with information derived from the lexicon and any annotation provided by a stochastic parser.

2 Previous Work

Grammars of Czech take a paradigmatic perspective, treating AVFs as an exclusively morphological phenomenon (Karlík et al., 1995; Cvrček et al., 2010; Komárek et al., 1986), glossed over without describing their syntagmatic and word-order properties. In Komárek et al. (1986), components of AVFs are assigned a particular grammatical meaning (person, number, tense, mood, voice) but their syntactic status is not specified.

The syntagmatic approach has been introduced to Czech by Veselovská (2003) and Veselovská and Karlík (2004), who analyze past tense and periphrastic passive within the Minimalist Program. A non-transformational account was pursued by Karel Oliva in an HPSG-inspired prototype grammar checker of Czech (Avgustinova et al., 1995). HPSG and LFG have been used to account for similar phenomena in closely related Polish, where the border between morphology and syntax is even less apparent than in Czech: all forms of the past tense and conditional auxiliaries are floating suffixes, attached either directly to the *l*-participle, or to some other preceding word. In the following, we briefly review several proposals for Polish, with an extension to Czech.

Based on the analysis of similar phenomena in West European languages, Borsley (1999) proposes two structures for modelling Polish AVFs: (i) classic VP complementation where the auxiliary is a subject-raising verb selecting a phrasal complement headed by an *l*-participle (Fig. 1), and (ii) flat structures where the auxiliary subcategorizes for an *l*-participle and its complements (Fig. 2).[6] The former is used for future tense while the latter for present conditional and past tense. This distinction is motivated by the ability or inability of the auxiliary to be preceded by the associated *l*-participle and its complements: while the future auxiliary allows for VP-preposing, the other auxiliaries are prohibitive in this respect.

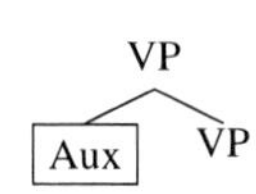

Figure 1: VP complementation.

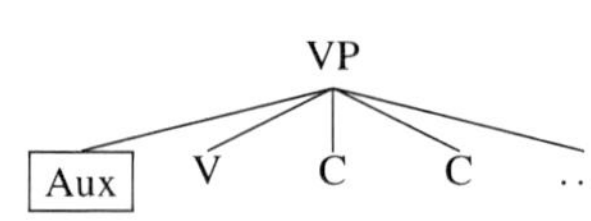

Figure 2: Flat structure.

Kupść (2000) follows Borsley (1999) but rejects the flat structure for past tense and present conditional as it makes incorrect predictions with respect to clitic climbing. Instead, she assumes VP complementation for all AVFs.

Kupść and Tseng (2005) argue against the unified treatment of AVFs. Only the future tense auxiliary behaves like a full syntactic word. In contrast, the forms of conditional auxiliary, albeit syn-

[4] See, e.g., Pollard and Sag (1994).

[5] See http://www.sfs.uni-tuebingen.de/hpsg/archive/projects/trale/. For more details see Jelínek et al. (2014).

[6] Heads are denoted by boxed nodes in the figures.

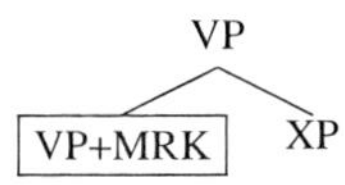

Figure 3: Local agreement marker.

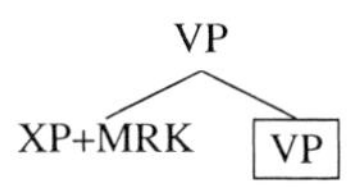

Figure 4: Nonlocal agreement marker.

tactic words, are clitics and thus subject to specific word order constraints (dependencies on various clitic hosts). Past tense is viewed as a simple tense and the past tense agreement markings are treated as inflectional elements, even if they are not attached to the *l*-participle. This analysis builds on (i) an observation that agreement markings are much more closely bound to the preceding word than conditional clitics, and (ii) the fact that there are no agreement markings used in the third person. As a result, the *l*-participle becomes the head of the whole structure. In order to ensure that the agreement marking appears somewhere in the structure the head acts as its trigger, carried by an agreement marker, either the head itself (Fig. 3), or some other preceding element (Fig. 4).

In light of diachronic and comparative considerations, Tseng and Kupść (2006) and Tseng (2009) extend the analysis of Kupść and Tseng (2005) to other Slavic languages, including Czech. The Czech past auxiliary forms are at the same time syntactic words and clitics with a restricted distribution (2nd position, cannot be negated). Moreover, the 2nd person singular clitic *-s* is similar to the Polish floating suffixes, suggesting that the head is the *l*-participle. As a result, the analysis of the Polish past tense can be applied to Czech with only a slight modification: the agreement markings are carried (mostly) by syntactic rather than morphological elements. No changes are proposed for the analysis of the Czech conditional either, where the only complication is the separable ending *-s* in the 2nd person singular (*bys*). However, the extremely restricted distribution of this phenomenon (only in combination with the *si* and *se* reflexives, resulting in the *sis* and *ses* forms) does not motivate treating Czech conditional structures like Polish past tense structures. The authors admit that the analysis based on the standard VP complementation is equally possible.

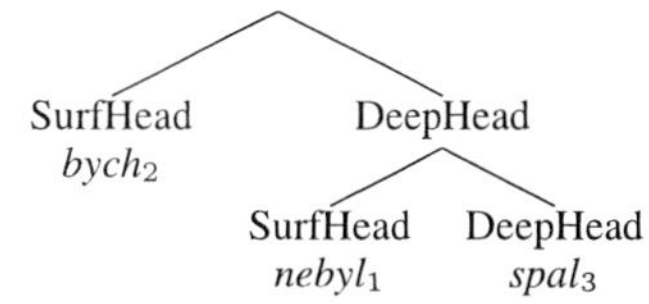

Figure 5: Structure of *nebyl bych spal* 'I wouldn't have slept'.

3 Our Approach

3.1 Two Types of Heads: Surface and Deep

In addition to strictly linguistic criteria for an optimal analysis of AVFs, our choice of the core representation format was influenced by the treebank design, which should allow for the derivation of syntactic structure and categorial labels of various shapes and flavours to be used in queries, responses and exported data. Adopting a uniform analysis for all AVFs simplifies the task. Each AVF is represented as a syntactic phrase with two constituents: a surface head daughter representing the auxiliary, and a deep head daughter representing the auxiliary's VP complement, which includes the content verb.[7] Multiple auxiliaries within a single AVF are surface heads within recursively embedded deep heads (see Fig. 5).[8]

3.2 Modifications of the HPSG Signature

HPSG represents linguistic data as typed feature structures. Words and phrases are subtypes of *sign*, a structure representing their form, meaning and combinatorial properties. Fig. 6 shows a simplified representation of an English sentence *dogs bark*. Types are in italics, attributes in upright capitals, boxed numbers indicate identity of values.

Each word consists of two parts: PHONOLOGY for the analyzed string and SS (SYNSEM) for its paradigmatic analysis. Phrases have two additional attributes: SD (SUBJECT-DAUGHTER) and HD (HEAD-DAUGHTER). The value of SS has L (LOCAL) as its single attribute; its NON-LOCAL counterpart, used for discontinuous constituents, is not relevant for our example. The CAT (CATEGORY) attribute specifies (i) morphosyntactic properties of the expression as its HEAD features and (ii) its VALENCY. The CONT (CONTENT) attribute is responsible for semantic interpretation.

[7] Cf. Przepiórkowski (2007) for an equivalent distinction between syntactic and semantic heads.

[8] The node labels in Fig. 5 are actually feature structure attributes modelling phrasal daughters, abbreviated as SH and DH in Fig. 7.

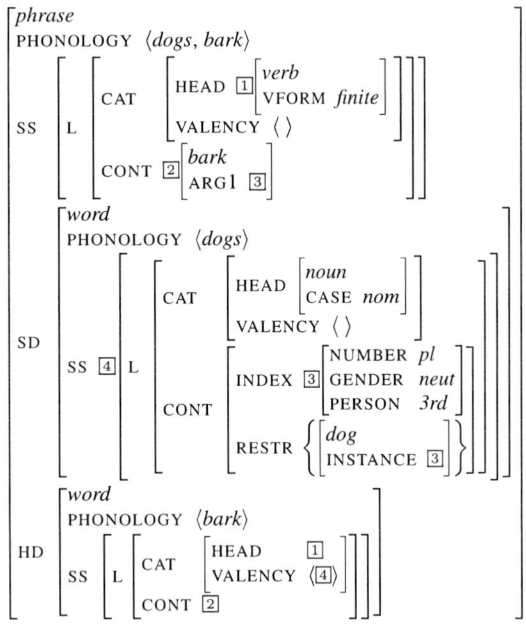

Figure 6: An HPSG representation of a sentence.

Some values are shared due to Head Feature Principle – HFP, projecting features of the head daughter to its phrasal mother, Valency Principle – ValP, a general valency satisfaction mechanism, and Semantics Principle. Morphosyntactic categories of the noun relevant for pronominal reference are the properties of CONTENT's INDEX, while those of the verb relevant for agreement are specified indirectly, as properties of its subject. For languages with rich morphology, NP-internal agreement and null subjects, such as Czech, other arrangements of morphosyntactic and valency features have been proposed.

In addition to the introduction of surface and deep heads, the standard HPSG signature has been modified in two main aspects: (i) at least in the current version, attributes such as LOCAL and HEAD are missing to simplify annotation of extensive data – discontinuities are treated as word order variations and head features are the value of CATEGORY; and (ii) the signature is extended by introducing a cross-clasification of morphological and morphosyntactic categories along three dimensions: morphological (inflectional), syntactic and semantic (lexical).[9] This is useful especially for word classes where classification criteria in the three dimensions do not coincide, such as numerals and pronouns. Their standard definitions are based on semantic criteria, but otherwise cardinal numerals and personal pronouns behave like nouns, whereas ordinal numerals and possessive pronouns behave like adjectives. The cross-classification can also be used to model some regular derivational relations, e.g., deverbal nouns and adjectives (inflectional classes) are derived from verbs (lexical class).

[9]See Rosen (2014) for more details.

3.3 Representing Analytic Categories

To accommodate AVFs, the 3D classification has been extended by an *analytic* dimension. The AC attribute specifies categories appropriate to the AVF as a whole. A verbal AC includes three basic properties: TENSE, MOOD and VOICE. Their values are encoded in the lexical specifications of function words, including the deep head's contribution, which is mediated through the valency frame of the auxiliary, including the content verb's ALEMMA. The rest is the task of ValP and HFP. More specifically, the surface head and its mother share their head features, including the analytic categories, and their deep valency frames – the deep structure is thus available in the phrasal category. Since AC is a head feature, tense, mood and voice are projected from the auxiliary as the surface head of the AVF.

3.4 An Example

The mechanism is illustrated in Figs. 5 and 7, using the past conditional form of the verb *spát* 'to sleep' (5).[10]

(5) *nebyl* *bych* *spal*
be.PTCP.M.SG.NEG be.COND.1SG sleep.PTCP.M.SG
'I wouldn't have slept'

Past conditional consists of the finite conditional auxiliary (*bych*), the *l*-participle form of the 'to be' auxiliary (*nebyl*) and the *l*-participle of the content verb (*spal*).[11]

[10]Fig. 5 ignores word order, which is specified within the PHON list of the phrase.

[11]Past conditional may include additional *l*-participle auxiliaries with the meaning unchanged: an iterative and a plain form (6). Passive past conditional, where two *l*-participle auxiliaries are obligatory (7), shows that the iterative is used to avoid two identical *l*-participles.

(6) *nebyl* *bych* *býval*
be.PTCP.M.SG.NEG be.COND.1SG be.PTCP.M.SG.ITER
(*byl*) *spal*
(be.PTCP.M.SG) sleep.PTCP.M.SG
'I wouldn't have slept'

The auxiliary *bych* is the surface head of the entire structure (see Fig. 5). Its sister phrase, i.e., *nebyl spal*, is the deep head, consisting of *nebyl* and *spal* as the surface and the deep head daughter. The auxiliary *bych* takes a single *l*-participle, unspecified as a content verb or auxiliary (see Fig. 8 below). This distinction, related to the interpretation of tense and/or voice of the AVF, is handled by grammar – see (8)–(12) below. In our example, the conditional auxiliary takes an auxiliary form *nebyl*, which in turn can take another *l*-participle as part of (i) indicative pluperfect (as in *byl spal*, 'he had slept'), or (ii) past conditional, as in our example. It is the presence or absence of the conditional auxiliary that identifies the structure as conditional or indicative. The substructure *nebyl spal* determines its tense as past, the resulting phrase is thus identified as past conditional.

The binary tree shown in Fig. 5 is represented as a feature structure of the *sdheaded* type (i.e., a surface/deep-headed phrase) in Fig. 7. The structure is similar to that in Fig. 6, except for the additions and some abbreviations: PH stands for PHONOLOGY, SH for the surface head daughter, DH for the deep head daughter, C for CATEGORY and COMPS for non-subject valency.[12]

The C attribute consists of three parts, representing three aspects of the category: analytic in AC, inflectional in IC and lexical in LC.[13] The AC attribute includes the lemma of the content verb (ALEMMA, shared as [2] with the lexical deep head and all its deep head projections), its mood, polarity (*minus* due to the negated auxiliary *nebyl*), tense and voice (*actv* for active). As in ALEMMA, [3] shows that the lexical deep head shares AVOICE with its projections. AMOOD and ATENSE are unspecified, because they can be determined only when the AVF is evaluated as a whole. E.g., the embedded DH phrase *nebyl spal* can be either part of indicative pluperfect or past conditional and the content verb participle *spal* can be part of past or pluperfect indicative, pluperfect indicative, present conditional or past conditional.

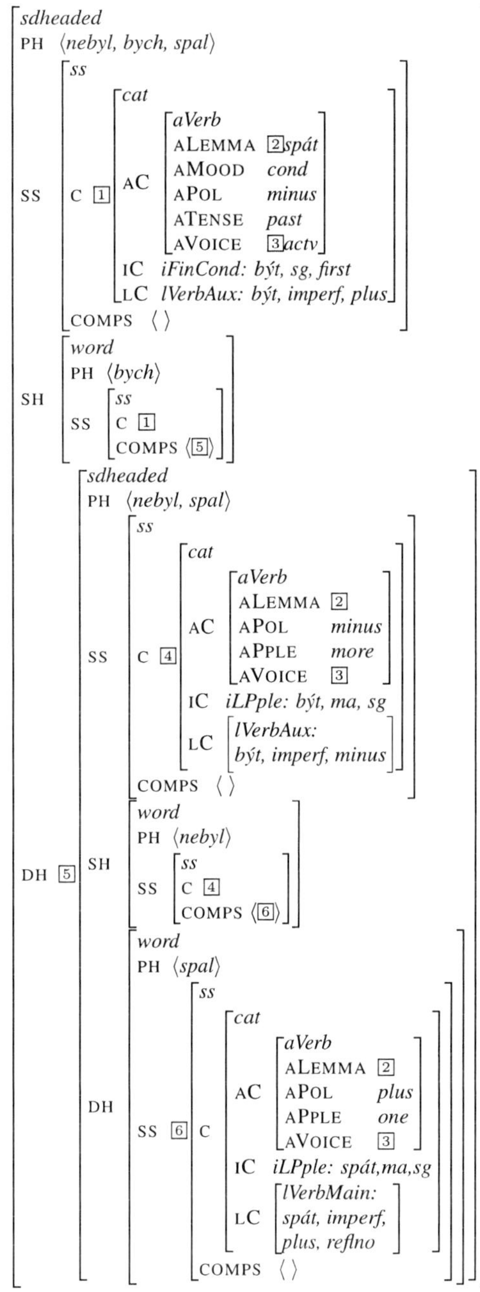

Figure 7: Analysis of *nebyl bych spal*.

Values of the other two attributes IC and LC are abbreviated: the categorial type is followed by a list of attribute values. More importantly, they refer only to the surface head of the phrase. They are obtained from the input parse. The grammar checks that some of them (person, number, also gender) agree with corresponding values in the

(7) *byl* *bych* *býval* /
be.PTCP.M.SG be.COND.1SG be.PTCP.M.SG.ITER /
?byl *dopaden*
be.PTCP.M.SG catch.PASS.M.SG
'I would have been caught'

[12] Subject valency, specified by a separate attribute, SUBJ, is not shown in Fig. 7.

[13] sC for the syntactic aspect is omitted for brevity.

rest of the predicate and/or in the subject.

Inflectional properties of the surface head as the finite conditional auxiliary (*iFinCond*) are *first* person *s*ingular of the lemma *být*. As the value of LC shows, *bych* is an *imperf*ective positive (*plus*) form of the verb *být*.

The top-level SS part, concerning the entire phrase, is followed by two daughters: (i) SH *bych*, whose categorial properties are identified with those of the whole phrase ([1], due to HFP), and whose single valency is identified with the SS part of its deep head sister ([5]); and (ii) DH *nebyl spal*. As for AC, the negative polarity *minus* as the value of APOL is due to the negative form *nebyl*. The rather technical APPLE attribute specifies the number of *l*-participles (*more*) and helps to determine AMOOD and ATENSE. The attributes IC and LC refer only to the *l*-participle (*iLPple*) *nebyl* as the surface head of the embedded phrase in singular masculine animate. LC (the lexical category) states that *nebyl* is a negative form of the *imperf*ective auxiliary *být*.

The COMPS (non-subject valency) list is empty – the phrase *nebyl spal* is saturated. It is made up of DH, the content verb *spal*, and SH, the auxiliary participle *nebyl*, whose C is shared with that its mother's C ([4]) and whose single item on the COMPS list ([6]) is identified with its deep head sister, the content verb's SS. The categorial features of the content verb are specified in SS|C. The form is positive (APOL *plus*) and the phrase *spal* consists of the single form (APPLE *one*). As above, the values of the IC and LC attributes refer to the form *spát* itself: lemma = *spát*, masculine animate form (*ma*), *imperf*ective voice, polarity positive (*plus*), non-reflexive (*reflno*) content verb (*lVerbMain*). The intransitive content verb has no non-subject valency – the COMPS list is empty.

Representations of AVFs are built from: (i) skeletal phrase structures, converted from dependency trees produced by the parser, including morphosyntactic information about the terminals, and (ii) valency of auxiliaries (except for subject, valency of content verbs are irrelevant for analytic predicates).

3.5 Lexical Entries for the Auxiliaries

The forms *bych* and *nebyl*, used in Fig. 7, are derived from lexical entries shown in Figs. 8 and 9. The entries stand for all forms of the conditional auxiliary and *l*-participle.

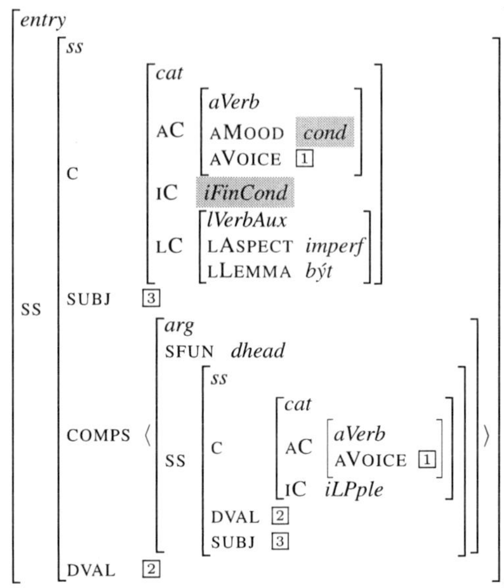

Figure 8: Lexical entry for the conditional auxiliary (e.g., *bych*).

Fig. 8 describes the conditional auxiliary irrespective of person or number, i.e., including *bych*. The value of C determines the *cond*itional mood (in AMOOD) for the whole AVF. Its voice is the same as the voice of its *l*-participle complement and of the entire structure. Inflectional category is finite conditional and lexically a form of the imperfective auxiliary *být* (*lVerbAux*). The valency (COMPS) specifies an *l*-participle (*iLPple*) whose deep valency is shared with that of *bych* itself. The subject of *bych* is also shared with that of its complement, including a potentially null subject. The lexical entry for the form *nebyl* in Fig. 9 differs from the entry for *bych* in the following respects: (i) no value of mood is present (there is no AMOOD in the AC attribute), (ii) the type of the IC attribute is *iLPle*, i.e., the form *nebyl* is an *l*-participle, and (iii) there is an SC (syntactic category) attribute whose *sLPple* value states that the form is a syntactic participle rather than *iFinPlain*, reserved for 3rd person *l*-participles.

3.6 Constraints for the Analytic Categories

Additional specifications are due to constraints of the grammar. Deep and surface heads share their ALEMMAS (8), deep head shares AVOICE with its auxiliary (9), *l*-participle surface head is marked as APPLE:*more* if the deep head is also an *l*-participle (10), tense is determined by the mood and num-

$$\begin{bmatrix} \textit{entry} \\ \text{SS} \begin{bmatrix} \textit{ss} \\ \text{C} \begin{bmatrix} \textit{cat} \\ \text{AC} \begin{bmatrix}\textit{aVerb}\\ \text{AVOICE } \boxed{1}\end{bmatrix} \\ \text{IC } \textit{iLPple} \\ \text{LC} \begin{bmatrix}\textit{lVerbAux}\\ \text{LASPECT } \textit{imperf} \\ \text{LLEMMA } \textit{být}\end{bmatrix} \\ \text{SC } \textit{sLPple}\end{bmatrix} \\ \text{SUBJ } \boxed{3} \\ \text{COMPS } \left\langle \begin{bmatrix} \textit{arg} \\ \text{SFUN } \textit{dhead} \\ \text{SS} \begin{bmatrix} \textit{ss} \\ \text{C} \begin{bmatrix}\textit{cat}\\ \text{AC}\begin{bmatrix}\textit{aVerb}\\ \text{AVOICE } \boxed{1}\end{bmatrix} \\ \text{IC } \textit{iLPple}\end{bmatrix} \\ \text{DVAL } \boxed{2} \\ \text{SUBJ } \boxed{3}\end{bmatrix}\end{bmatrix}\right\rangle \\ \text{DVAL } \boxed{2}\end{bmatrix}\end{bmatrix}$$

Figure 9: Lexical entry for the past auxiliary *l*-participle (e.g., *nebyl*).

ber of the *l*-participles (11), polarity of the entire AVF is positive unless any of its constituents is negated (12).

Using the same mechanism with different attributes, prepositions and conjuctions as surface heads can model the AC of prepositional phrases and subordinate clauses.

$$(8)\quad \textit{sdheaded} \rightarrow \begin{bmatrix} \text{SH}|..\text{ALEMMA } \boxed{1} \\ \text{DH}|..\text{ALEMMA } \boxed{1} \end{bmatrix}$$

$$(9)\quad \begin{bmatrix} \textit{sdheaded} \\ \text{SH}|..\text{LC } \textit{lVerbAux} \end{bmatrix} \rightarrow \begin{bmatrix} \text{SH}|..\text{AVOICE } \boxed{1} \\ \text{DH}|..\text{AVOICE } \boxed{1} \end{bmatrix}$$

$$(10)\quad \begin{bmatrix} \textit{sdheaded} \\ \text{SH}|..\text{LC } \textit{lVerbAux} \\ \text{SH}|..\text{SC } \textit{sLPple} \\ \text{DH}|..\text{SC } \textit{sLPple} \end{bmatrix} \rightarrow \begin{bmatrix} \text{SH}|..\text{APPLE } \textit{more} \end{bmatrix}$$

$$(11)\quad \begin{bmatrix} \textit{sdheaded} \\ \text{SH}|..\text{LC } \textit{lVerbAux} \\ \text{SH}|..\text{IC } \textit{iFin} \\ \text{DH}|..\text{SC } \textit{sLPple} \end{bmatrix} \rightarrow \begin{bmatrix} \text{SH}|..\text{AMOOD } \boxed{1} \\ \text{SH}|..\text{ATENSE } \boxed{2} \\ \text{DH}|..\text{APPLE } \boxed{3} \end{bmatrix}$$
$$\begin{array}{llllll} & \textit{mood\_tense}(& \boxed{1}, & \boxed{2}, & \boxed{3} &) \\ & \textit{mood\_tense}(& \textit{ind}, & \textit{past}, & \textit{one} &) \\ \wedge & \textit{mood\_tense}(& \textit{ind}, & \textit{plusq}, & \textit{more} &) \\ & \textit{mood\_tense}(& \textit{cond}, & \textit{pres}, & \textit{one} &) \\ & \textit{mood\_tense}(& \textit{cond}, & \textit{past}, & \textit{more} &) \end{array}$$

$$(12)\quad \begin{bmatrix} \textit{sdheaded} \\ \text{SH}|..\text{LC } \textit{lVerbAux} \\ \text{DH}|..\text{SC } \textit{sLPple} \end{bmatrix} \rightarrow \begin{bmatrix} \text{DH}|..\text{APOL } \boxed{1} \\ \text{SH}|..\text{LPOL } \boxed{2} \\ \text{SH}|..\text{APOL } \boxed{3} \end{bmatrix}$$
$$\begin{array}{llllll} & \textit{polarity}(& \boxed{1}, & \boxed{2}, & \boxed{3} &) \\ \wedge & \textit{polarity}(& \textit{bool}, & \textit{minus}, & \textit{minus} &) \\ & \textit{polarity}(& \textit{minus}, & \textit{plus}, & \textit{minus} &) \\ & \textit{polarity}(& \textit{plus}, & \textit{plus}, & \textit{plus} &) \end{array}$$

4 Discussion

We presented a uniform and compact approach to the annotation of AVFs, supporting effective search options in a treebank. Information about an AVF as a whole is contained in its analytic category (AC, Fig. 7) in the phrasal node representing this form (Fig. 5). E.g., content verbs in past conditional can be retrieved by a straightforward query quoting appropriate values of the ACAT attributes. The entire AVF, including auxiliaries, is retrieved when the selection is extended by all surface and deep heads along the analytic projection of the content verb.

This is an advantage over an approach adopted, e.g., in the Prague Dependency Treebank (PDT).[14] On its *analytic level*,[15] auxiliaries are immediate dependents of a content verb (unless coordination is involved) and sisters of dependents of other types. Thus it is not easy to identify AVFs and their type or to infer their properties, e.g., as a response to a query. On the PDT's *tectogrammatical level* the auxiliaries are absent: an AVF is represented as a single complex node, but components of the complex node on the analytic level can be recovered since the representations on the two levels are interlinked. However, the corpus annotated on the tectogrammatical level is too small for many research tasks.

AVFs can have a complex internal syntax. If there is a single auxiliary for two or more coordinated content verbs (e.g., in *Já jsem přišel a viděl.* 'I came and saw'), the two content verbs as well as the predicate are identified as active past indicative forms. On the other hand, such structures are very difficult to identify on the PDT analytic layer. Searching, e.g., for all present conditionals, requires a complex query, based on detailed knowledge of the PDT representation.

The automatically determined analytic categories can be projected to a different annotation format, including PDT or CoNLL-U.[16] At the very least, the annotation of content verbs can be extended by analytically determined specification of mood, tense and voice. In addition to theoretical interest, some NLP applications may profit from the identification of AVFs as a distinctive unit with specific properties. While a certain lan-

[14] http://ufal.mff.cuni.cz/pdt3.0

[15] Note that *analytic level* denotes a *a level of surface syntax* rather than anything related to AVFs.

[16] http://universaldependencies.github.io/docs/format.html

guage tends to express morphological meanings analytically, using auxiliaries and other function words, a different (synthetic) language may avoid AVFs. Identification of such equivalent units may improve the quality of parallel texts alignment and machine translation. Similarly, a parser trained on texts where such units are identified can produce better results.

The first release of a part of the Czech National Corpus annotated in the style of the PDT analytic level is due soon. A pilot treebank including the proposed annotation of analytic categories will follow, supplemented by the formal grammar and lexicon. The planned size is in the order of tens of millions of words. The annotation will include analytic categories and other information added by the grammar and the lexicon, or a flag identifying a failure in the application of the grammar and its possible reason, while the annotation will retain only information from the parser. At present, the grammar and the lexicon are developed and tested on a sample of 1000 sentences from the PDT annotation manual,[17] covering a wide range of linguistic phenomena. A proper evaluation is previewed on a larger sample extracted from real corpus texts.

Acknowledgments

This research was supported by the Grant Agency of the Czech Republic, grant no. 13-27184S.

References

Tania Avgustinova, Alla Bémová, Eva Hajičová, Karel Oliva, Jarmila Panevová, Vladimír Petkevič, Petr Sgall, and Hana Skoumalová. 1995. Linguistic problems of Czech. Project Peco 2924. Technical report, Charles University, Prague.

Robert D Borsley. 1999. Auxiliaries, verbs and complementizers in Polish. *Slavic in Head-Driven Phrase Structure Grammar*, pages 29–59.

Václav Cvrček, Vilém Kodýtek, Marie Kopřivová, Dominika Kováříková, Petr Sgall, Michal Šulc, Jan Táborský, Jan Volín, and Martina Waclawičová. 2010. *Mluvnice současné češtiny*. Karolinum, Praha.

Mary Dalrymple. 1999. Lexical-functional grammar. In Rob Wilson and Frank Keil, editors, *MIT Encyclopedia of the Cognitive Sciences*. The MIT Press.

Jan Hajič, Jarmila Panevová, Eva Buráňová, Zdeňka Urešová, and Alla Bémová. 1999. A Manual for Analytic Layer Annotation of the Prague Dependency Treebank. Technical report, ÚFAL MFF UK, Prague.

Tomáš Jelínek, Vladimír Petkevič, Alexandr Rosen, Hana Skoumalová, Přemysl Vítovec, and Jiří Znamenáček. 2014. A grammar-licensed treebank of Czech. In Verena Henrich, Erhard Hinrichs, Daniël de Kok, Petya Osenova, and Adam Przepiórkowski, editors, *Proceedings of TLT13*, pages 218–229, Tübingen.

Petr Karlík, Marek Nekula, and Zdenka Rusínová. 1995. *Příruční mluvnice češtiny*. Lidové noviny, Praha.

Miroslav Komárek, Jan Kořenský, Jan Petr, and Jarmila Veselková, editors. 1986. *Mluvnice češtiny 2 – Tvarosloví*. Academia, Praha.

Anna Kupść and Jesse Tseng. 2005. A New HPSG Approach to Polish Auxiliary Constructions. In Stefan Müller, editor, *Proceedings of HPSG12*, CSLI Publications, pages 253–273. University of Lisbon.

Anna Kupść. 2000. *A HPSG Grammar of Polish Clitics*. Ph.D. thesis, Atelier national de Reproduction des Thèses.

Carl J. Pollard and Ivan A. Sag. 1994. *Head-Driven Phrase Structure Grammar*. University of Chicago Press, Chicago.

Adam Przepiórkowski. 2007. On heads and coordination in valence acquisition. In Alexander Gelbukh, editor, *CICLing 2007*, pages 50–61, Berlin. Springer.

Alexandr Rosen. 2014. A 3D taxonomy of word classes at work. In Ludmila Veselovská and Markéta Janebová, editors, *Complex Visibles Out There. Proceedings of OLINCO 2014*, volume 4, pages 575–590, Olomouc. Palacký University.

Jesse Tseng and Anna Kupść. 2006. A cross-linguistic approach to Slavic past tense and conditional constructions. *Proceedings of FDSL6*.

Jesse Tseng. 2009. A formal model of grammaticalization in Slavic past tense constructions. *Current Issues in Unity and Diversity of Languages*, pages 749–762.

Ludmila Veselovská and Petr Karlík. 2004. Analytic passives in Czech. *Zeitschrift für Slawistik*, pages 163–235.

Ludmila Veselovská. 2003. Analytické préteritum a opisné pasivum v češtině: dvojí způsob saturace silného rysu <+v> hlavy v*. *Sborník filozofické fakulty Masarykovy Univerzity*, pages 161–177.

Gert Webelhuth, editor. 1995. *Government and Binding Theory and the Minimalist Program*. Blackwell Publishers, Oxford, UK.

[17] Hajič et al. (1999).

Resolving Entity Coreference in Croatian with a Constrained Mention-Pair Model

Goran Glavaš and **Jan Šnajder**
Text Analysis and Knowledge Engineering Lab
Faculty of Electrical Engineering and Computing, University of Zagreb
Unska 3, 10000 Zagreb, Croatia
{goran.glavas, jan.snajder}@fer.hr

Abstract

Being able to identify that different mentions refer to the same entity is beneficial for applications such as question answering and text summarization. In this paper, we propose the first model for entity coreference resolution for Croatian. We enforce transitivity constraints with integer linear programming on top of pairwise decisions produced by the supervised mention-pair model. Experimental results show that the proposed model significantly outperforms two different rule-based baselines, reaching performance of 74.4% MUC score and 77.6% B^3 score.

1 Introduction

Entity coreference resolution, the task of recognizing mentions in text that refer to the same real-world entity, has been one of the central tasks of natural language processing (NLP) for decades (Grosz et al., 1983; Connolly et al., 1997; Ponzetto and Strube, 2006). Coreference resolution owes this attention to numerous applications that could greatly benefit from the ability to identify different mentions of the same entity, such as relation extraction (Shinyama and Sekine, 2006), question answering (Vicedo and Ferrández, 2000; Zheng, 2002), and text summarization (Bergler et al., 2003; Steinberger et al., 2007).

Despite being easy to define, coreference resolution is considered to be a rather difficult task, primarily because it heavily relies on external knowledge (e.g., for resolving *"U.S. President"* and *"Barack Obama"*, one needs to know that Obama is the president of the USA) (Markert et al., 2003; Durrett and Klein, 2014).

Although machine learning-based approaches to anaphora and coreference resolution for English appeared almost two decades ago (Connolly et al., 1997), for many languages, including the majority of Slavic languages, no coreference resolution systems exist, mainly due to the lack of annotated corpora required for developing such systems.

In this paper, we present a coreference resolution model for Croatian. Our model enforces transitivity of coreference relations via integer linear programming (ILP) optimization over a set of binary coreference decisions made by the supervised mention-pair model (McCarthy and Lehnert, 1995). To the best of our knowledge, this is the first work on coreference resolution for Croatian, and one of the first efforts in coreference resolution for Slavic languages in general.

2 Related Work

Early computational approaches to coreference resolution for English were rule-based and heavily influenced by computational theories of discourse such as *focusing* and *centering* (Sidner, 1979; Grosz et al., 1983). As annotated coreference corpora became available, primarily within the Message Understanding Conferences (MUC-6 and MUC-7), research focus shifted towards supervised machine learning models. The first learning-based coreference resolution approach dates back to Connolly et al. (1997).

The mention-pair model is essentially a binary coreference classifier for pairs of entity mentions, introduced by Aone and Bennett (1995) and McCarthy and Lehnert (1995). It is still at the core of most coreference resolution systems, despite its obvious inability to enforce the transitivity inherent to the coreference relation and the fact that it requires an additional clustering algorithm to build the coreference clusters. Interestingly enough, more complex models such as entity-mention model (McCallum and Wellner, 2003; Daumé III and Marcu, 2005; Yang et al., 2008a) and ranking models (Iida et al., 2003; Yang et al., 2008b), designed to remedy for the shortcomings of the mention-pair model,

Proceedings of the 5th Workshop on Balto-Slavic Natural Language Processing, pages 17–23,
Hissar, Bulgaria, 10–11 September 2015.

failed to demonstrate a significant performance improvements over the simple mention-pair model.

Besides for English, there is a significant body of work on coreference resolution for other major languages, including Spanish (Palomar et al., 2001; Sapena et al., 2010), Italian (Kobdani and Schütze, 2010; Poesio et al., 2010), German (Versley, 2006; Wunsch, 2010), Chinese (Converse, 2006; Kong and Zhou, 2010), Japanese (Iida et al., 2003; Iida, 2007), and Arabic (Zitouni et al., 2005; Luo and Zitouni, 2005).

On the other hand, research on coreference resolution for Slavic languages has been quite limited, mainly due to the non-existence of manually annotated corpora. The exceptions are the work done for Polish, (Marciniak, 2002; Matysiak, 2007; Kopec and Ogrodniczuk, 2012), Czech (Linh et al., 2009), and Bulgarian (Zhikov et al., 2013). In particular, Kopec and Ogrodniczuk (2012) demonstrate that a rule-based coreference resolution system for Polish significantly outperforms state-of-the-art machine learning models for English, suggesting that the coreference resolution model benefits from morphological complexity of Polish.

In this work, we present a mention-pair coreference resolution model for Croatian. Our model accounts for transitivity of coreference relations by encoding transitivity constraints as an ILP optimization problem. Our constrained mention-pair model reaches a performance of 77.6% B^3 score, which is significantly above the state-of-the-art performance for English. This supports the claim that rich morphological information facilitates coreference resolution.

3 Dataset Annotation

Supervised coreference models require a manually annotated dataset. We next describe how we compiled a coreference resolution dataset for Croatian.

3.1 Annotation Guidelines

Although coreference in most cases relates to both mentions referring to exactly the same real-world entity (i.e., identity relation), coreference may also relate to several near-identity relations between two mentions (Recasens et al., 2010); e.g., one mention may be referring to part of the entity to which the other mention refers. Arguably the most important step prior to annotating the coreference resolution dataset is to determine the identity and near-identity relations that hold between different mentions of the same real-world entity. Considering that Croatian is a highly inflectional language, we adopt the coreference relation type scheme for inflectional languages proposed by Ogrodniczuk et al. (2013). This scheme includes the following coreference relation types (an instantiation of each of the relation types is given in Table 1):

- IDENTITY relation covers the most common case of coreference where both mentions refer to exactly the same real-world entity;
- HYPER-HYPONYM relation refers to cases where one mention is a hypernym of the other mention (but both mentions still refer to the same entity);
- MERONYMY relation is present where one mention refers to the part of the entity to which the other mention refers;
- METONYMY is a relation in which one of the mentions, although referring to the same entity as the other mention, is expressed via a phrase that typically denotes a different entity;
- ZERO ANAPHORA is a relation where one of the mentions is expressed implicitly in the form of a hidden subject.

Annotators were instructed to annotate instances of all of the aforementioned coreference relation types. They were instructed to link each mention to its closest previous coreferent mention in the text. Entity mentions that are not being part of at least one coreference relation were ignored.

3.2 Annotation Workflow

Six annotators participated in the annotation task. The corpus used for annotation comprised of articles from the Croatian news collection "Vjesnik". Annotators used an in-house developed annotation tool and were provided detailed annotation guidelines. We first asked the annotators to annotate a calibration set consisting of 15 news articles. We then discussed the disagreements and resolved them by consensus.

After calibration, we conducted two rounds of annotation. In each of the rounds we paired the annotators (pairings were different between the rounds), so that we have each document annotated by exactly two annotators. In both rounds, each pair of annotators was assigned 45 news articles, but each annotator annotated the documents independently. After each of the two annotations rounds, we measured the average pairwise agreement and observed that it reached 70% of accuracy. The fol-

Coreference type	Example
IDENTITY	***Premijer*** *je izjavio da* ***on*** *nije odobrio taj zahtjev.* (**The Prime Minister** said **he** didn't grant that request.)
HYPER-HYPONYM	*Ivan je kupio novi* ***automobil.*** ***Taj Mercedes*** *je čudo od auta.* (Ivan bought a new **car**. **That Mercedes** is an amazing car.)
MERONYMY	*Od* ***jedanaestorice rukometaša*** *danas je igralo samo njih* ***osam.*** (Only **eight** out of **eleven handball players** played today.)
METONYMY	***Dinamo Zagreb*** *je jučer pobijedio Cibaliju.* ***Zagrepčani*** *su postigli tri pogotka.* (**Dinamo Zagreb** defeated Cibalia yesterday. **Zagreb boys** scored three goals.)
ZERO ANAPHORA	***Marko*** *je išao u trgovinu.* ***Kupio*** *je banane.* (**Marko** went to the store. [He] **bought** bananas.)

Table 1: Coreference relation types.

lowing were the main causes of disagreement: (1) different pairing of mentions (80%), (2) disagreement in mention extent (16.7%), and (3) different coreference type assigned (3.3%).

The entire annotation procedure yielded a dataset consisting of 270 news articles (a total of 147,000 tokens), annotated with almost 13,000 coreference relations.[1] Expectedly, the IDENTITY relation is by far the most frequent one in the dataset, accounting for 87% of all coreference annotations, followed by MERONYMY (7%) and ZERO ANAPHORA (4%). Given the prevalence of the IDENTITY relation in our dataset, in this work we focus on extracting only coreference relations of that particular type.

4 Constrained Mention-Pair Model

At the core of our approach is a mention-pair model, i.e., a binary classifier that, given two entity mentions, predicts whether they corefer. To produce clusters of coreferent mentions, a mention-pair model needs to be coupled with two additional components: (1) a heuristic for the generation of mention-pair instances (as forming all possible pairs of mentions would result in a dataset that would be heavily skewed towards the negative class) and (2) a method for ensuring the transitivity of the coreference relation and the clustering of coreferent mentions (as the set of individual binary decisions may conflict the transitivity property of the coreference relation).

4.1 Creating Training Instances

In this work, we generate training instances using the heuristic proposed by Ng and Cardie (2002), which is, in turn, the extension of the approach by Soon et al. (2001). We thus create a positive instance between a mention m_j and its closest preceding mention m_i, and negative instances between m_j and all the mentions in between m_i and m_j $(m_{i+1}, \ldots, m_{j-1})$. However, if the mention m_j is non-pronominal and m_i is pronominal, then we create the positive instance by pairing m_j with its closest preceding non-pronominal mention, instead of with m_i.

4.2 Mention-Pair Model

Our mention pair model is a supervised classifier that predicts whether an IDENTITY coreference relation holds for a given pair of mentions. The classifier is based on a set of binary and numeric features, each comparing two entity mentions. Most of these features or their variants have been proposed in previous work for English and other languages. The features can be roughly grouped into four categories: string-matching features, overlap features, grammatical features, and distance-based features.

String-matching features compare the two entity mentions on the superficial string level (without any linguistic preprocessing of the mentions):

- Indication whether the two mention strings fully match (f_1);
- Indication whether one mention string contains the other (f_2);
- Length of the longest common subsequence between the mentions (f_3);
- Edit distance (i.e., Levenshtein distance) between the mentions (f_4).

Overlap features quantify the overlap between the mentions in terms of tokens these mentions share:

- Indications whether there is at least one matching word, lemma, and stem between the tokens of the two mentions (f_4, f_5, and f_6);
- Relative overlap between the mentions, mea-

[1] A part of this dataset is freely available; cf. Section 5.

sured as the number of content lemmas (nouns, adjectives, verbs, and adverbs) found in both mentions, normalized by the token length of both mentions (f_7).

Grammatical features encode some grammatical properties and aim to indicate grammatical compatibility of the two mentions:

- Indication whether the first and second mentions are pronominal mentions, respectively (f_8 and f_9);
- Indication whether the mentions match in gender (f_{10}). Morphosyntactic descriptors for Croatian content words, including the information on gender and number, are obtained with the lemmatization tool for Croatian (Šnajder et al., 2008);
- Indication whether the mentions match in number (f_{11}).

Distance-based features indicate how far apart the two mentions are in the text (the pronominal references cannot be too far from the closest coreferent noun-phrase mention):

- Distance between the mentions in the number of tokens (f_{12});
- Distance between the mentions in the number of sentences (f_{13});
- Indication whether the two mentions are in the same sentence (f_{14});
- Indication whether the two mentions are adjacent, i.e., whether there are any other entity mentions in between them (f_{15});
- Number of other mentions in between the mentions at hand (f_{16}).

Given that our original feature space is relatively small (i.e., several orders of magnitude smaller than the number of instances in the training set), we chose as the learning algorithm the support vector machines (SVM) with the radial-basis function (RBF) kernel that maps the training instances into a high-dimensional feature space.

4.3 Enforcing Transitivity

The IDENTITY coreference relation is inherently transitive. However, by making only the local pairwise decisions, the mention-pair model does not guarantee global (i.e., document-level) coherence of its decisions with respect to the transitivity of the IDENTITY coreference relation. Thus, we need a separate mechanism to ensure that the transitivity between individual pairwise decisions holds. In this work, we enforce transitivity as a set of linear constraints in the integer linear programming (ILP) optimization setting. We aim to maximize the objective function, which is a linear combination of mention-pair classifier confidences for individual pairwise decisions, by taking into account the linear transitivity constraints at the same time.

Objective function. Let $M = \{m_1, \ldots, m_n\}$ be the set of all entity mentions in a single news article, let P be the set of all mention pairs considered by the pairwise classifier, $P = \{(m_i, m_j) \mid m_i, m_j \in M, i < j\}$, let $r(m_i, m_j)$ be the mention-pair classifier's decision for mentions m_i and m_j, so that $r(m_i, m_j) \in \{-1, 1\}$), and let $C(m_i, m_j)$ be the confidence of the binary mention-pair classifier ($0.5 \leq C(m_i, m_j) \leq 1$). The objective function is then defined as follows:

$$\sum_{(m_i,m_j)\in P} x_{ij} \cdot r(m_i, m_j) \cdot C(m_i, m_j)$$

where x_{ij} is the binary label variable indicating whether the mentions m_i and m_j corefer.

Transitivity constraints. For all triplets of entity mentions (m_i, m_j, m_k) for which all three pairs (m_i, m_j), (m_j, m_k), and (m_i, m_k) exist, we enforce the following linear transitivity constraints:

$$\begin{aligned} x_{ij} + x_{jk} - x_{ik} &\leq 1, \\ x_{ij} + x_{ik} - x_{jk} &\leq 1, \\ x_{jk} + x_{ik} - x_{ij} &\leq 1, \\ \forall\{(m_i, m_j), (m_j, m_k), (m_i, m_k)\} &\subseteq P \end{aligned}$$

Clustering. After the ILP optimization, we obtain transitively coherent coreference relations, which allows us to derive the clusters of coreferent mentions simply by computing the transitive closure upon those relations.

5 Evaluation

We split the manually annotated dataset consisting of 270 documents into a train set containing 220 documents and a test set with 50 documents.[2] We optimized the hyperparameters of our SVM mention-pair model (C and γ) by means of 10-folded cross validation. We then trained the model with the optimal hyperparameters on the entire train set and evaluated that model on the test set.

[2]The test set is available from `http://takelab.fer.hr/crocoref`

Model	MUC			B^3		
	P	R	F_1	P	R	F_1
OVERLAP	81.0	42.9	54.1	75.7	54.5	61.4
GENDNUM	55.2	39.0	45.4	59.8	50.5	54.3
MP-MORPH	90.6	61.1	72.1	86.2	67.3	74.6
MP	89.4	**64.7**	74.2	84.0	**70.1**	75.4
MP+ILP	**91.9**	63.5	**74.4**	**90.6**	68.7	**77.6**

Table 2: Coreference resolution performance.

Baselines. We compare the performance of our transitively coherent mention-pair model against two different baseline models. The OVERLAP baseline classifies two mentions as coreferent if they share at least one content word. The GENDNUM baseline links each mention to the closest preceding mention with which it matches in gender and number. Standard closest-first clustering (Soon et al., 2001) is applied for both baselines.

Results. We show the performance of our mention-pair model, both without (MP) and with (MP+ILP) enforcing transitivity, along with the performance of both baselines in Table 2. We evaluate all models in terms of two standard evaluation measures for coreference resolution – MUC score and B^3 score. In order to evaluate the contribution of morphological features, we additionally evaluate the mention-pair model but excluding all features relying on morphological preprocessing (MP-MORPH).

Results show that the supervised mention-pair model significantly outperforms both reasonable rule-based baselines. When morphological features are not used, the model exhibits a slightly lower performance, although the difference is not substantial. Enforcing transitivity in an ILP setting marginally improves the overall MUC score, but yields notable 2-point improvement in B^3 score. Precision is consistently higher than recall for all models and both evaluation metrics, which is consistent with the coreference resolution results for other languages (Lee et al., 2011; Kobdani and Schütze, 2011).

Overall, our results are over 10 points higher than the state-of-the-art performance for English (Lee et al., 2011) and comparable (higher MUC and lower B^3 score) to the best results obtained for Polish (Kopec and Ogrodniczuk, 2012), suggesting that coreference resolution may be easier task for morphologically complex languages.

Error analysis. In an attempt to identify the most common types of errors, we manually analyzed the errors made by the supervised mention-pair model. The vast majority of false negatives originate from mention pairs where external knowledge is necessary for inferring coreference, e.g., *željezni kancelar* (iron chancellor) and *Bismarck*). Other common causes of false negatives include abbreviations, e.g., *DS* and *Demokratski savez* (Democratic Alliance), and distant pronominal anaphora (i.e., when an anaphoric pronoun is far away from its preceding coreferent mention). Most false positives stem from non-coreferent mentions with substantial lexical overlap, e.g., *Društvo hrvatskih književnika* (Croatian Writers' Association) and *svečanosti u Društvu hrvatskih književnika* (ceremonies at the Croatian Writers' Association). A significant number of false positives are due to a pronominal mention being close to some non-coreferent noun-phrase mention.

6 Conclusion

We presented the first coreference resolution model for Croatian. We built a supervised mention-pair model for recognizing identity coreference relations between entity mentions and augmented it with transitivity constraints enforced via ILP optimization. We demonstrated the effectiveness of the model by showing that it substantially outperforms two rule-based baselines. Enforcing transitivity improves the B^3 score.

Manual error analysis revealed that most errors are due to the lack of external knowledge necessary for inferring coreference. Thus, we plan to extend the model with knowledge-based features obtained from external knowledge sources like Wikipedia. Furthermore, as we currently use no syntactic information, we intend to incorporate dependency relations as features.

In this work we focused on resolving identity coreference between gold event mentions. With the goal of building an end-to-end coreference resolution system for Croatian, our future efforts will focus on the development of a mention detection model. We will also consider near-identity relations like meronymy and zero anaphora.

Acknowledgments

We thank Matija Hanževački for his assistance in guiding the annotation process. We also thank the anonymous reviewers for their useful comments.

References

Chinatsu Aone and Scott William Bennett. 1995. Evaluating automated and manual acquisition of anaphora resolution strategies. In *Proceedings of the 33rd Annual Meeting on Association for Computational Linguistics*, pages 122–129.

Sabine Bergler, René Witte, Michelle Khalife, Zhuoyan Li, and Frank Rudzicz. 2003. Using knowledge-poor coreference resolution for text summarization. In *Proceedings of the Document Understanding Conference*, pages 85–92.

Dennis Connolly, John D Burger, and David S Day. 1997. A machine learning approach to anaphoric reference. In *New Methods in Language Processing*, pages 133–144.

Susan Converse. 2006. *Pronominal Anaphora Resolution in Chinese*. Ph.D. thesis.

Hal Daumé III and Daniel Marcu. 2005. A large-scale exploration of effective global features for a joint entity detection and tracking model. In *Proceedings of the conference on Human Language Technology and Empirical Methods in Natural Language Processing*, pages 97–104.

Greg Durrett and Dan Klein. 2014. A joint model for entity analysis: Coreference, typing, and linking. *Transactions of the Association for Computational Linguistics*, 2:477–490.

Barbara J Grosz, Aravind K Joshi, and Scott Weinstein. 1983. Providing a unified account of definite noun phrases in discourse. In *Proceedings of the 21st Annual Meeting on Association for Computational Linguistics*, pages 44–50.

Ryu Iida, Kentaro Inui, Hiroya Takamura, and Yuji Matsumoto. 2003. Incorporating contextual cues in trainable models for coreference resolution. In *Proceedings of the Conference of the European Chapter of the Association for Computational Linguistics (EACL '03) Workshop on The Computational Treatment of Anaphora*, pages 23–30.

Ryu Iida. 2007. *Combining Linguistic Knowledge and Machine Learning for Anaphora Resolution*. Ph.D. thesis.

Hamidreza Kobdani and Hinrich Schütze. 2010. SUCRE: A modular system for coreference resolution. In *Proceedings of the 5th International Workshop on Semantic Evaluation*, pages 92–95.

Hamidreza Kobdani and Hinrich Schütze. 2011. Supervised coreference resolution with SUCRE. In *Proceedings of the Fifteenth Conference on Computational Natural Language Learning: Shared Task*, pages 71–75.

Fang Kong and Guodong Zhou. 2010. A tree kernel-based unified framework for Chinese zero anaphora resolution. In *Proceedings of the Conference on Empirical Methods in Natural Language Processing*, pages 882–891.

Mateusz Kopec and Maciej Ogrodniczuk. 2012. Creating a coreference resolution system for Polish. In *LREC*, pages 192–195.

Heeyoung Lee, Yves Peirsman, Angel Chang, Nathanael Chambers, Mihai Surdeanu, and Dan Jurafsky. 2011. Stanford's multi-pass sieve coreference resolution system at the CoNLL-2011 shared task. In *Proceedings of the Fifteenth Conference on Computational Natural Language Learning: Shared Task*, pages 28–34.

Nguy Giang Linh, Václav Novák, et al. 2009. Comparison of classification and ranking approaches to pronominal anaphora resolution in Czech. In *Proceedings of the 10th Annual Meeting of the Special Interest Group on Discourse and Dialogue*, pages 276–285.

Xiaoqiang Luo and Imed Zitouni. 2005. Multilingual coreference resolution with syntactic features. In *Proceedings of the Conference on Human Language Technology and Empirical Methods in Natural Language Processing*, pages 660–667.

Malgorzata Marciniak. 2002. Anaphor binding for Polish. In *Proceedings of the 4th Discourse Anaphora and Anaphor Resolution Colloquium*.

Katja Markert, Malvina Nissim, and Natalia Modjeska. 2003. Using the web for anaphora resolution. In *Proceedings of the 10th Conference of the European Chapter of the Association for Computational Linguistics (EACL '03) Workshop on the Computational Treatment of Anaphora*, pages 39–46.

Ireneusz Matysiak. 2007. Information extraction systems and nominal anaphora analysis needs. In *Proceedings of the International Multiconference on Computer Science and Information Technology*, pages 183–192.

Andrew McCallum and Ben Wellner. 2003. Toward conditional models of identity uncertainty with application to proper noun coreference.

Joseph F McCarthy and Wendy G Lehnert. 1995. Using decision trees for coreference resolution. In *Proceedings of the 14th International Joint Conference on Artificial Intelligence*, pages 1050–1055.

Vincent Ng and Claire Cardie. 2002. Improving machine learning approaches to coreference resolution. In *Proceedings of the 40th Annual Meeting on Association for Computational Linguistics*, pages 104–111.

Maciej Ogrodniczuk, Magdalena Zawisławska, Katarzyna Głowińska, and Agata Savary. 2013. Coreference annotation schema for an inflectional language. In *Computational Linguistics and Intelligent Text Processing*, pages 394–407. Springer.

Manuel Palomar, Antonio Ferrández, Lidia Moreno, Patricio Martínez-Barco, Jesús Peral, Maximiliano Saiz-Noeda, and Rafael Muñoz. 2001. An algorithm for anaphora resolution in Spanish texts. *Computational Linguistics*, 27(4):545–567.

Massimo Poesio, Olga Uryupina, and Yannick Versley. 2010. Creating a coreference resolution system for Italian. In *LREC*, pages 713–716.

Simone Paolo Ponzetto and Michael Strube. 2006. Exploiting semantic role labeling, wordnet and wikipedia for coreference resolution. In *Proceedings of the Human Language Technology Conference of the North American Chapter of the Association of Computational Linguistics*, pages 192–199.

Marta Recasens, Eduard H Hovy, and Maria Antònia Martí. 2010. A typology of near-identity relations for coreference (NIDENT). In *LREC*, pages 149–156.

Emili Sapena, Lluís Padró, and Jordi Turmo. 2010. RelaxCor: A global relaxation labeling approach to coreference resolution. In *Proceedings of the 5th International Workshop on Semantic Evaluation*, pages 88–91.

Yusuke Shinyama and Satoshi Sekine. 2006. Preemptive information extraction using unrestricted relation discovery. In *Proceedings of the Human Language Technology Conference of the North American Chapter of the Association of Computational Linguistics*, pages 304–311.

Candace Lee Sidner. 1979. *Towards a Computational Theory of Definite Anaphora Comprehension in English Discourse*. Ph.D. thesis.

Jan Šnajder, Bojana Dalbelo Bašić, and Marko Tadić. 2008. Automatic acquisition of inflectional lexica for morphological normalisation. *Information Processing & Management*, 44(5):1720–1731.

Wee Meng Soon, Hwee Tou Ng, and Daniel Chung Yong Lim. 2001. A machine learning approach to coreference resolution of noun phrases. *Computational linguistics*, 27(4):521–544.

Josef Steinberger, Massimo Poesio, Mijail Kabadjov, and Karel Ježek. 2007. Two uses of anaphora resolution in summarization. *Information Processing & Management*, 43(6):1663–1680.

Yannick Versley. 2006. A constraint-based approach to noun phrase coreference resolution in German newspaper text. In *In Proceedings of Konferenz zur Verarbeitung Naturlicher Sprache*, pages 143–150.

José Vicedo and Antonio Ferrández. 2000. Importance of pronominal anaphora resolution in question answering systems. In *Proceedings of the 38th Annual Meeting on Association for Computational Linguistics*, pages 555–562.

Holger Wunsch. 2010. *Rule-Based and Memory-Based Pronoun Resolution for German: A Comparison and Assessment of Data Sources*. Ph.D. thesis, Universität Tübingen.

Xiaofeng Yang, Jian Su, Jun Lang, Chew Lim Tan, Ting Liu, and Sheng Li. 2008a. An entity-mention model for coreference resolution with inductive logic programming. In *ACL*, pages 843–851.

Xiaofeng Yang, Jian Su, and Chew Lim Tan. 2008b. A twin-candidate model for learning-based anaphora resolution. *Computational Linguistics*, 34(3):327–356.

Zhiping Zheng. 2002. Answerbus question answering system. In *Proceedings of the Second International Conference on Human Language Technology Research*, pages 399–404.

Valentin Zhikov, Georgi Georgiev, Kiril Simov, and Petya Osenova. 2013. Combining POS tagging, dependency parsing and coreferential resolution for Bulgarian. In *RANLP*, pages 755–762.

Imed Zitouni, Jeff Sorensen, Xiaoqiang Luo, and Radu Florian. 2005. The impact of morphological stemming on Arabic mention detection and coreference resolution. In *Proceedings of the ACL Workshop on Computational Approaches to Semitic Languages*, pages 63–70.

Evaluation of Coreference Resolution Tools for Polish from the Information Extraction Perspective

Adam Kaczmarek
Institute of Computer Science
University of Wrocław
Wrocław, Poland
akaczmarek@cs.uni.wroc.pl

Michał Marcińczuk
Department of Computational Intelligence
Wrocław University of Technology
Wrocław, Poland
michal.marcinczuk@pwr.edu.pl

Abstract

In this paper we discuss the performance of existing tools for coreference resolution for Polish from the perspective of information extraction tasks. We take into consideration the source of mentions, i.e., gold standard vs mentions recognized automatically. We evaluate three existing tools, i.e., IKAR, Ruler and Bartek on the KPWr corpus. We show that the widely used metrics for coreference evaluation (B^3, MUC, CEAF, BLANC) do not reflect the real performance when dealing with the task of semantic relations recognition between named entities. Thus, we propose a supplementary metric called PARENT, which measures the correctness of linking between referential mentions and named entities.

1 Introduction

In this paper we approach the problem of coreference resolution and its evaluation metrics. We consider this problem from a slightly different perspective—not as a simple clustering problem, but rather as a problem of extracting information from text. We make an observation that not every mention carries equal amount of information, e.g., when considering a pronoun resolution problem there are usually a few named entities that can be assigned to real world objects and relatively larger amount of pronouns that carry almost no information about the object they are referring to, without resolving the coreference with the named entity. Thus we do not want to treat named entities and pronouns equally as in the case below. We can imagine a document with two named entities, for simplicity each with equal count of n pronouns in gold coreferential clusters:

$$\{\text{Romeo}, \text{he}_1, \text{he}_2, \ldots, \text{he}_n\}$$
$$\{\text{Juliet}, \text{she}_1, \text{she}_2, \ldots, \text{she}_n\}$$

and two possible system responses, one with two pronouns interchanged between coreferential clusters:

$$\{\text{Romeo}, \mathbf{she_1}, \text{he}_2, \ldots, \text{he}_n\}$$
$$\{\text{Juliet}, \mathbf{he_1}, \text{she}_2, \ldots, \text{she}_n\}$$

and the second with the named entities interchanged:

$$\{\mathbf{Juliet}, \text{he}_1, \text{he}_2, \ldots, \text{he}_n\}$$
$$\{\mathbf{Romeo}, \text{she}_1, \text{she}_2, \ldots, \text{she}_n\}$$

According to the measures which do not distinguish between types of mentions and are based only on the similarity of clusters, these two responses are scored equally. However, from information extraction perspective the first answer is almost correct, while the second gives us totally incorrect information about both named entities. Thus we propose a supplementary method to score the performance of coreference resolution systems with respect to different types of mentions.

2 Related Work

We will present here work related to this topic in a two-way manner: first by introducing the coreference evaluation metrics and second describing current tools for coreference resolution for Polish.

2.1 Evaluation

Coreference evaluation is a widely studied problem in the literature. Starting from 1995 with the introduction of the MUC evaluation metric (Vilain et al., 1995) that calculates a score based on

Proceedings of the 5th Workshop on Balto-Slavic Natural Language Processing, pages 24–33,
Hissar, Bulgaria, 10–11 September 2015.

the missing/wrong links between the coreference chains according to a minimal amount of such links needed to be added or removed to transform the system response into the key coreference chains. This approach leads to a counter-intuitive result in the case of merging large chains, when keeping the *recall* equal to 100% and dropping the *precision* only by a small amount independent from the size of improperly merged chains. This metric was followed by the B^3 score (Bagga and Baldwin, 1998) developed as an attempt to address some drawbacks of the MUC evaluation metric. In this metric *precision* and *recall* are calculated as an average score for every mention in the text. This metric, unlike MUC, takes into account singletons but is vulnerable to multiple singletons causing *precision* to increase. To overcome the disadvantages of MUC and B^3, Luo (2005) proposed a metric called CEAF. This metric uses an one-to-one mapping between the gold and the system coreference clusters mapping. The most important feature is that this metric can be considered as interpretable—the score reflects a percentage of mentions assigned to the correct clusters. However, it is still sensitive to the singletons and in some cases the correct links can be ignored. One of the latest metrics is BLANC—a metric based on the Rand index for clustering, which was introduced in the original form by Recasens and Hovy (2011). It focuses on the relations between every single pair of mentions—both coreferential and non-coreferential. The final values of *precision*, *recall* and F_1 are calculated as means of respective values for coreferential and non-coreferential links separately. This metric solves the problem of singletons and takes into account the size of the clusters. In the original form BLANC assumes that the mentions in the gold standard data and in the system response are the same. Luo et al. (2014) proposed a modified version of BLANC, called BLANC-SYS, which can handle imperfect mention recognition. This modification also introduced a joint way of scoring the mention detection in conjunction with the coreference resolution.

Twinless Mentions

Simultaneously to the development of the BLANC metric there were several observations made on the problematic nature of the *twinless* mentions[1] occurring due to imperfect mention detection in end-to-end coreference resolution systems. Cai and Strube (2010) addressed this problem for metrics considering only the coreferential relations between mentions. Additionally, they distinguished *twinless* singletons, which are not connected by any coreferential relation.

Evaluation from Applications Perspective

Holen (2013) made some critical observations on the nature of commonly used evaluation metrics, claiming that the loss of information value—an important factor in the perception of coreference resolution—is not addressed good enough in the current evaluation metrics. Some of the issues with different levels of informativeness of mentions were addressed by Chen and Ng (2013). The main idea was to extend the existing metrics with link weights that would reflect the informativeness of certain types of relations. These enhancements provided a more accurate way of scoring coreference results, however, making them less intuitive and harder to interpret. Tuggener (2014) presented an approach that considers coreference results as mention chains and scores every mention according to whether it has a correct direct antecedent. As an extension of this approach he proposed to consider the relations to the closest preceding nouns, e.g., two pronouns are not really useful for higher level applications of coreference resolution. The final proposition was to determine the so-called *anchor mentions* for each key coreference chain and to measure the score as the harmonic mean of the score for detection of these *anchor mentions* and the score for resolving mentions to *anchor mentions* that were found by the system.

2.2 Coreference Resolution for Polish

For Polish there were several approaches to coreference resolution—we took into consideration three tools implementing different approaches to this problem: a rule-based mention-pair system Ruler (Ogrodniczuk and Kopeć, 2011), a machine learning-based mention-pair system Bartek (Kopeć and Ogrodniczuk, 2012) based on the BART framework (Versley et al., 2008) and a machine learning-based entity-mention system IKAR (Broda et al., 2012a). However, these approaches were based on two different definitions of coreference: IKAR considers the coreference as a relation between a mention and a certain named entity. On

[1] A twinless mention is a mention which occurs only in the gold standard data or in the system response.

the other hand, Ruler and Bartek were designed to resolve the coreference relations between any two mentions.

3 IKAR with a Zero-Anaphora Baseline

The task of zero anaphora resolution in Polish was ignored in most of the studies as a non-trivial problem. To be able to fully compare these algorithms we needed first to implement a method for zero-anaphora resolution in IKAR. We made an approach to prepare a zero-anaphora resolution baseline based on the previous work made in IKAR. The main motivation for this baseline approach is the fact that, as stated by Kaczmarek and Marcińczuk (2015), Polish zero subjects carry at least the same amount of grammatical information as pronouns (gender, number and person), so we can approach the problem of zero-anaphora similarly to the pronoun coreference.

3.1 IKAR Approach to Coreference Resolution

In the current approach IKAR divides the coreference resolution problem into four subcategories of coreferential relations, each pointing to a named entity, but originating from different types of mentions, namely: named entities, agreed noun phrases, personal pronouns and zero subjects. The coreference resolution mechanism for each type (except zero subjects) was originally implemented in IKAR as a C4.5 decision tree classifier[2] (Quinlan, 1993) utilizing different sets of features. The coreference is resolved in entity-mention manner, where discourse entities are introduced by named entities, what means that for each mention we perform a binary classification of pairs consisting of the considered mention and a preceding named entity. In the final step the relations are disambiguated to avoid assigning one mention to many different entities. The disambiguation is based on the number of mentions assigned to given entity and on the distance to the mention.

3.2 Naïve Zero-Anaphora in IKAR

The classifier for recognition of pronoun and zero-anaphora links uses the *pronounlink* features which take into consideration the grammatical agreement (person, number, gender) and consider either a direct coreference relation from the pronoun/zero subject to a named entity or a coreference relation to an agreed phrase that is semantically similar to the named entity. This semantic similarity is calculated using a wordnet[3] distance between the phrase's head and a synset inferred from the type of named entity.

4 PARENT Metric

To address the problem with non-intuitive results from an information extraction perspective, we propose a supplementary measure called PARENT (Performance of Anaphora Resolution to ENTities) that will reflect the amount of correct information returned by a coreference resolution system.

4.1 Defining and Referring Mentions

For the purpose of our scoring metric we introduce concepts of *defining* and *referring* mentions. The *defining* mentions are mentions which we consider as self-defining, i.e., carrying enough information to be identified as real-world objects. The *referring* mentions are those mentions which do not hold this property. All mentions in a document can be divided into two disjoint subsets: *defining* mentions and *non-defining* mentions.

$$M_{all} = M_{defining} \cup M_{non\text{-}defining}$$

$$M_{defining} \cap M_{non\text{-}defining} = \varnothing$$

The *non-defining* mention subset is then defined as a union of *referring* mentions that we are particularly interested in and *ignored* mentions which we do not want to consider in the scoring procedure, for the purpose of scoring different variants of coreference resolution (e.g., pronoun resolution or zero subject coreference resolution in a isolation).

$$M_{non\text{-}defining} = M_{referring} \cup M_{ignored}$$

$$M_{referring} \cap M_{ignored} = \varnothing$$

The split into $M_{defining}$, $M_{referring}$ and $M_{ignored}$ should be made on the basis of some criteria which will be taken as a parameter for the scoring algorithm. The split criteria must be also independent from the gold mention annotation, as it can be applied to the system response as well. For example,

[2]IKAR uses an implementation from the Weka software (Hall et al., 2009).

[3]A wordnet for Polish called Słowosieć (Maziarz et al., 2012) was used.

$$\{\underbrace{\text{Romeo}}_{defining}, \underbrace{\text{he}_1, \ldots \text{he}_n}_{referring}, \underbrace{\text{boy, young man} \ldots}_{ignored}\}$$

(a) Mention split 1 – noun phrases are ignored.

$$\{\underbrace{\text{Romeo}}_{defining}, \underbrace{\text{he}_1, \ldots \text{he}_n, \text{boy, young man} \ldots}_{referring}\}$$

(b) Mention split 2 – no mentions are ignored.

Figure 1: Examples of mentions split.

if one want to evaluate the performance of linking pronouns with proper names, then the *defining* set will contain proper names, the *referring* set will contain pronouns and the *ignored* set will contain the remaining mentions (i.e., noun phrases) (see Figure 1a). In another scenario (see Figure 1b) one may want to evaluate the performance of linking non-proper names with proper names. Then, the *defining* set will contain proper names (as in the first example) and the *referring* set will contain all the remaining mentions (i.e., pronouns, noun phrases). The *ignored* set will remain empty.

4.2 Precision and Recall

The existing cluster-based metrics for coreference evaluation do not make distinction between the *defining* and *referring* mentions. However, as shown in section 1, from the perspective of information extraction the links between *referring* and *defining* mentions are much more important than the links between *referring* mentions only. Taking into account this assumption we will define precision and recall as follows.

First, we want to relate the *recall* to finding a relation between a *referring* mention m_r and at least one *defining* mention m_d from the same gold coreferential cluster. We are interested in connecting the *referring* mentions to the proper discourse entities introduced by the *defining* mentions which are coreferential with the *referring* mentions in the gold standard data. This way we infer additional information about the entities based on the context of the *referring* mentions. For that purpose it is sufficient for each *referring* mention m_r to have a coreferential link with only one m_d from its gold standard cluster.

Second, we want the *precision* to reflect the ambiguity of information extracted from the coreference resolution system response, i.e., for a *referring* mention m_r we want to penalize situations when m_r is assigned to a *defining* mention from a cluster which does not contain the m_r. The applied penalty is meant to be proportional to the distinct number of entities (represented by their *defining* mentions) assigned to each *referring* entity. This will address situations when the system returns non-existent coreferential links between either two *defining* mentions or between a *defining* and a *referring* mention. We also want the *precision* and the *recall* to be interpretable in following way:

- *Precision* should indicate the ratio of correct relations between *referring* mentions and entities to all relations between *referring* mentions and entities returned by the system

- *Recall* should indicate the ratio of correct relations between *referring* mentions and entities to all relations between *referring* mentions and entities that are expected to be found basing on the gold standard data.

4.3 Description

Intuitively this metric works on links between two predefined groups of mentions. Additionally we map all the *defining* mentions occurring in the same gold cluster into one entity about which we will extract information based on the coreferential relations with *referring* mentions. We do not want to penalize missing some of the defining mention links in cases when a gold cluster contains multiple defining mentions and relate the score to ambiguity of found links. We also do not want to consider the correctness of links between the *non-defining* mention pairs, because these relations do not give us any valuable information.

A *true positive* (*tp*) will be a correct relation between a *referring* mention and a *defining* mention from the same gold coreference cluster (redundant relations between the *referring* mention and other *defining* mentions from the same gold cluster will be ignored).

A *false positive* (fp) will be an incorrect relation between a *referring* mention and a *defining* mention from different gold coreference clusters (redundant relations between the *referring* mention and other *defining* mentions from the same gold cluster will be ignored).

A *false negative* (fn) will be a pair of a *referring* mention m_r and a *defining* mention, such that no *defining* mention from the gold coreferential cluster containing m_r are found.

4.4 Formal Definition

Formally we will denote the gold set of clusters as C^{key} and i-th gold cluster C_i^{key} will be defined as follows:

$$C_i^{key} = \{\underbrace{m^i_{d_1} \dots m^i_{d_l}}_{defining}, \underbrace{\underbrace{m^i_{r_1} \dots m^i_{r_n}}_{referring}, \underbrace{m^i_{z_l} \dots m^i_{z_k}}_{ignored}}_{non-defining}\}$$

The gold cluster constitutes an *entity*. We will introduce the notation of equivalence classes with respect to the coreference relations to denote the *entity* that given mention belongs to according to the gold standard clusters:

$$[\![m]\!]^{key} = C_i^{key} \text{ such that } m \in C_i^{key}$$

We will define a gold relation set G as follows:

$$G = \{(m^i_{r_l}, C_i^{key}) | \forall C_i^{key} \in C^{key} \forall m^i_{r_l} \in C_i^{key}$$

This set contains pairs of a *referring* mention and the gold cluster it belongs to, one for each *referring* mention, defining mapping from the mentions to the entities they should indicate.

The system set of clusters will be denoted by C^{sys} and the relation set based on the system response will be defined as follows:

$$S = \{ (m^i_{r_l}, [\![m^i_{d_k}]\!]^{key}) | \forall C_i^{sys} \in C^{sys} \forall m^i_{r_l} \in C_i^{sys} \quad \forall m^i_{d_k} \in C_i^{sys}\}$$

This set contains pairs of a *referring* mention and an *entity* it indicates, represented by the gold clusters containing *defining* mentions that are marked by the system as coreferential with the *referring* mention.

Then we can define *precision* and *recall* as follows:

$$precision = \frac{TP}{TP + FP} = \frac{|G \cap S|}{|S|}$$

$$recall = \frac{TP}{TP + FN} = \frac{|G \cap S|}{|G|}$$

Twinless Mentions

The PARENT metric is also designed to jointly score mention detection with coreference resolution. The problem of *twinless* mentions is treated like Cai and Strube (2010) did—the *twinless* singletons are removed from both gold and system clusters, as we consider only coreferential links between mentions. *Defining* mentions produced by the system, which are not present in the gold data but they were linked with other mentions, are added to the gold data as singletons. This is done because they can produce *false positives* and they must be added to the gold data in order to be included in the evaluation. In other case, those *false positives* would be ignored. The rest of *twinless* non-singleton mentions are left as they are.

4.5 Specific Case Analysis

Here we discuss some specific cases to illustrate the methodology of PARENT scoring:

- a missing link between *defining* mentions—as long as we can correctly connect referring mention with one *defining* mention it is enough, so these missing links should not have negative impact on neither *precision* nor *recall*;
- a missing link between a *referring* mention and a *defining* mention will decrease the *recall* by a unit value;
- an incorrect link between *defining* mentions referring to different entities (clusters) in the gold standard data—this type of error will decrease the *precision* proportionally to the number of entities represented by *defining* mentions in the system cluster and to the number of *referring* mentions.

Given a system response cluster C_j^{sys}, for each *referring* mention m_r in this cluster we will increase the *true positives* value for this cluster (tp_j) by one if there is a *defining mention* in this cluster that is coreferential with m_r in the gold standard data and we will increase the value of *true and false positives* for this cluster ($tp_j + fp_j$) by the number of entities. So the final precision for such cluster will be equal to:

$$\frac{\sum_{m^j_{r_l} \in C_j^{sys}} \mathbb{1}_{\exists m^j_{d_k} \in C_j^{sys}, (m^j_{r_l}, [\![m^j_{d_k}]\!]^{key}) \in G}}{entities_j \times referring_j}$$

where

$$entities_j = |\{[\![m^j_{d_k}]\!]^{key} : \forall m^j_{d_k} \in C_j^{sys}\}|$$

and

$$referring_j = |\{m^j_{r_l} : \forall m^j_{r_l} \in C_j^{sys}\}|$$

- an incorrect link between a *referring* mention and a *defining* mention will decrease *precision* by a value proportional to the number of entities assigned to this mention by the system being scored (analogously to the previous case);

- an one-cluster solution with only gold mentions will be scored with $recall = 100\%$ (all relations between referring mentions and entities are found) and precision inversely proportional to the number of entities, i.e.:

$$precision = \frac{1}{\#entities} = \frac{1}{|C^{key}|}$$

- an one-cluster solution with invented mentions $I = \{i_1, \dots i_m\}$ will have lower precision calculated as:

$$precision = \frac{|R|}{(|R| + |I|) \times |C^{key}|}$$

  where R is a set of all *referring* mentions from the gold clusters;

- an all-singleton solution will have both *precision* and *recall* equal to 0.

4.6 The Problem of Split

The PARENT metric is parametrized with the definitions of *defining* and *referring* mentions. This task may occur to be not as easy as it seems due to the fact that it may not be exactly clear how to conclusively describe mentions that are informative enough. Therefore, we left these definitions to be introduced as a parameter to the PARENT metric to allow an introduction of custom definitions of *defining* and *referring* mentions. That possibility is also important for testing only certain parts of coreference resolution systems.

4.7 A Case Study for Metric Comparison

Here we present a case study, which show the advantage of the PARENT metric over other cluster-based metrics. Figure 2 contains a visualization of a gold standard (Figure 2a) and a response returned by a system (Figure 2b). The squares represent *defining* mentions (which are named entities in this case) and the remaining shapes represent *referring* mentions (the circles—pronouns and diamonds—nouns). The blue, red and green color represents groups of mentions referring to the same entity. The system response contains

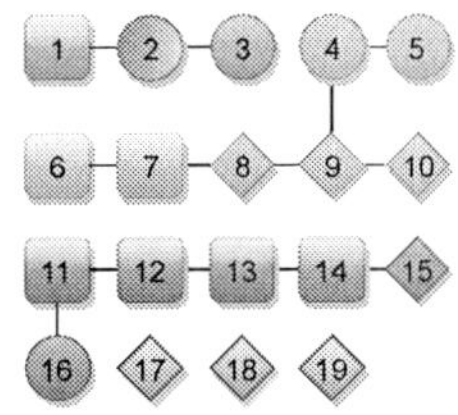

(a) Gold standard

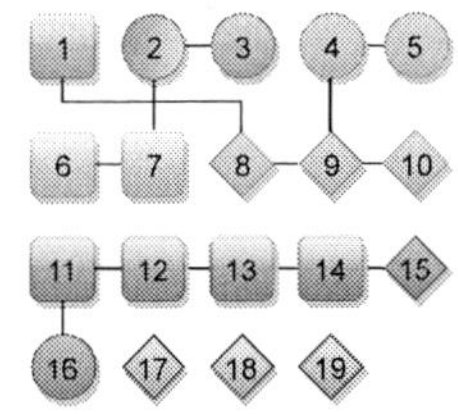

(b) System response.

Figure 2: Examples of mentions split.

incorrect links between $\{2, 3\}$ and $\{6, 7\}$, and $\{4, 5, 8, 9, 10\}$ and $\{1\}$. As can be seen in Table 1 the cluster-based metrics (MUC, B^3, CEAFE, CEAFM, BLANC) scored the response over 70% of F-measure. However, from the perspective of information extraction, the response is not so useful, as most of the *referring* mentions were incorrectly linked with the *defining* mentions—only two (15 and 16) out of nine *referring* mentions were correctly linked with their *defining* mentions. The linguistically aware metrics presented by Chen and Ng (2013) (LMUC, LB^3, LCEAFE, LCEAFM)[4] scored between 30% and 70%—the values are a bit more accurate than their counterparts. According to PARENT the response was scored only 22.2% and the value is much more accurate.

5 Evaluation

We evaluated the following tools for Polish coreference resolution: IKAR, Bartek and Ruler. The results for IKAR were obtained for several different configuration settings. We tested it on the gold standard mentions and on the mentions that were automatically added by simply annotating all the agreed phrases and pronouns, and by using Minos (Kaczmarek and Marcińczuk, 2015) for the detection of zero subject verbs. Bartek and Ruler were tested on the same corpus but with system mentions annotated by their own system for automatic mention annotation, i.e., MentionDetector (Kopeć, 2014). For the evaluation we used 10-fold cross validation on the KPWr corpus (see next section). IKAR was trained for each fold on the training part. For Bartek and Ruler we used the pre-trained models distributed with the tools.

[4] We used the following weights: $w_{nam} = 1$, $w_{nom} = 0$, $w_{pron} = 0$ and $w_{sing} = 10^{-38}$—the weights are set to 0 except for the relations between named entities and other mentions and a small weight of 10^{-38} for singletons. This is the closest configuration to PARENT.

	MUC	B^3	CEAFE	CEAFM	LMUC	LB^3	LCEAFE	LCEAFM	BLANC	PARENT
F_1	80.0%	74.5%	80.8%	78.9%	30.8%	47.4%	66.7%	30.8%	76.6%	22.2%

Table 1: Comparison of different metrics for a sample system response.

5.1 KPWr Corpus

We used a subcorpus of the KPWr corpus (Broda et al., 2012b) version 1.1. It contains 689 documents with a total of 27 452 links (14 141 of them are links other than zero-anaphora). The links were manually annotated between four types of mentions: named entities, agreed nominal phrases, pronouns and zero subjects.

5.2 PARENT Configuration

We used a split, where the set of *defining* mentions contains named entities and the set of *referring* mentions contains nouns, pronouns and zero subjects.

5.3 Impact of Automatic Mention Detection

In the previous study the results of coreference resolution of IKAR were only measured on the gold set of mentions. Here we want to present the impact of the automatic mention detection on the performance of this tool. To simulate the environment with automatically detected mentions we considered as mentions all the hand-annotated agreed noun phrases and all words tagged as personal pronouns using WCRFT tagger (Radziszewski, 2013) and used Minos (Kaczmarek and Marcińczuk, 2015) to annotate potential zero subjects. The results shown in Table 2 indicate a decrease of precision for coreference resolution with automatically detected mentions—particularly significant is the loss of precision for PARENT metric that is several times higher than for BLANC.

5.4 Modifications due to BLANC-SYS

We performed the evaluation using the reference implementation of the coreference scorer (Pradhan et al., 2014). However, due to the fact that we wanted to measure how these systems are capable of recognizing proper coreferential relations even with imperfect mentions detected—for IKAR we mostly recognize much more mentions than are needed and we can omit only some zero subjects—we use a specific evaluation setting. Namely we compare the system results with the gold standard corpus that is modified by adding all system-invented mentions as singletons. This is done due to the fact that in the most recent version of BLANC-SYS metric we are penalized for finding incorrect *non-coreferential* links either between *twinless* singleton mentions in the system response or connecting them to the gold standard mentions. So basically we are penalized for not finding coreference relations where they do not occur. This is due to the fact that BLANC-SYS is intended to jointly score coreference resolution with mention detection. However for information extraction tasks we do not infer any information from singleton mentions and we are basically focused on relations between phrases, so such an approach is not suitable from this perspective.

5.5 PARENT and BLANC Result Comparison

In Table 2 we present results of IKAR with different settings of the mention detection and scores for PARENT and BLANC. We show results for IKAR without zero anaphora baseline (*NonZero*) and with it (*All*). The results for *All* and *NonZero* mention settings are however not directly comparable due to the evaluation setting for *NonZero* mentions that scores only the coreferential relations between named entities, agreed noun phrases and pronouns, excluding zero-anaphora. We can also observe that for each configuration we got much lower scores for PARENT than BLANC. That indicates that although the coreference resolution system can recognize partial coreference clusters quite well it does not necessarily mean that the information extracted from its result is as reliable as the BLANC score would indicate. In a real-world scenario, where the mentions must be automatically recognized beforehand, IKAR does not resolve the links between defining mentions and referring mentions properly. Only 11% of the those links are correct. Also the recall drops by more than half from 66% to only 32%. In the context of information extraction for named entities it is a very low result.

5.6 Algorithm Comparison

In Table 3 we present results of these three systems measured with the BLANC and PARENT metrics. The configuration of PARENT metric was similar

Mentions	Metric	Precision	Recall	F_1
Gold NZ	BLANC	69.02%	71.38%	70.11%
Gold NZ	PARENT	34.94%	30.78%	32.73%
NonZero	BLANC	56.12%	70.18%	58.62%
NonZero	PARENT	7.15%	30.26%	11.57%
Gold All	BLANC	69.94%	67.71%	68.73%
Gold All	PARENT	31.10%	33.95%	32.46%
All	BLANC	57.99%	66.35%	60.39%
All	PARENT	11.09%	32.26%	16.50%

Table 2: IKAR results for different settings.

Algorithm	Mentions	Precision	Recall	F_1
IKAR	NonZero	7.15%	30.26%	11.57%
IKAR	All	11.09%	32.26%	16.50%
Bartek	NonZero	13.49%	5.29%	7.60%
Bartek	All	17.67%	4.89%	7.66%
Ruler	NonZero	14.77%	5.10%	7.59%
Ruler	All	14.07%	3.00%	4.95%

Table 3: Evaluation of the tools for coreference resolution for Polish with the PARENT metric.

to this presented in section 5.2 for the *All* mention setting. For the *NonZero* mention setting we excluded from *referring* mentions all zero-anaphora similarly to what was done for BLANC evaluation in section 5.5. The lower results for Bartek and Ruler can be explained by the fact that these algorithms were not tuned to recognize relations to named entities.

6 Conclusions

We faced the fact that the current state-of-the-art coreference metrics do not take into account various level of mention informativeness. To deal with this problem we introduced a new metric called PARENT[5] that is designed to measure the ability of coreference resolution system to retrieve information about entities in the text. In contrast to the enhanced metrics presented by Chen and Ng (2013), PARENT is not as generic, however, it gives intuitive and interpretable results for given kinds of coreference relations. PARENT is also independent from the number of the correct/incorrect *defining* mentions and from the size of clusters, while these metrics are influenced by size of clusters as well as by counts of the *defining* mentions. In comparison to the approach presented by Tuggener (2014), PARENT is not constrained by the assumption that the coreferential relations must be interpreted either as relations to the closest preceding noun or to a single *anchor mention* for a cluster what makes it more robust in case of imperfect mention detection. PARENT also seems to be more generic by allowing a flexible definition of *defining* and *referring* mentions. The main difference between PARENT and the other metrics is that PARENT treats all *defining* mentions from a *gold* cluster as one object and does not require more than one relation between a *referring* mention and such an object that can be as set of *defining* mentions. Being aware of some drawbacks of PARENT method (e.g., the score does not reflect reliably the coreference resolution quality between defining mentions) we will advise to use it as a complementary score for one of state-of-the-art metrics for scoring coreference systems.

The results for coreference resolution for Polish reported in the literature were optimistic. However, when dealing with an information extraction task, where the linking between defining mentions and referring mentions is much more important than between referring mentions only, the performance drops significantly. The best results we obtained were 17.67% of precision for the Bartek system and 32.26% of recall for IKAR measured using the proposed metric PARENT. This shows, that for information extraction tasks oriented on named entities, like recognition of semantic relations between named entities (Marcińczuk and Ptak, 2012), the performance of coreference resolution systems for Polish needs a significant improvement.

Acknowledgement Work financed by the Polish Ministry of Science and Higher Education, a program in support of scientific units involved in the development of a European research infrastructure for the humanities and social sciences in the scope of the consortia CLARIN ERIC and ESS-ERIC, 2015-2016. One of the authors is receiving Scholarship financed by European Union within European Social Fund.

References

Amit Bagga and Breck Baldwin. 1998. Algorithms for scoring coreference chains. In *In The First International Conference on Language Resources and Evaluation Workshop on Linguistics Coreference*, pages 563–566.

Bartosz Broda, Łukasz Burdka, and Marek Maziarz. 2012a. IKAR: An Improved Kit for Anaphora Resolution for Polish. In Martin Kay and Christian

[5]The PARENT metric evaluation was implemented as a part of Liner2 toolkit (Marcińczuk et al., 2013).

Boitet, editors, *COLING 2012, 24th International Conference on Computational Linguistics, Proceedings of the Conference: Demonstration Papers, 8-15 December 2012, Mumbai, India*, pages 25–32. Indian Institute of Technology Bombay.

Bartosz Broda, Michał Marcińczuk, Marek Maziarz, Adam Radziszewski, and Adam Wardyński. 2012b. KPWr: Towards a Free Corpus of Polish. In Nicoletta Calzolari, Khalid Choukri, Thierry Declerck, Mehmet Uğur Doğan, Bente Maegaard, Joseph Mariani, Jan Odijk, and Stelios Piperidis, editors, *Proceedings of LREC'12*. ELRA.

Jie Cai and Michael Strube. 2010. Evaluation metrics for end-to-end coreference resolution systems. In *Proceedings of the 11th Annual Meeting of the Special Interest Group on Discourse and Dialogue*, SIGDIAL '10, pages 28–36, Stroudsburg, PA, USA. Association for Computational Linguistics.

Chen Chen and Vincent Ng. 2013. Linguistically aware coreference evaluation metrics. In *Sixth International Joint Conference on Natural Language Processing, IJCNLP 2013, Nagoya, Japan, October 14-18, 2013*, pages 1366–1374.

Mark Hall, Eibe Frank, Geoffrey Holmes, Bernhard Pfahringer, Peter Reutemann, and Ian H. Witten. 2009. The weka data mining software: An update. *SIGKDD Explor. Newsl.*, 11(1):10–18, November.

Gordana Ilic Holen. 2013. Critical reflections on evaluation practices in coreference resolution. In Lucy Vanderwende, Hal Daumé III, and Katrin Kirchhoff, editors, *HLT-NAACL*, pages 1–7. The Association for Computational Linguistics.

Adam Kaczmarek and Michał Marcińczuk. 2015. Heuristic algorihtm for zero subject detection in Polish (to be published). In *Text, Speech and Dialogue*, Lecture Notes in Artificial Intelligence. Springer Berlin / Heidelberg.

Mateusz Kopeć and Maciej Ogrodniczuk. 2012. Creating a Coreference Resolution System for Polish. In *Proceedings of the Eighth International Conference on Language Resources and Evaluation, LREC 2012*, pages 192–195, Istanbul, Turkey. ELRA.

Mateusz Kopeć. 2014. Zero subject detection for Polish. In *Proceedings of the 14th Conference of the European Chapter of the Association for Computational Linguistics, volume 2: Short Papers*, pages 221–225, Gothenburg, Sweden. Association for Computational Linguistics.

Xiaoqiang Luo, Sameer Pradhan, Marta Recasens, and Eduard H. Hovy. 2014. An extension of BLANC to system mentions. In *Proceedings of the 52nd Annual Meeting of the Association for Computational Linguistics, ACL 2014, June 22-27, 2014, Baltimore, MD, USA, Volume 2: Short Papers*, pages 24–29.

Xiaoqiang Luo. 2005. On coreference resolution performance metrics. In *In Proc. of HLT/EMNLP*, pages 25–32. URL.

Michał Marcińczuk, Jan Kocoń, and Maciej Janicki. 2013. Liner2—A Customizable Framework for Proper Names Recognition for Polish. In Robert Bembenik, Łukasz Skonieczny, Henryk Rybiński, Marzena Kryszkiewicz, and Marek Niezgódka, editors, *Intelligent Tools for Building a Scientific Information Platform*, volume 467 of *Studies in Computational Intelligence*, pages 231–253. Springer.

Michał Marcińczuk and Marcin Ptak. 2012. Preliminary Study on Automatic Induction of Rules for Recognition of Semantic Relations between Proper Names in Polish Texts. In Petr Sojka, Aleš Horák, Ivan Kopeček, and Karel Pala, editors, *Text, Speech and Dialogue*, volume 7499 of *Lecture Notes in Computer Science*, pages 264–271. Springer Berlin Heidelberg.

Marek Maziarz, Maciej Piasecki, and Stanisław Szpakowicz. 2012. Approaching plWordNet 2.0. In *Proceedings of the 6th Global Wordnet Conference*, Matsue, Japan, January.

Maciej Ogrodniczuk and Mateusz Kopeć. 2011. Rule-based coreference resolution module for Polish. In *Proceedings of the 8th Discourse Anaphora and Anaphor Resolution Colloquium (DAARC 2011)*, pages 191–200, Faro, Portugal.

Sameer Pradhan, Xiaoqiang Luo, Marta Recasens, Eduard H. Hovy, Vincent Ng, and Michael Strube. 2014. Scoring coreference partitions of predicted mentions: A reference implementation. In *Proceedings of the 52nd Annual Meeting of the Association for Computational Linguistics, ACL 2014, June 22-27, 2014, Baltimore, MD, USA, Volume 2: Short Papers*, pages 30–35.

J. Ross Quinlan. 1993. *C4.5: Programs for Machine Learning*. Morgan Kaufmann Publishers Inc., San Francisco, CA, USA.

Adam Radziszewski. 2013. A tiered CRF tagger for Polish. In H. Rybiński M. Kryszkiewicz M. Niezgódka R. Bembenik, Ł. Skonieczny, editor, *Intelligent Tools for Building a Scientific Information Platform: Advanced Architectures and Solutions*. Springer Verlag.

Marta Recasens and Eduard H. Hovy. 2011. BLANC: implementing the rand index for coreference evaluation. *Natural Language Engineering*, 17(4):485–510.

Don Tuggener. 2014. Coreference resolution evaluation for higher level applications. In *Proceedings of the 14th Conference of the European Chapter of the Association for Computational Linguistics, volume 2: Short Papers*, pages 231–235, Gothenburg, Sweden, April. Association for Computational Linguistics.

Yannick Versley, Simone Paolo Ponzetto, Massimo Poesio, Vladimir Eidelman, Alan Jern, Jason Smith, Xiaofeng Yang, and Alessandro Moschitti. 2008. Bart: A modular toolkit for coreference resolution. In *Proceedings of the 46th Annual Meeting of the Association for Computational Linguistics on Human Language Technologies: Demo Session*, HLT-Demonstrations '08, pages 9–12, Stroudsburg, PA, USA. Association for Computational Linguistics.

Marc Vilain, John Burger, John Aberdeen, Dennis Connolly, and Lynette Hirschman. 1995. A model-theoretic coreference scoring scheme. In *Proceedings of the 6th Conference on Message Understanding*, MUC6 '95, pages 45–52, Stroudsburg, PA, USA. Association for Computational Linguistics.

Open Relation Extraction for Polish: Preliminary Experiments

Jakub Piskorski
Linguistic Engineering Group
Polish Academy of Sciences
Jakub.Piskorski@ipipan.waw.pl

Abstract

This paper presents preliminary experiments on Open Relation Extraction for Polish. In particular, a variant of a prior-art algorithm for open relation extraction for English has been adapted and tested on a set of articles from Polish on-line news. The paper provides initial evaluation results, which constitute the point of departure for in-depth research in this area.

1 Introduction

While traditional Information Extraction (IE) systems are tailored to the extraction of predefined set of target relations (Appelt, 1999), an Open Information Extraction (OIE) system focuses on the extraction of non predefined, domain-independent relations from texts. The main drive behind the emergence of the OIE paradigm comes from the need to scale IE methods to the size and diversity of the Web (Etzioni et al., 2008).

Analogously to traditional IE, OIE systems deploy either machine-learned extraction patterns, hand-crafted heuristics or a combination of both of them. TEXTRUNNER (Etzioni et al., 2008) was the first OIE system based on a ML approach, where the OIE paradigm was introduced. WOE (Wu and Weld, 2010) is an extension of TEXTRUNNER, where the *Wikipedia* corpus was exploited as training data to boost the coverage. (Etzioni et al., 2011; Fader et al., 2011) introduced REVERB, the first linguistically-lightweight OIE system based on heuristics, which initially identifies verb phrases and light verb constructions that express relations, and subsequently extracts the relations' arguments in the left/right context thereof. (Mausam et al., 2012) and (Del Corro and Gemulla, 2013) are examples of hybrid systems that deploy dependency parsing. Relatively little work has been reported on OIE for non-English languages, e.g., (Gamallo et al., 2012) presents an approach based on dependency parsing and provides evaluation figures for non-English languages. An extensive overview of research and open problems in OIE is provided in (Xavier et al., 2015).

This paper reports on preliminary experiments on developing a scalable linguistically lightweight OIE approach to extraction of arbitrary binary relations from Polish texts. We are particularly interested in extraction of relations from on-line news. Although the recently reported OIE techniques for extracting binary relations from English texts are advancing rapidly, they might not be directly applicable to languages such as Polish with various phenomena that complicate both IE and OIE tasks (Przepiórkowski, 2007), e.g., relatively free word order, rich morphology (including complex proper noun declension paradigm), syncretism of forms (i.e., single form may fulfill different grammatical functions: subject/object), zero anaphora and existence of pro-drop pronouns. To our best knowledge, the only work on OIE for Polish has been reported in (Wróblewska and Sydow, 2012), where a dependency parsing-based approach to binary relation extraction has been introduced. The main difference of the aforementioned work vs. ours is that the former focuses solely on the extraction of relations that hold between named entities of certain type, whereas in the presented work we do not introduce such limitations. Secondly, we deliberately intend to approach the OIE problem in an incremental manner, i.e., start explorations with as linguistically-poor methods as possible and identify the phenomena/issues that complicate the task at hand most before elaborating more sophisticated solutions, whereas the work described in (Wróblewska and Sydow, 2012) deploys relatively linguistically sophisticated chain of NLP modules, including a dependency parser, which might prohibit applying it

Proceedings of the 5th Workshop on Balto-Slavic Natural Language Processing, pages 34–39,
Hissar, Bulgaria, 10–11 September 2015.

on Web-scale corpora. Finally, although the evaluation results reported in (Wróblewska and Sydow, 2012) are promising, they only refer to a limited number of preselected relation types (e.g., *'born in*), thus making a direct comparison difficult.

2 Simple Relation Extraction for Polish

In order to start explorations on OIE for Polish we developed SREP (Simple Relation Extractor for Polish) that extracts binary relations from free texts in Polish in a form of triples `(arg1,relation,arg2)`, e.g., (*prezydent Komorowski,spotkał się z,lekarzem*) (president Komorowski, met with, the doctor). SREP is to a large extent a direct adaptation of REVERB (i.e., it borrows the main idea), an open relation extractor for English (Fader et al., 2011). It first identifies candidate relation phrases that satisfy certain syntactic and lexical constraints, and subsequently finds for each such phrase potential NP arguments. In a third (optional) step, a set of generic lexico-syntactic patterns for extracting binary relations is applied to capture specific phenomena and harder-to-tackle constructions in Polish. In case the application of such a pattern covers a larger text span than a text span corresponding to a relation extracted at an earlier stage then the latter is discarded. All identified relation extractions are assigned a confidence score and the ones, for which confidence is higher than a prespecified threshold are returned by the system.

A more detailed description of SREP is given below. In order to create some of the resources described below a *Training Corpus* consisting of ca. 1200 sentences randomly selected from a larger collection of on-line Polish news (*News Corpus*), consisting of 20 MB of text was used.[1].

1. **Pre-processing:** SREP takes as input a sequence of sentences and performs tokenization and morphological analysis thereof. For obtaining part-of-speech information we use *Polimorf* (Woliński et al., 2012), a freely available morphological dictionary for Polish, consisting of circa 6.7 million word forms, including proper names.

2. **Relation Phrase Extraction:** Relation phrase candidates are extracted using a small-scale POS-based regular grammar consisting of 6 patterns, which appeared frequently in the training corpus, e.g., patterns like:

```
1. "nie" V (V)?
2. V (V)? N? "się"? PREP
```

The second pattern covers for instance the phrase *urodził się w* (was born in) or *zawarł umowę z* (made a deal with). In order to eliminate implausible relation phrases a 'stop' list of phrases[2] is used (e.g., it contains the phrase *niż do* - meaning "bow down to" (something) or "than to", where the second interpretation is more prevalent and is not used to express relations. If any pair of matches overlap or are adjacent then they are merged into a single relation phrase. Each extracted relation phrase is associated with a confidence score that depends on the rule that has triggered the extraction and also other parameters, e.g., length of the extraction. For instance, the second pattern above is less reliable than the first one, hence it is associated with a lower confidence. Confidence score for a given pattern has been computed based on the fraction of 'correct' extractions it produced in the training corpus.

3. **Noun Phrase Recognition:** Analogously to Step 2 NPs are extracted subsequently using 8 POS-based patterns, where each pattern is associated with a confidence score, computed in a similar manner as above, e.g., the pattern `(Adj)+ N (Adj)+`[3] is less reliable than `N+`.

4. **Argument Extraction:** For each relation phrase *rel* identified in Step 2, the nearest noun phrase *X* to the left of *rel* is identified, which is neither a pronoun nor WHO-adverb. Analogously, the nearest noun phrase *Y* to the right of *rel* is identified. In case such *X* and *Y* could be found the system returns (*X,rel,Y*) triple as an extraction. Each such extraction is assigned a confidence score, which is the product of the confidence of extracting the constituents of the relation triple.

[1] The news articles were gathered using Europe Media Monitor (*emm.newsbrief.eu*), a multilingual news aggregation engine.

[2] This list consist of circa 400 entries and was created based on frequency analysis of application of the aforementioned grammar on the news corpus.

[3] Adjectives may appear in Polish both on the left and right of a noun in a noun phrase.

5. **Application of Lexico-Syntactic patterns (Optional):** A set of 12 generic lexico-syntactic patterns for extracting binary relations is applied optionally at this stage, many of which are intended to cover either more complex constructions or phenomena typical for Polish.[4] In particular, the patterns rely on previously computed relation phrases in Step 2. Some sample patterns are given below (in a simplified form), where `REL` refers to the relation phrases extracted in Step 2.

```
1. NP-1 REL-1 NP-2, "który" REL-2
   NP-2
    -> (NP-1,REL-1,NP-2)
       (NP-2,REL-2,NP-3)

2. NP-1 "to" NP-2 PREP NP-3
   -> (NP-1,NP-2 PREP,NP-3)

3. PREP NP(GEN)-1 REL NP-2
   -> (NP-2,REL-1 PREP, NP(GEN)-1)

4. NP-1 REL NP-2 ("," or CONJ) REL-2
   NP-3
   -> (NP-1,REL,NP-2)
      (NP-1,REL-2,NP-3)
```

The first pattern extracts two relations from a text fragment that includes a relative clause (starting with the word *który* - which), whereas the second pattern covers relations that are not expressed using verbs[5], e.g., *Oborniki to miasto w Wielkopolsce* (Oborniki is a city in Wielkopolska) is covered by this rule and results in the extraction of (*Oborniki,miasto w,Wielkopolsce*). The third pattern covers a specific construction, in which the relation phrase is not a continuous sequence of tokens, that turns to occur frequently in Polish, e.g., *Do Polski przyjechał prezydent USA* (To Poland has arrived president of USA). Finally, the fourth pattern extracts relations from a particular elliptical construction, e.g., from the sentence *Lech wygrał z Legią i przegrał z Ruchem* (Lech won with Legia and lost to Ruch). Analogously to Step 4, each pattern is assigned a confidence score, which reflects the fraction of correct extractions this pattern triggered on the sentences in the training corpus.

[4]Analogously to Step 2, the patterns for Step 5 were created via identification of the most prevalent constructions in the test corpus.

[5]The word '*to*' is a pronoun (meaning either 'it' or 'this') that can be used to express 'is-a' relation in Polish.

The creation and testing of all underlying linguistic resources mentioned above, i.e., the patterns, took 3-4 days for a single person.

3 Evaluation

Four instances of the algorithm sketched in 2 have been evaluated: SREP (the algorithm without Step 5), SREP-PAT (the algorithm with Step 5), SREP-OV (the algorithm without Step 5, where the text fragments from which relation triples are extracted may overlap, e.g., two relations are extracted from the same text fragment), and SREP-PAT-OV (the algorithm with Step 5, where the text fragments from which relations are extracted may overlap). The rationale of including 'OV' variants was to estimate the number of potentially missed extractions by the base versions of the algorithm.

3.1 Test Corpus

In order to create the Test Corpus 238 sentences (either first or second sentence) from on-line news articles in Polish published during May 2015 were randomly selected using the *Europe Media Monitor*. These sentences cover various domains, including economy, finances, world and local politics, sports, culture and crisis situations. The main motivation behind the selection of initial sentences was due to our particular interest in the extraction of relations related to the main events of the news articles (Tanev et al., 2008). Figure 1 shows the histogram for sentences length in the test corpus. Nearly 50% of the sentences consists of 15 or more tokens which reflects the complexity level.

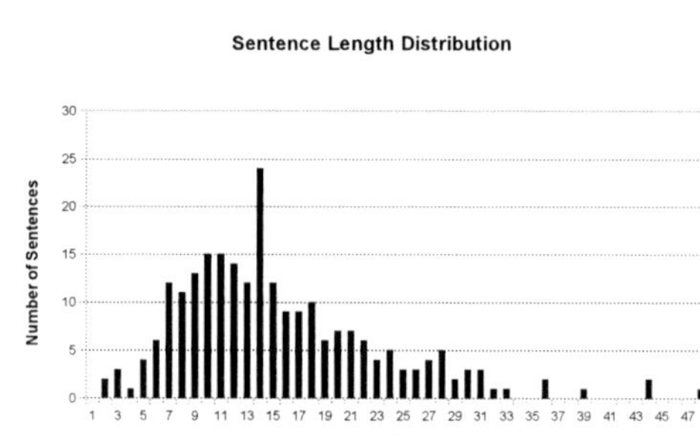

Figure 1: Sentence length distribution.

For each sentence in the test corpus 'to-be-extracted' relation triples were manually created. This task was accomplished by one human annotator. In total 616 relation triples were annotated, i.e., on average there are more than two relations per sentence. It is important to note that n-nary (where $n > 3$) relations (e.g., *X* took place in *Y* at *Z*) were annotated as $n-1$ triples accordingly: (*X,took place in, Y*) and (*X,took place at,Z*). For instance, for the sentence '*Lechia Gdańsk okazała się znacznie lepsza od APOEL-u Nikozja i pokonała go w meczu sparingowym aż 4:1 (1:0)*' (Lechia Gdańsk turned out to be significantly better than APOEL Nicosia and defeated it in a friendly match 4:1 (1:0)) in the test corpus the following two annotations[6] are made:

```
(Lechia Gdańsk,okazała się lepsza od,
 APOEL-u Nikozja)
```

```
(Lechia Gdańsk,pokonała,APOEL-u Nikozja)
```

The system does not lemmatize the arguments, i.e., the arguments in the returned triples are 1:1 copy of the surface forms in the text, e.g., *APOEL-u Nikozja* instead of *APOEL Nikozja*.

3.2 Experiments

Figure 2 shows the precision-recall curves for the *exact relation extraction task*[7] for the four configurations: SREP, SREP-PAT, SREP-OV and SREP-PAT-OV (see 2), computed by varying the confidence threshold. Somewhat unsurprisingly, one can observe that the overall results for exact matching are rather poor, in particular as regards recall. The version of the algorithm that includes the application of generic lexico-syntactic patterns (SREP-PAT) performs better than the version without (SREP) in terms of both recall and precision. Furthermore, one can observe a small boost in recall (at the cost of lowering precision figures) when 'overlapping' was allowed (SREP-PAT-OV), which indicates an area where improvement could be made.

In order to have a more in-depth picture of the error types we have computed precision-recall curves for the subtask of exact relation extraction task, namely, the *relation phrase extraction task*, which are depicted in Figure 3. One can observe significant improvement as regards both precision and recall vs. extracting entire relations, in particular for SREP and SREP-PAT configurations, for which the figures still lag behind the ones reported for relation phrase extraction for English (Fader et al., 2011) but are getting closer.

[6]One corresponding to 'being better' and one to 'winning a match' relation.

[7]Relation phrase and both arguments have to be identical with the corresponding annotation in the test corpus.

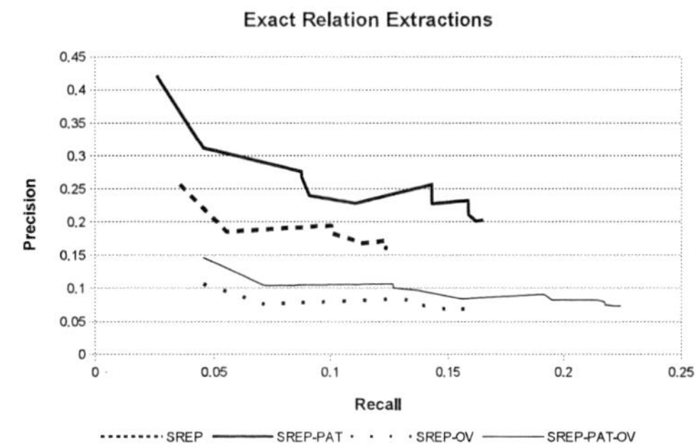

Figure 2: Precision-Recall curves for the exact relation extraction task.

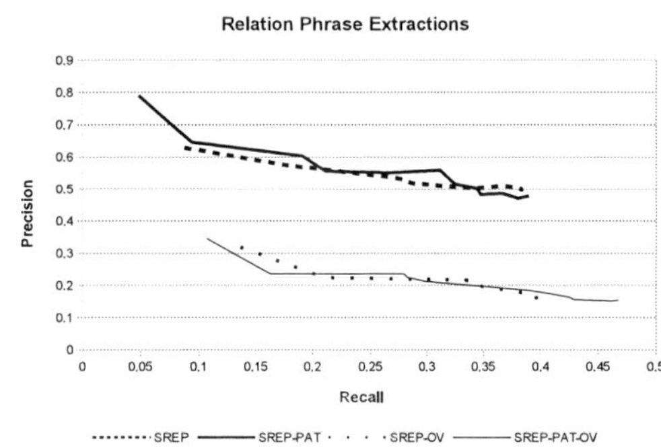

Figure 3: Precision-Recall curves for the relation phrase extraction task.

One can also conclude from Figure 3 that a significant number of errors stems from non correct extraction of the arguments of a relation. To study the problem more thoroughly we also computed the precision-recall curves for the *fuzzy relation extraction task*, in which an extracted triple (*X,rel,Y*) is considered to be correct if *rel* is identical with the corresponding value in the test corpus, whereas *X* and *Y* are similar to the corresponding values in the test corpus, i.e., the string distance between the extracted values and the correct ones in the test corpus is relatively small. For the purpose of computing string distance we used the *longest common substrings* distance metric (Navarro, 2001). Figure 4 presents the precision-recall curves for the fuzzy extraction task, where SREP-PAT-FUZZY-2 curve corresponds to a variant of fuzzy matching, in which relation phrase may also slightly differ from the relation phrase in the test corpus. Although both precision and recall figures are higher vs. figures for exact relation matching, there is an indication (cf. Figure 3) that there is still a fraction of extracted relations for which the extraction of at least one of the arguments entirely failed, i.e., the error is not related to mismatching left/right boundary of the NP representing the argument.

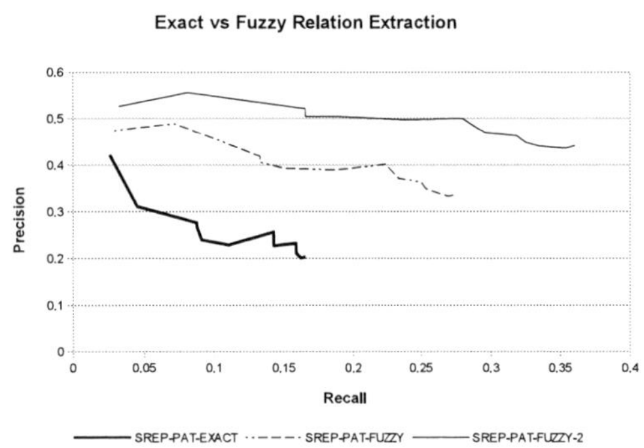

Figure 4: Fuzzy vs. exact relation extraction.

The analysis of the errors for the SPAT-PAT-FUZZY-2 configuration (i.e., errors that go beyond simple mismatching of the left/right boundaries of the text pieces that are to be extracted (both arguments and relation phrases)), revealed that: 34.8% of the errors are related to the extraction of triples that do not represent relations at all; 23.3% of the errors are due to the failure of extracting the first argument correctly (subject of the predicate); 14.0% of the errors are due to extracting *arg1* as *arg2* and vice versa; 7.0% of errors constitute errors, in which *arg2* is wrongly extracted; whereas remaining errors cover issues related to more significant mismatch of left/right margin of *arg1*, *arg2* or the relation phrase itself.

The main cause of missed relations was due to, i.a.,: (a) relation phrase not being present in the text between arguments (36.7%); (b) non-contiguous relation phrase structure (28.3%)[8]; (c) non-matching of POS-based patterns for detection of relation phrases (10.4%); and (d) non handling of constructions, in which arguments of the relations are "embraced" in verbs (8.9%)[9].

[8] Although some of the patterns in Step 5 of the algorithm do cover such cases.

[9] Polish is a null-subject language. No mechanism for detecting null-subjects was used.

4 Conclusions and Outlook

We presented initial experiments on developing a linguistically-lightweight tool for open relation extraction for Polish that is an adaptation of an existing approach to open relation extraction for English. An evaluation carried out on a small set of sentences randomly extracted from Polish online news and a coarse-grained error analysis revealed that: (a) precision/recall figures for relation phrase extraction are promising, although a significant part of errors is due to extracting triples that do not represent any relations (ca. 35%), (b) performance of the extraction of relation arguments needs to be significantly improved as this is the main cause of errors, although, the observed errors did not result only from incorrect NP boundary detection[10], but also due to errors of different nature, e.g., extracting *arg1* as *arg2* and vice versa (14%).

We believe that the work in progress reported in this paper constitutes useful source of knowledge for researchers aiming at working on OIE for Slavic languages. In particular, the linguistically-poor approach to open relation extraction and the accompanying performance figures presented here could serve as a baseline to use against which to compare more sophisticated solutions.

Apart from improving the overall approach and fine-tuning the underlying resources, future work could possibly encompass integration of a mechanism to: (a) aid detecting argument boundaries, e.g., as the one in (Etzioni et al., 2011) and (b) decompose sentence into parts that belong together (Bast and Haussmann, 2013), but without deploying linguistically sophisticated tools, e.g., dependency parsers, in case one is interested in developing a Web-scale solution. Most likely, some of the identified problems could be tackled through the deployment of additional linguistic processing modules for Polish, e.g., a named-entity recognition component (Savary and Piskorski, 2011) could be used to improve NP boundary detection, while deployment of even a rudimentary co-reference resolution mechanism (Broda et al., 2012) could potentially help to handle zero anaphora to increase the recall. Finally, instead of relying on full-form lexica for computing POS information, full-fledged POS taggers could be deployed (Piasecki, 2007; Acedański, 2010; Radziszewski, 2013).

[10] It constitutes one of the core problems while developing IE solutions for Polish.

Acknowledgments

We are indebted to Hristo Tanev from the Joint Research Centre of the European Commission, who provided the corpus of news articles in Polish.

References

Szymon Acedański. 2010. A morphosyntactic Brill tagger for inflectional languages. In Hrafn Loftsson, Eiríkur Rögnvaldsson, and Sigrún Helgadóttir, editors, *IceTAL*, volume 6233 of *Lecture Notes in Computer Science*, pages 3–14.

Douglas E. Appelt. 1999. Introduction to information extraction. *AI Commun.*, 12(3):161–172.

Hannah Bast and Elmar Haussmann. 2013. Open information extraction via contextual sentence decomposition. In *Proceedings of ICSC'13*, pages 154–159.

Bartosz Broda, Łukasz Burdka, and Marek Maziarz. 2012. Ikar: An improved kit for anaphora resolution for Polish. In Martin Kay and Christian Boitet, editors, *COLING 2012, 24th International Conference on Computational Linguistics, Proceedings of the Conference: Demonstration Papers*, pages 25–32.

Luciano Del Corro and Rainer Gemulla. 2013. Clausie: Clause-based open information extraction. In *Proceedings of the 22nd International Conference on World Wide Web*, WWW '13, pages 355–366.

Oren Etzioni, Michele Banko, Stephen Soderland, and Daniel S. Weld. 2008. Open information extraction from the web. *Commun. ACM*, 51(12):68–74, December.

Oren Etzioni, Anthony Fader, Janara Christensen, Stephen Soderland, and Mausam Mausam. 2011. Open information extraction: The second generation. In *Proceedings of the Twenty-Second International Joint Conference on Artificial Intelligence - Volume Volume One*, IJCAI'11, pages 3–10.

Anthony Fader, Stephen Soderland, and Oren Etzioni. 2011. Identifying relations for open information extraction. In *Proceedings of the Conference on Empirical Methods in Natural Language Processing*, EMNLP '11, pages 1535–1545, Stroudsburg, PA, USA.

Pablo Gamallo, Marcos Garcia, and Santiago Fernández-Lanza. 2012. Dependency-based open information extraction. In *Proceedings of the Joint Workshop on Unsupervised and Semi-Supervised Learning in NLP*, ROBUS-UNSUP '12, pages 10–18.

Mausam, Michael Schmitz, Robert Bart, Stephen Soderland, and Oren Etzioni. 2012. Open language learning for information extraction. In *Proceedings of the 2012 Joint Conference on Empirical Methods in Natural Language Processing and Computational Natural Language Learning*, EMNLP-CoNLL '12, pages 523–534.

Gonzalo Navarro. 2001. A guided tour to approximate string matching. *ACM Comput. Surv.*, 33(1):31–88.

Maciej Piasecki. 2007. Polish tagger TaKIPI: Rule based construction and optimisation. *Task Quarterly*, 11(1–2):151–167.

Adam Przepiórkowski. 2007. Slavonic information extraction and partial parsing. In *Proceedings of the Workshop on Balto-Slavonic Natural Language Processing: Information Extraction and Enabling Technologies*, ACL 2007, pages 1–10.

Adam Radziszewski. 2013. A tiered CRF tagger for Polish. In H. Rybiński M. Kryszkiewicz M. Niezgódka R. Bembenik, Ł. Skonieczny, editor, *Intelligent Tools for Building a Scientific Information Platform: Advanced Architectures and Solutions*. Springer Verlag.

Agata Savary and Jakub Piskorski. 2011. Language resources for named entity annotation in the national corpus of Polish. *Control and Cybernetics*, 40(2):361–391.

Hristo Tanev, Jakub Piskorski, and Martin Atkinson. 2008. Real-time news event extraction for global crisis monitoring. In *Proceedings of the 13th International Conference on Natural Language and Information Systems: Applications of Natural Language to Information Systems*, NLDB '08, pages 207–218.

Marcin Woliński, Marcin Miłkowski, Maciej Ogrodniczuk, and Adam Przepiórkowski. 2012. Polimorf: a (not so) new open morphological dictionary for Polish. In Nicoletta Calzolari (Conference Chair), Khalid Choukri, Thierry Declerck, Mehmet Ugur Dogan, Bente Maegaard, Joseph Mariani, Asuncion Moreno, Jan Odijk, and Stelios Piperidis, editors, *Proceedings of the Eight International Conference on Language Resources and Evaluation (LREC'12)*, pages 860–864, Istanbul, Turkey.

Alina Wróblewska and Marcin Sydow. 2012. DEBORA: dependency-based method for extracting entity-relationship triples from open-domain texts in Polish. In *Foundations of Intelligent Systems - 20th International Synposium (ISMIS) 2012, Macau, China, December 4-7, 2012, Proceedings*, pages 155–161.

Fei Wu and Daniel S. Weld. 2010. Open information extraction using Wikipedia. In *Proceedings of the 48th Annual Meeting of the Association for Computational Linguistics*, ACL '10, pages 118–127.

Clarissa Castellã Xavier, Vera Lúcia Strube de Lima, and Marlo Souza. 2015. Open information extraction based on lexical semantics. *Journal of the Brazilian Computer Society*, 21(4).

Regional Linguistic Data Initiative (ReLDI)

Tanja Samardžić
Corpus Lab
URPP Language and Space
University of Zurich
tanja.samardzic@uzh.ch

Nikola Ljubešić
Dept. of Information and Communications Sciences
Faculty of Humanities and Social Sciences
University of Zagreb
nljubesi@ffzg.hr

Maja Miličević
Dept. of General Linguistics
Faculty of Philology
University of Belgrade
m.milicevic@fil.bg.ac.rs

1 Introduction

Regional Linguistic Data Initiative is a two-year institutional partnership between research units in Switzerland, Serbia and Croatia, funded by the Swiss National Science Foundation grant No. 160501.[1] The partners in the project are the authors of this article. The goal of the partnership is two-fold. First, we will collect and distribute various kinds of linguistic data and tools to support empirical research on Croatian and Serbian. Second, we will organise didactic activities and establish a regional community of researches who will use these data and tools in their research and teaching. In this paper, we describe the key components of the partnership.

2 The Infrastructure

The collected data and tools are mostly managed through the infrastructure at the University of Zurich. In collaboration with the S3IT support service, we have set up a virtual server running most of the software used in the project:

- WordPress for the main project website / access point for data and tools
- WebAnno for collaborative manual annotation of language corpora
- NoSketch Engine for searching corpora
- R and Python for data processing
- EdX for online courses

We also use a public GitHub repository to share the source code of specialised NLP tools and the related documentation.

3 Online Content

We collect and distribute two main kinds of data and tools: a natural language processing set and an experimental set. Both sets of resources are associated with courses and tutorials.

[1] http://p3.snf.ch/project-160501

3.1 NLP Resources and Tools

The natural language processing set consists of Croatian and Serbian corpora, morphological dictionaries and processing tools. While such resources and tools already exist for both languages (Vitas et al., 2003; Agić et al., 2008), they are mostly inaccessible to researches outside the groups that develop them. Our aim is to compile and distribute resources that will be available to all interested researches.

Corpora include smaller manually annotated samples[2] and large automatically annotated corpora (Ljubešić and Klubička, 2014); annotation will be improved and enriched in the course of the project. Free existing morphological dictionaries[3] are extended inside the project in a semi-automated fashion (Ljubešić et al., in press). Tools currently include a state-of-the-art part-of-speech tagger and lemmatiser reaching a new best performance for both languages (~91% for full morphosyntactic annotation and ~97% for lemmatisation). Development of tools for other kinds of analysis (dependency syntax, semantic role labelling) is planned for the remainder of the project. In addition to the standard tools, we provide a set of scripts for extracting corpus data commonly needed for quantitative linguistic analysis (e.g., for extracting and comparing frequency lists), and scripts for format conversion and file handling. Special emphasis is placed on detailed documentation of all resources.

The presented resources and tools for Croatian are currently more developed than those for Serbian. We take advantage of the large structural and lexical overlap between the two languages to develop Serbian resources starting from the existing Croatian ones.

[2] https://github.com/ffnlp/sethr

[3] https://svn.code.sf.net/p/apertium/svn/languages/apertium-hbs/

Proceedings of the 5th Workshop on Balto-Slavic Natural Language Processing, pages 40–42,
Hissar, Bulgaria, 10–11 September 2015.

3.2 Linguistic Experimental Data

Another important empirical trend in language science concerns experimental research. Linguists increasingly rely on sampling and statistical processing of human judgements about and their reactions to linguistic phenomena (acceptability judgements, reading times, etc.; see e.g., Kraš and Miličević (in press)). Currently, such empirical data tend to be used only within the studies for which they are collected. Through our partnership, experimental data for Croatian and Serbian will be collected and their wider distribution and reuse encouraged. Both instruments (stimuli lists) and results will be included. Papers published based on the given stimuli and results will serve as documentation. Similar initiatives are still rare in linguistics (but see Marsden and Mackey (2014) for instruments in second language acquisition research), so our work in this domain is largely pioneering even beyond the regional context.

3.3 Online Courses and Tutorials

One of the major obstacles to a wider use of both corpus and experimental linguistic data is a lack of skills required for obtaining and analysing them. Despite the growing demand, experimental design, data manipulation and statistical analysis are not yet covered in standard linguistic curricula. An important part of our initiative is thus devoted to online courses and tutorials.

The educational component of the project is intended to equip the interested researchers with the skills needed to fully exploit the resources shared through our initiative. The courses are based on the current teaching activities of the three partners. They cover issues in three main domains:

- Methodological: general principles of experimental design, corpus-based studies, statistical analysis, basics of machine learning
- Theoretical: the role of data in language science, corpus annotation as a form of linguistic analysis
- Technical: data processing with R and Python, data visualisation, use of annotation tools and other NLP resources

All courses will include exercises in which participants will have an opportunity to use the data and tools collected within the project. The courses will emphasise the points in common between the analysis of corpus and experimental data.

4 Activities in the Region

The work on creating a regional research community will be centred around four three-day workshops, two in Belgrade and two in Zagreb, which are planned for the second project year. The targeted participants are graduate students and researchers at universities and institutes, joined by professionals from companies that work with linguistic data.

All four workshops will be composed of invited talks, tutorials given by the project partners (based on the online courses), and a range of activities geared towards encouraging exchange and networking between the participants. Each workshop will have two invited speakers – internationally recognised experts in linguistics or NLP who have worked on Croatian and/or Serbian. Tutorials will have the form of live classes based on the online materials, with hands-on sessions and practical exercises. Exchange and networking will take place during panel discussion and social events. To facilitate participant mobility within the region, we will offer a number of small grants covering travel and accommodation costs.

Different activities will be undertaken to advertise the workshops, promoting at the same time the project goals: the project website (currently under construction), local media, social media, and presentations at various academic events.

5 Expected Outcomes

The partnership is expected to result in a community of researchers working with linguistic data in a shared empirical framework, exchanging ideas, and adhering to common research quality standards. Some of the contacts established through the initiative are expected to result in research collaborations that will extend beyond the duration of the partnership; these collaborations should bring about new research ideas and new projects.

The data and training provided through the initiative are expected to increase the competitiveness of researchers from the region in the international context. The initiative will also help researches contribute to the study of language beyond their specific subject languages.

Finally, Regional Linguistic Data Initiative is expected to help establishing contacts between researchers and professionals in the domain of language technology, identifying common interests and potential for collaboration.

References

Željko Agić, Marko Tadić, and Zdravko Dovedan. 2008. Improving part-of-speech tagging accuracy for Croatian by morphological analysis. *Informatica*, 32(4):445–451.

Tihana Kraš and Maja Miličević. in press. *Eksperimentalne metode u istraživanjima usvajanja drugoga jezika*. Filozofski fakultet, Rijeka.

Nikola Ljubešić and Filip Klubička. 2014. {bs,hr,sr}WaC – web corpora of Bosnian, Croatian and Serbian. In *Proceedings of the 9th Web as Corpus Workshop (WaC-9)*, pages 29–35, Gothenburg, Sweden. Association for Computational Linguistics.

Nikola Ljubešić, Miquel Esplà-Gomis, Filip Klubička, and Nives Mikelić Preradović. in press. Predicting inflectional paradigms and lemmata of unknown words for semi-automatic expansion of morphological lexicons. In *Proceedings of Recent Advances in Natural Language Processing*, Hissar, Bulgaria.

Emma Marsden and Alison Mackey. 2014. IRIS: A new resource for second language research. *Linguistic Approaches to Bilingualism*, (4):125–130.

Duško Vitas, Cvetana Krstev, Ivan Obradović, Ljubomir Popović, and Gordana Pavlović-Lažetić. 2003. An overview of resources and basic tools for processing of Serbian written texts. In *Proceedings of the Workshop on Balkan Language Resources, 1st Balkan Conference in Informatics*, pages 97–104, Thessaloniki, Greece.

CoCoCo: Online Extraction of Russian Multiword Expressions

Mikhail Kopotev[1] **Llorenç Escoter**[2] **Daria Kormacheva**[1]
Matthew Pierce[2] **Lidia Pivovarova**[2] **Roman Yangarber**[2]
[1]University of Helsinki, Department of Modern Languages
[2]University of Helsinki, Department of Computer Science

Abstract

In the CoCoCo project we develop methods to extract multi-word expressions of various kinds—idioms, multi-word lexemes, collocations, and colligations—and to evaluate their linguistic stability in a common, uniform fashion. In this paper we introduce a Web interface, which provides the user with access to these measures, to query Russian-language corpora. Potential users of these tools include language learners, teachers, and linguists.

1 Introduction

We present a system that automatically extracts selectional preferences from a corpus. For a given word, the system finds its selectional preferences, both lexical and grammatical, using algorithms described in (Kopotev et al., 2013; Kormacheva et al., 2014). The system[1] is developed as a part of CoCoCo Project: *Collocations, Colligations, and Corpora*. The system has two important features. First, it allows users to identify selectional preferences, based on a large underlying corpus on-line, in real time, rather than relying on pre-computed lists of multi-word expressions (MWEs). Second, it treats MWEs of various kinds—idioms, multi-word lexemes, collocations and colligations—in a uniform fashion, returning MWEs of all these types in response to a given query.

These features make the system useful for studying a wide variety of linguistic phenomena, depending on the queries formulated by users. For example, in response to a query such as "preposition plus any following word," the system may produce on output a list of nominal *cases* that can be used with (are governed by) the preposition;

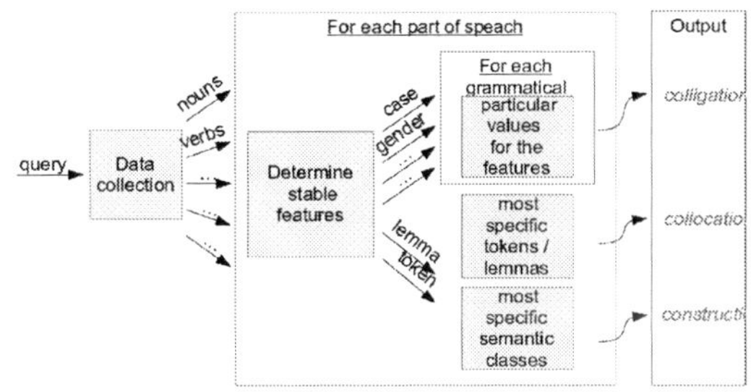

Figure 1: System overview.

or a list of most stable phrases with this preposition; or both. The list may contain idioms or collocations that a learner must memorise by rote. The quality of the algorithm is: F-measure 92% for the grammatical preferences task (Kopotev et al., 2013), average precision 24.25% for the lexical preferences though it depends on the queries: for some queries precision is much higher, up to 75% (Kormacheva et al., 2014). An expert linguist may use the system, e.g., to find patterns of use of the so-called "second genitive" case.[2] All queries are processed using the same algorithm; there is no difference between these use-cases in terms of implementation. The system currently works with Russian-language data, but in principle the algorithms and the user interface (UI) can be applied to other typologically similar languages.

From the theoretical perspective, we follow the recent *constructional grammar* approach, where the language is considered as a *constructicon* (Goldberg, 2006), i.e., an inventory of constructions or patterns that predefine both the grammatical and the lexical selectional preferences of words. Distinguishing *collocations*, i.e., "co-occurrences of words" from *colligations*, i.e., "co-occurrence of word forms with grammatical phe-

[1]Accessible at
http://corpussearch.cs.helsinki.fi

[2]This case in many instances syncretizes with the normal ("first") genitive, but in many instances does not—it behaves like the partitive case in some languages (e.g., Finnish).

Proceedings of the 5th Workshop on Balto-Slavic Natural Language Processing, pages 43–45,
Hissar, Bulgaria, 10–11 September 2015.

nomena" (Gries and Divjak, 2009) is not always a simple task. There is no clear distinction between various types of word combinations, since they can be simultaneously a collocation and a colligation—this type of MWE is called *collostruction* in (Stefanowitsch and Gries, 2003). Thus our main focus is to find "the underlying cause" for the frequent co-occurrence of certain words: whether it is due to their morphological categories, or to lexical compatibility, or both.

2 Program Overview

The general overview of the system is shown in Figure 1. The system takes as input a query—an N-gram (currently of length 2–4)—where one of the positions is a sought variable, and all positions may have additional, optional grammatical constraints. The constraints may include certain properties, e.g., part of speech (POS), or case, etc. Thus, the query is a pattern. The aim is to find the most stable lexical and grammatical features that match this pattern.

The algorithm finds all words in the corpus that match the pattern, and first groups them according to their POS. Then, for every POS, the system determines the most stable features, which include grammatical categories (case, gender, etc.), tokens, and lemmas. To find the most stable features we exploit the difference between the distribution of the feature values in the pattern vs. distribution in the corpus overall, using a measure based on Kullback-Leibler Divergence (Kopotev et al., 2013).

Having specified the most stable categories, we compute various frequencies to find particular values for these categories (Kormacheva et al., 2014). In this step, grammatical categories are processed separately from tokens and lemmas, since tokens and lemmas have significantly different distributional properties than grammatical categories. The output of the system are colligations and collocations for a given pattern. The combinations of the pattern with the most stable *semantic* classes (constructions) are currently not included in the current version of the on-line tool.

Currently we use two corpora: a (manually) morphologically disambiguated sub-corpus of the Russian National Corpus (Rakhlina, 2005) and the Russian Internet Corpus (Sharoff and Nivre, 2011). The former contains approximately 6 million tokens; from this corpus it is possible to get

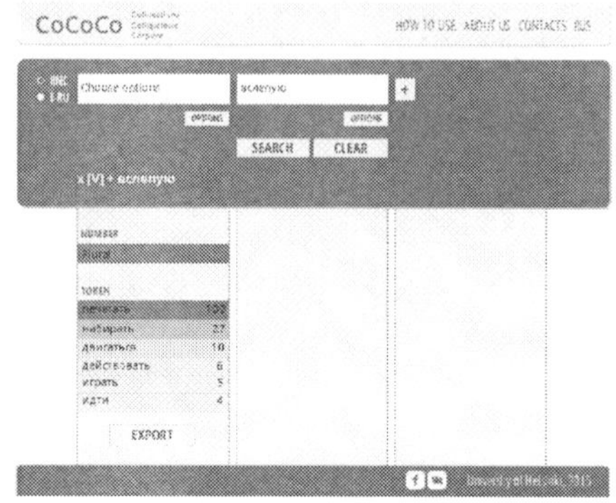

Figure 2: On-line interface.

selectional preferences for the most frequent Russian words. The latter corpus contains almost 150 million tokens and is automatically annotated; this corpus may be used to investigate selectional preferences for less frequent words.

3 User Interface

We have implemented a simple graphical interface (GUI) to construct query patterns and obtain results as ordered lists of grammatical and lexical features, Figure 2. Although we show to the user only several most significant results, the algorithm needs to find in the corpus all possible combinations for a given pattern. Since the corpora are large, these would be impossible to manage using plain-text search. Thus, all bi-grams and tri-grams from a corpus are stored in a MySQL database; for the Russian Internet corpus we removed from the data all bi-grams and trigrams that appear in the corpus only once. We use indexing and database optimisation to be able to process user queries on the fly.

The interface has an "Export" function for downloading the complete system output, i.e., the full list of examples matching the pattern in the corpus, ordered according to the measures developed for this task. This output is organized as a set of files in CSV format; these files can be viewed in a spreadsheet, e.g., by users without advanced computational skills. We expect that the export function will be used by professional linguists, while language learners will find that the GUI provides sufficient information for their needs.

Some other functions, such as, for example, batch processing of a set of queries, are currently developed as a command line script and not available for the users outside the CoCoCo team. We plan to include them into future versions of the interface.

Acknowledgements

The CoCoCo project is partially financed by the BAULT research community (University of Helsinki) and Centre for International Mobility CIMO (Finland). We would like to thank E. Rakhilina, O. Lyashevskaya and S. Sharoff for providing corpora for this project. We thank Ekaterina Nironen for help with Web site design.

References

Adele Goldberg. 2006. *Constructions at work: The nature of generalization in language*. Oxford University Press, USA.

Stefan Th. Gries and Dagmar Divjak. 2009. Behavioral profiles: a corpus-based approach to cognitive semantic analysis. *New Directions in Cognitive Linguistics*, pages 57–75.

Mikhail Kopotev, Lidia Pivovarova, Natalia Kochetkova, and Roman Yangarber. 2013. Automatic detection of stable grammatical features in N-grams. In *9th Workshop on Multiword Expressions (MWE 2013), NAACL HLT 2013*, pages 73–81.

Daria Kormacheva, Lidia Pivovarova, Mihail Kopotev, et al. 2014. Automatic collocation extraction and classification of automatically obtained bigrams. In *Workshop on Computational, Cognitive, and Linguistic Approaches to the Analysis of Complex Words and Collocations (CCLCC 2014)*.

Ekaterina Rakhlina, editor. 2005. *Nacionalnyj korpus russkogo jazyka 2003–2005*.

Serge Sharoff and Joakim Nivre. 2011. The proper place of men and machines in language technology: Processing Russian without any linguistic knowledge. *Komputernaja lingvistika i intellektualnye tekhnologii: Po materialam Mezhdunarodnoj konferencii Dialog(Bekasovo, 25-29 maja 2011)*, pages 591–604.

Anatol Stefanowitsch and Stefan Th. Gries. 2003. Collostructions: Investigating the interaction of words and constructions. *International Journal of Corpus Linguistics*, 8(2):209–243.

E-law Module Supporting Lawyers in the Process of Knowledge Discovery from Legal Documents

Marek Kozłowski
National Information Processing Institute

Maciej Kowalski
National Information Processing Institute

Maciej Kazuła
National Information Processing Institute

{marek.kozlowski,maciej.kowalski,maciej.kazula}@opi.org.pl

Abstract

E-law module is the web application which works mainly as the set of information retrieval and extraction tools dedicated for the lawyers. E-law module consists of following tools: (1) document search engine; (2) context oriented search engine plugin; (3) legal phrase oriented machine translation; (4) document meta-tagger; (5) verdict finder. Machine translation, document meta-tagger and verdict finder tools are available for the general public. Other tools are restricted and are accessible after logging into the module.

1 Introduction

E-law module is being built by the CTI (Center of Information Technologies for the Social Science) consortium, which is granted with the European funds. The main goal of the consortium is to build innovative hardware and software infrastructure for lawyers, sociologists, psychologists and other humanists.

The consortium consists of three members: Cardinal Stefan Wyszyski University in Warsaw, Military Institute of Aviation Medicine, and National Information Processing Institute (OPI).

OPI as a member of the consortium is responsible for delivering software infrastructure, namely three modules: (1) E-law[1] – module supporting lawyers with text mining functionalities e.g., as classifiers, machine translation or search engines, (2) E-survey[2] – module responsible for creating questionnaires in a drag-and-drop wizard mode and sending them to respondents, (3) E-analytics[3] – module supporting social sciences researchers in performing the qualitative analysis for various data (statistical tools, predicative and simulation methods).

E-law module consists of following tools: (1) document search engine (2) context-oriented search engine plugin (3) legal phrase oriented machine translation (4) document meta-tagger (5) verdict finder.

2 Approach

2.1 Document Search Engine

During the project, 2 million legal documents have been downloaded from various, Polish and foreign European, open databases. Only the metadata about documents were collected: title, summary, depositors, date, keywords etc. The search engine retrieves results using Apache Lucene index[4] and well defined filters. For building the Lucene index, different analyzers depending on the language were used. Morfologik[5] analyzer was used for Polish, Standard analyzer was used for other languages.

2.2 Context Oriented Search Engine Plugin

We expanded our search engine with the plugin, which finds all relevant contexts for the query and cluster results (documents) according to the contexts. Most of currently used IR (Information Retrieval) approaches are based on lexico-syntactic analysis of text and they are mainly focused on words occurrences. Two main flaws of the approach are: inability to identify documents using different wordings and lack of context-awareness, which leads to retrieval of unwanted documents. Knowledge of an actual meaning of a polysemous word can improve the quality of the information retrieval process. However, the current generation

[1] `http://eprawo-test.opi.org.pl/`

[2] `http://esurvey-test.opi.org.pl/`

[3] `http://eanalytics-test.opi.org.pl/`

[4] `https://lucene.apache.org`

[5] It provides dictionary driven lemmatization filter and analyzer for the Polish Language, driven by the Morfologik library `https://github.com/morfologik`

Proceedings of the 5th Workshop on Balto-Slavic Natural Language Processing, pages 46–48,
Hissar, Bulgaria, 10–11 September 2015.

of search engines still lack an effective way to address the issue of lexical ambiguity. In a recent study (Sanderson, 2008) conducted using WordNet and Wikipedia as sources of ambiguous words it was reported that around 3% of Web queries and 23% of the most frequent queries are ambiguous. In the previous years, Web clustering engines (Carpineto et al., 2009) have been proposed as a solution to the issue of lexical ambiguity in IR. These systems group search results, by providing a cluster for each specific topic of the input query.

In the module presented, a novel result clustering method has been introduced, which exploits rule association mining in order to create coherent clusters of results concerning different subtopics. The core part is a frequent term sets mining method identifying closed frequent termsets using CHARM algorithm (Zaki and Hsiao, 2002). Discovered frequent termsets are hierarchized and used for building labeled trees of patterns.

2.3 Legal Phrase Oriented Machine Translation

One of the key features of E-law module was to aid law-related people with translating legal phrases from Polish to English and vice-versa.

The created translation system uses parallel bilingual data (Polish and English). The total amount of Polish-English data is approximately 42.000.000 pairs of words, phrases, sentences and whole documents (different granularity), incorporated from sources e.g., EUPARL, TED, CURIA, EURLEX.

The process starts from the data alignment based on the PoS oriented floating window of the correspondent block of text. Next there is processed final translation as follows: (1) Input phrase split by tokenizer into n-grams of the predefined maximum size; (2) Each n-gram is taken as a query to Lucene index and corresponding result text block is narrowed down using data alignment method. (3) Each result block is processed by the tokenizer (point 1) and stored in a sorted list. (4) Translation uses replacement by most frequent n-grams, starting from the longest n-grams.

Presented solution cannot compete against currently working SMT solutions like Joshua and Moses (up to 0.20 higher BLEU than the described solution) (Koehn, 2005; Machado and Hilario, 2014). Although the simplicity and little amount of RAM necessary makes this approach useful.

2.4 Document Meta-Tagger

Document Meta-Tagger is a tool, which assigns the high-level keywords to the text using the external knowledge resources i.e., BabelNet. BabelNet[6] is both a multilingual, encyclopedic dictionary with lexicographic and encyclopedic coverage of terms and a semantic network, connecting concepts and named entities in a very large network of semantic relations, called Babel synsets. Each BabelNet synset represents a given meaning and contains all the synonyms, which express that meaning in a range of different languages. BabelNet 3.0 covers and is obtained from the automatic integration of Wikipedia, WordNet, Wiktionary and Wikidata (Navigli and Ponzetto, 2012). The meta-tagger presented works on BabelNet synsets. It performs tokenization as the first step, removing stop-words, lower-casing, lemmatization and PoS tagging. We only persist the noun-phrases, because there are the most informative ones. Next we use the BabelNet API in order to disambiguate phrases. The result of the disambiguation step is the most probable synset. Each synset has it's categories (like Wikipedia categories describing articles). Within the text, all synsets are gathered and the most frequent categories of the synsets are retrieved as the meta-tags.

2.5 Verdict Finder

This tool refers to information extraction(IE). IE deals with unstructured or semi-structured machine-readable documents. The most popular tasks in IE are: named entity recognition, coreference and relationship identification, table extraction or the terminology extraction.

In the legal judgments we are interested in extracting article's legal numbers, which were used as the law references.

The IE is performed as follows: (1) Judgments processing using Apache Tika. (2) Article's legal numbers extraction using regular expressions, which come from the retrieved content files.

For each document the vector of legal article's numbers is build. Such vector representation is used in order to find similar verdicts. Similarity between vectors is measured by the Jaccard metric. The 10 most similar ones are returned as the potentially similar judgments.

[6] http://babelnet.org

References

Mark Sanderson. 2008. Ambiguous queries: test collections need more sense. *Proceedings of SIGIR*, pages 499–506. ACM, New York.

Claudio Carpineto, Stanislaw Osinski, Giovanni Romano and David Weiss. 2009. A survey of web clustering engines. *ACM Computing Surveys 41(3)*, pages 1–38. ACM, New York.

Mohammed Zaki and Ching Hsiao. 2002. CHARM: An efficient algorithm for closed itemset mining. *Proceedings 2002 SIAM Int. Conf. Data Mining*, pages 457–472. Arlington.

Roberto Navigli and Simone Ponzetto. 2012. The Automatic Construction, Evaluation and Application of a Wide-Coverage Multilingual Semantic Network. *Artificial Intelligence*, pages 217–250.

Maria Jose Machado and Hilario Leal Fontes. 2014. Moses for Mere Mortals. Tutorial. https://github.com/jladcr/Moses-for-Mere-Mortals/blob/master/Tutorial.pdf.

Philipp Koehn. 2005. Europarl: A parallel corpus for statistical machine translation. *MT Summit*, pages 79–86.

Experiments on Active Learning for Croatian Word Sense Disambiguation

Domagoj Alagić and **Jan Šnajder**
Text Analysis and Knowledge Engineering Lab
Faculty of Electrical Engineering and Computing, University of Zagreb
Unska 3, 10000 Zagreb, Croatia
{domagoj.alagic, jan.snajder}@fer.hr

Abstract

Supervised word sense disambiguation (WSD) has been shown to achieve state-of-the-art results but at high annotation costs. Active learning can ameliorate that problem by allowing the model to dynamically choose the most informative word contexts for manual labeling. In this paper we investigate the use of active learning for Croatian WSD. We adopt a lexical sample approach and compile a corresponding sense-annotated dataset on which we evaluate our models. We carry out a detailed investigation of the different active learning setups, and show that labeling as few as 100 instances suffices to reach near-optimal performance.

1 Introduction

Word sense disambiguation (WSD) is the task of computationally determining the meaning of a word in its context (Navigli, 2009). WSD is considered one of the central tasks of natural language processing (NLP). A number of NLP applications can benefit from WSD, most notably machine translation (Carpuat and Wu, 2007), information retrieval (Stokoe et al., 2003), and information extraction (Markert and Nissim, 2007; Hassan et al., 2006; Ciaramita and Altun, 2006). At the same time, WSD is also considered a very difficult task; the difficulty arises from the fact that WSD relies on human knowledge and that it lends itself to different formalizations (e.g., the choice of a sense inventory) (Navigli, 2009).

The two main approaches to WSD are knowledge-based and supervised. Knowledge-based approaches rely on lexical knowledge bases such as WordNet. The drawback of knowledge-based approaches is that the construction of large-scale lexical resources requires a tremendous effort, rendering such approaches particularly cost-ineffective for smaller languages. On the other hand, supervised approaches do not rely on lexical resources and generally outperform knowledge-based approaches (Palmer et al., 2001; Snyder and Palmer, 2004; Pradhan et al., 2007). However, supervised methods instead require a large amount of hand-annotated data, which is also extremely expensive and time-consuming to obtain. Interestingly enough, Ng (1997) estimates that a wide coverage WSD system for English would require a sense-tagged corpus of 3200 words with 1000 instances per word. Assuming human throughput of one instance per minute (Edmonds, 2000), this amounts to an immense effort of 27 man-years.

One way of addressing the lack of manually sense-tagged data is to rely on semi-supervised learning (Abney, 2007), which, along with a smaller set of labeled data, also makes use of a typically much larger set of unlabeled data. A related technique is that of *active learning* (Olsson, 2009; Settles, 2010). However, what differentiates active learning from ordinary semi-supervised learning is that the former requires subsequent manual labeling. The underlying idea is to minimize the annotation effort by dynamically selecting the most informative unlabeled instances, i.e., the most informative contexts of a polysemous word to be manually labeled.

In this paper we address the WSD task for Croatian using active learning (AL). Croatian is an under-resourced language, lacking large-scale lexical resources and sense-annotated corpora. Our ultimate goal is to develop a cost-effective WSD system with a reasonable coverage for the most frequent Croatian words. As a first step towards that goal, in this paper we present a preliminary, small-scale but thorough empirical study using different AL setups. We adopt the lexical sample evaluation setup and evaluate our models on a chosen set of polysemous words. The contribution of our work is two-fold.

Proceedings of the 5th Workshop on Balto-Slavic Natural Language Processing, pages 49–58,
Hissar, Bulgaria, 10–11 September 2015.

First, we present a small sense-annotated dataset – the first such dataset for Croatian – which we also make freely available for research purposes. Secondly, we investigate in detail the performance of various AL models on this dataset and derive preliminary findings and recommendations. Although our focus is on Croatian, we believe our results generalize to other typologically similar (in particular Slavic) languages.

The rest of the paper is organized as follows. In the next section, we give a brief overview of AL-based WSD. In Section 3, we describe the manually sense-annotated dataset for Croatian. In Section 4, we describe the AL-based WSD models, while in Section 5 we present and discuss the experimental results. Lastly, Section 6 concludes the paper and outlines future work.

2 Related Work

WSD is a long-standing problem in NLP. A number of semi-supervised WSD methods have been proposed in the literature, including the use of external sources for the generation of sense-tagged data (McCarthy et al., 2004), 2004), use of bilingual corpora (Li and Li, 2004), label propagation (Niu et al., 2005), and bootstrapping (Mihalcea, 2004; Park et al., 2000).

Focusing on AL approaches to WSD, one of the first attempts is that of Chklovski and Mihalcea (2002). Their Open Mind World Expert system collected sense-annotated data over the web, which were later used for the Senseval-3 English lexical sample task (Mihalcea et al., 2004). The system employs the so-called committee-based sampling: the instances to be labeled are selected based on the disagreement between the labels assigned by two different classifiers.

Chen et al. (2006) experiment with WSD for five frequent English verbs. Unlike Chklovski and Mihalcea, they use uncertainty-based sampling coupled with a maximum entropy learner, and a rich set of topical, collocational, syntactic, and semantic features. Their results show that, given a target accuracy level, AL can reduce the number of training instances by half when compared to labeling randomly selected instances. Their analysis also reveals that careful feature design and generation is necessary to fully leverage the AL potential.

Additionally, a number of studies focus on issues specific to AL for WSD. Zhu and Hovy (2007) consider the class imbalance problem, which is typical for WSD due to skewness in sense distribution. They analyze the effect of resampling techniques and show that bootstrap-based oversampling of underrepresented senses improves classifier performance. Another important issue of AL is the stopping condition. Zhu and Hovy (2007) propose a stopping criterion based on the classifier confidence, Wang et al. (2008) propose a minimum expected error strategy, while Zhu et al. (2008a) propose classifier-change as a stopping criterion. Finally, Zhu et al. (2008b) propose sampling methods for generating a representative initial training set, as well as selective sampling method for alleviating the problem of outliers.

All of the above cited work addresses WSD for English, whereas our work focuses on Croatian. Similar to Chen et al. (2006), we use uncertainty-based sampling but combine it with an SVM model. In contrast to Chen et al. (2006), we opt for simple, readily available features derived from co-occurrences. We study three sampling methods in this work, but leave the issues of stopping criterion and class imbalance for future work.

Croatian is a Slavic language, and WSD for Slavic languages seems not to have received much attention so far. Notable exceptions are (Baś et al., 2008; Broda and Piasecki, 2009) for Polish and (Lyashevskaya et al., 2011) for Russian. WSD for Bulgarian, Czech, Serbian, and Slovene has been considered in a cross-lingual setup by Tufiş et al. (2004) and Ide et al. (2002). Bakarić et al. (2007) analyze the discriminative strength of co-occurring words for WSD of Croatian nouns. Additionally, Karan et al. (2012) consider a problem dual to WSD, namely synonymy detection. To the best of our knowledge, our work is the first reported work on active learning for WSD for a Slavic language.

3 Dataset

In this work we adopt the lexical sample style evaluation, i.e., we select a set of words and sample sentences from a corpus containing these words. We next describe how we compiled and sense-annotated the sample.

3.1 Corpus and Preprocessing

To compile a sense-annotated dataset for our experiments, we sample from a Croatian web corpus hrWaC[1] (Ljubešić and Klubička, 2014), containing 1.9M tokens, annotated with lemma, morphosyntax and dependency syntax tags.

For the sense inventory, we initially adopted the Croatian wordnet (CroWN) compiled by Raffaelli et al. (2008). Although of a limited coverage (10k synsets, compared to 200k synsets of Princeton WordNet), CroWN was a good starting point for word selection and sense definition for this task.

To keep the annotation effort manageable, similarly to (Chen et al., 2006), we decided to limit ourselves to six words: two nouns, two verbs, and two adjectives. We selected these by first compiling a list of polysemous words from CroWN that occur at least 1000 times in hrWaC. We then decided to discard words with more than three senses as our preliminary analysis revealed that CroWN senses of such words are potentially very difficult to differentiate. The problem of sense granularity of wordnets is a well-known issue (Edmonds and Kilgarriff, 2002), and in this study we wanted to avoid the problem by choosing words with as distinct senses as possible.[2] Research on sense granularity in the context of AL is warranted but is beyond the scope of this paper.

The final list of words is as follows: $okvir_N$ (frame), $vatra_N$ (fire), $brusiti_V$ (to rasp), $odlikovati_V$ (to award), lak_A (easy), and $prljav_A$ (dirty). For each of these words, we sampled 500 sentences from hrWaC, yielding a total of 3000 word instances. Note that 500 instances per word is well above the $75+15 \cdot n$ instances recommended by Edmonds and Cotton (2001), where n is the number of senses of the word.

3.2 Sense Annotation

To construct the sense-annotated dataset, we asked 10 annotators to label the senses of the selected words in sampled sentences. Each annotator was given 600 sentences to annotate, with 100 instances of each of the six words. To obtain a more reliable annotation, each instance was double-annotated, and we ensured that there is a uniform distribution across the annotator pairings.

For each word instance, the annotators were given a list of possible word senses (two or three) and an additional "none of the above" (NOTA) option. They were instructed to select a single sense, unless there is no adequate sense listed or the instance is erroneous (incorrect lemmatization or a spelling error). For each sense, we provided a gloss line and usage examples from CroWN.

The annotation guidelines were rather straightforward. In cases when more than a single sense apply, the annotators were asked to choose the one they deem more appropriate. The only issue that we felt deserved additional elaboration was the treatment of polysemous words in semantically opaque contexts (idioms and metaphors). In such contexts, the annotators were asked to choose the literate sense of a word, rather than to consider the idiomatic or metaphoric reading. For example, in sentence *Istarska kuhinja je dijamant koji treba brusiti* (*Istrian cuisine is a diamond that needs to be cut*), the verb *brusiti* (*to cut* in this example) is used in its literate sense (*to rasp*), although the whole phrase *brusiti dijamant* is used in a metaphorical sense, which in this case happens to be somewhat related to the *to hone* sense of *brusiti*.[3]

The total effort for annotating 6000 word instances (including double annotations) was 36 man-hours, i.e., a throughput of 22 seconds per word instance. We note that this is considerably lower than the one-minute-per-instance estimate of Edmonds (2000). One of the possible reasons for this difference might be the biased word selection process, which probably resulted in somewhat easier disambiguation tasks.

3.3 Inter-Annotator Agreement

We use Cohen's kappa to measure the inter-annotator agreement (IAA). We calculate the agreement for each word separately by averaging the agreements for each annotator pair that labeled that word. The per-word IAA is shown in Table 1. The average IAA across the six words is 0.761, which, according to Landis and Koch (1977) is considered a substantial agreement.

Two words that stand out in terms of IAA are *odlikovati* (high IAA) and *prljav* (low IAA). The former has two clearly distinguishable senses. The latter turned out to be problematic as the word is of-

[1] `http://nlp.ffzg.hr/resources/corpora/hrwac/`

[2] We are aware that selecting words with easily distinguishable senses results in a biased sample. However, we note that such a sample does not necessarily need to be *unrealistically* easy. One could argue that senses that are difficult to differentiate are not realistic to begin with, as they are not likely to be of practical interest in real-world NLP applications.

[3] The alternative strategy would be to exclude (ask the annotators to tag as NOTA) all instances with opaque contexts, under the justification that idioms and metaphors require a special treatment. We will investigate this strategy in future work.

Word	κ	Word	κ
okvir$_N$	0.795	*odlikovati*$_V$	**0.978**
vatra$_N$	0.704	*lak*$_A$	0.582
brusiti$_V$	0.816	*prljav*$_A$	0.690

Table 1: Cohen's κ for the six chosen words.

Word	Freq.	# Senses	Sense distr.	NOTA
okvir$_N$	141862	2	381 / 115	4
vatra$_N$	45943	3	244 / 106 / 141	9
brusiti$_V$	1514	3	205 / 262 / 27	7
odlikovati$_V$	15504	2	425 / 75	0
lak$_A$	15424	3	277 / 87 / 113	23
prljav$_A$	14245	2	228 / 187	85

Table 2: Statistics of the gold standard sample.

ten used as part of the idiomatic expression *prljavo rublje* (*dirty laundry*). According to our annotation guidelines, here *prljav* is used in its literal sense (*dirty*), as *dirty laundry* is an idiom (matters embarrassing if made public). Annotators often selected the other, "sordid" meaning of *prljavi*, probably because they felt it is more related to the meaning of the idiom. Another source of disagreement are the named entities *Prljavo kazalište* (a rock band) and *Prljavi Harry* (the movie *Dirty Harry*), in which the intended sense of *prljavo* is questionable.

3.4 Gold Standard Sample

The last step in data annotation was to manually resolve the disagreements and obtain a gold standard sample. While trying to resolve the disagreements, we noticed that a large number of them are systematic – most of the time, one of the two annotators chose the NOTA option. Upon closer inspection, we found that for the most of the six considered words the CroWN sense inventory was arguably incomplete. To overcome this problem, we decided to modify the CroWN sense inventory for the six considered words to get a reasonable sense coverage on our lexical sample. Using this revised sense inventory, we (the authors) resolved all the disagreements (a 6 man-hours effort). The statistics of the 3000-sentences gold standard sample is shown in Table 2. Sense inventory is given in Table 3. We make the dataset freely available.[4]

[4]http://takelab.fer.hr/cro6wsd

okvir (frame)	
#1	An environment to which the situation is related or whose influence it is exposed to.
#2	A structure that supports or contains something.
vatra (fire)	
#1	One of the four fundamental classical elements (along with water, air, and earth) according to Empedocles.
#2	The act of firing weapons or artillery at an enemy.
#3	A heat source for food preparation.
brusiti (to rasp)	
#1	Making something smooth using a file or a rasp.
#2	Gaining skill in something; taking quality, readiness, and specific knowledge and abilities to a high level.
#3	Increasing the level of eagerness/tension/excitement.
odlikovati (to award)	
#1	Having a certain characteristic, trait, feature.
#2	Giving something to someone, especially as a reward for an accomplishment.
lak (easy)	
#1	One that does not require a lot of effort to be carried out or understood.
#2	One that possesses a small physical mass.
#3	One that is not strong or intense.
prljav (dirty)	
#1	One that contains or produces stains or filth.
#2	One that is not morally pure.

Table 3: Sense inventory.

4 Models

4.1 Active Learning Setup

There are a number of different AL strategies; refer to Settles (2010) for a comprehensive overview. We employ the *pool-based strategy* (Lewis and Gale, 1994) using *uncertainty sampling*. This method uses a small set of labeled data L (the seed train set) and a large pool of unlabeled data U. The classifier is first trained on set L. After that, P (the pool size) instances are randomly sampled from U and the classifier is used to predict their labels. Next, from this set at most G (train growth size) instances are selected for which the classifier is the least confident about and an oracle (e.g., a human expert) is queried for their labels. Finally, the newly-labeled instances are added to the training set L and the process is repeated until a stopping criterion is met. The active learning loop is shown in Algorithm 1.

The motivation for the use of a pool is to reduce the computational cost associated with sense label prediction on the entire set of unlabeled instances

Algorithm 1: Active learning loop

L : initial training set
U : pool of unlabeled instances
P : pool sample size
G : train growth size
f : classifier
while *stopping criteria not satisfied* **do**
  $f \leftarrow train(f, L)$;
  $R \leftarrow randomSample(U, P)$
  $predictions \leftarrow predict(f, R)$
  $R \leftarrow sortByUncertainty(R, predictions)$
  $S \leftarrow selectTop(R, G)$
  $S \leftarrow oracleLabel(S)$
  $L \leftarrow L \cup S$
  $U \leftarrow U \setminus S$
end

U. In our experiments, U is relatively small, thus we decide to use the complete set U as the pool, $P = |U|$. This eliminates one source of randomness and allows us to focus on other, in our view, more important AL parameters.

Our experiments are focused on different uncertainty sampling methods. We therefore simulate a perfect oracle by providing the labels from the gold standard sample for each query. Furthermore, we ignore the stopping criterion issue and run the AL algorithm until the complete training set is utilized.

We consider three uncertainty sampling methods, i.e., methods for evaluating the informativeness of an unlabeled instance, as outlined below.

Least confident (LC). Trivially, the most informative instance is the one for which the prediction is the least confident:

$$x^*_{\text{LC}} = \underset{x}{\operatorname{argmax}} \left(1 - P_\theta(\hat{y}|x)\right) \tag{1}$$

where $\hat{y}$ stands for the class label with the highest posterior probability under the model θ.

Minimum margin (MM). An instance for which the difference between the posterior probabilities of two most probable class labels is maximal bears the most information:

$$x^*_{\text{MM}} = \underset{x}{\operatorname{argmin}} \left(P_\theta(\hat{y}_1|x) - P_\theta(\hat{y}_2|x)\right) \tag{2}$$

where $\hat{y}_1$ and $\hat{y}_2$ are the first and second most probable class labels under the model θ.

Maximum entropy (ME). Selects an instance whose vector of posterior class label probabilities has the maximum entropy:

$$x^*_{\text{ME}} = \underset{x}{\operatorname{argmax}} \Big(- \sum_i P_\theta(y_i|x) \log P_\theta(y_i|x)\Big) \tag{3}$$

4.2 Classifier and Features

As the core classifier in AL experiments, we use a linear Support Vector Machine (SVM) implemented in LIBSVM (Chang and Lin, 2011) library. To turn SVM confidence scores into probabilities over classes, we use the method proposed by Platt (1999), also implemented in the same library. Multiclass classification is handled using the *one-vs-one* scheme.

We opt for a simple model with readily available features. The simplest features are word-based context representations: given a sentence in which a polysemous word occurs, we compute its context vector by considering the words it co-occurs with in the sentence. We consider two context representations. First is a simple binary bag-of-words vector (BoW). In our case, the average dimension of a BoW vector is approximately 7000.

The second representation we use is the recently proposed skip-gram model, a neural word embedding method of Mikolov et al. (2013), which has shown to be useful on a series of NLP tasks. To obtain a context vector, we simply add up the skip-gram vectors of all the context words. The advantage of skip-gram representation over BoW is that it generates compact, continuous, and distributed vectors representations such that semantically related words tend to have similar vectors. This not only results in more effective context representations, but also allows for a better generalization, as context vectors of words unseen during training will be similar to vectors of semantically related context words used for training. We build the vectors from hrWaC using the `word2vec`[5] tool. We use 300 dimensions, negative sampling parameter set to 5, minimum frequency set to 100, and no hierarchical softmax.

5 Experimental Results

In this section we describe the AL experiments on our lexical sample dataset. We randomly split the dataset into a training and a test set: for each of the six words, we use 400 instances for training and 100 for testing.

5.1 Supervised Baseline

We compare our AL-based models against their fully supervised counterparts as baselines, i.e., linear SVM classifiers with either BoW or skip-gram context representations, denoted SVM-BoW and

[5]`https://code.google.com/p/word2vec/`

Word	MFS	SVM-BoW	SVM-SG
$okvir_N$	0.53	**0.92**	0.89
$vatra_N$	0.49	**0.91**	0.88
$brusiti_V$	0.53	0.85	**0.86**
$odlikovati_V$	0.85	**0.97**	**0.97**
lak_A	0.55	0.80	**0.81**
$prljav_A$	0.46	0.82	**0.88**
Average:	0.57	**0.88**	**0.88**

Table 4: Supervised models accuracy.

SVM-SG, respectively. In addition, we use the most frequent sense (MFS) as a baseline for the supervised models. Note that MFS has been generally proven to be a very strong baseline for WSD. We optimized the SVM regularization parameter C using 5-fold cross-validation on the training set.

Table 4 shows the results on the test set. Overall, the SVM models perform comparably well and outperform the MFS baseline by a wide margin. The models perform best on *odlikovati*, which was also the word with the highest IAA score (cf. section 3.2). The MFS baseline also performs quite well on this word due to its skewed sense distribution.

5.2 Active Learning Experiments

For AL experiments we use the same train-test split as before. The difference is that, for each word, the initial training set L is a randomly chosen subset of the full training set. In what follows, to obtain robust performance estimates, we run 50 trials of each experiment, each time random sampling anew the set L, and then averaging the results.

AL is governed by a number of parameters: the choice of the sampling method, train growth size G, and the size of the initial training set L. To more clearly show the effectiveness of AL, we set G to 1 and the size of the initial training set to 20, but elaborate on this choice later.

For the C parameter we use the same value as above, i.e., the value optimized using cross-validation on the entire training set. Arguably, this is not a realistic AL setup, as in practice the entire training is not labeled up front. In this work, however, we decided to simplify the setup as we observed that on our dataset the optimal C value is rather stable regardless of the training set size.

Learning curves. The purpose of AL is to reduce the labeling effort, i.e., to achieve a satisfactory level of accuracy with a smaller number of training instances. To analyze the effectiveness of AL WSD on our lexical sample, we compute the learning curves for SVM-BoW and SVM-SG and the three considered uncertainty sampling methods. The baselines are the learning curves obtained using random sampling (RAND). Fig. 1 shows the learning curves and the standard deviation bands.

The first thing we observe is that all uncertainty sampling methods outperform RAND. For example, when the training set reaches 100 instances, AL with uncertainty sampling outperforms RAND by $\sim$2% of accuracy for both SVM-BoW and SVM-SG models. In our view, this performance gain justifies the use of AL WSD on our dataset.

The second thing we observe is that the three uncertainty sampling methods generally perform comparably. However, the least confident (LC) and maximum margin (MM) methods slightly outperform the maximum entropy (ME) method in the 100–150 instances range.

The last thing we observe is that, with uncertainty sampling, labeling as few as 100 out of 400 training instances already gives $\sim$0.94% of maximum accuracy for SVM-BoW, while random sampling requires a training set of twice that size. Moreover, labeling 150 instances gives almost maximum accuracy for SVM-BoW. For SVM-SG, the effect of uncertainty sampling is even more pronounced – with 100 instances we already reach performance equivalent to that on the full training set. We conclude that AL WSD with SVM-SG reduces the number of training instances to 100 without any drop in performance.

Taking into account the previous observations, we decided to use the SVM-SG model and MM uncertainty sampling in subsequent experiments.

Parameter analysis. To investigate the impact of the initial training set size L and the train growth size G, we run a grid search with $L \in \{20, 50, 100\}$ and $G \in \{1, 5, 10\}$. For each pair of parameter values, we carry out 50 AL runs per word, each time using a random sample of size L as the initial training set. We thus obtain a total of 300 runs per parameter pair, which we average to produce corresponding learning curves. We compare the AL WSD performance in terms of the Area Under Learning Curve (ALC), which we define as a sum of classifier accuracy scores across the iterations of the AL algorithm, normalized by the number of iterations.

Table 5 shows the ALC scores for different parameter combinations. Expectedly, the larger the initial training set L, the more information is avail-

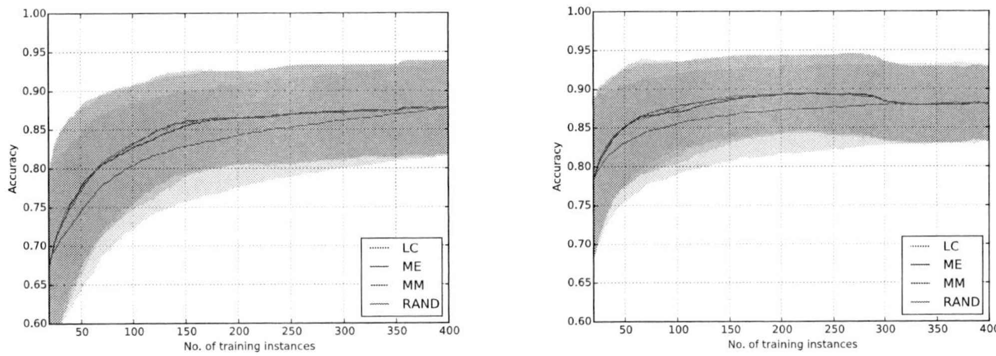

(a)

(b)

Figure 1: Learning curves for (a) SVM-BoW and (b) SVM-SG.

	G		
$\|L\|$	1	5	10
20	0.8794	0.8772	0.8760
50	0.8824	0.8819	0.8810
100	**0.8843**	0.8836	0.8833

Table 5: ALC scores across parameters for SVM-SG with MM sampling.

able to the learning algorithm up front. At the same time, using a train growth size G of one yields better models, as they are able to make more confident predictions on yet unlabeled instances in each iteration of the AL algorithm. Nonetheless, we observe that in our case these two AL parameters do not considerably affect the model performance.

Per word analysis. In the previous analyses we looked at learning curves averaged over the six words in our dataset. For a more detailed analysis, we turn to the learning curves of the individual words, shown in Fig. 2. We plot both the accuracy on the training set and the test set using the MM sampling method, as well as the RAND accuracy on the test set. Note that a large gap between the curves on the training set and test set indicates model overfitting.

The plots reveal that MM outperforms the RAND baseline for all six words. Moreover, the gain is most prominent for *vatra*, *lak*, and *brusiti*. On *odlikovati* the full maximum accuracy can already be reached with as few as 60 training instances. In contrast, the word *prljav* is a problematic one: the learning curve does not seem to get saturated even after 400 instances. This is probably due to the many NOTA labels for that words. The train-test curve gap is the largest for *lak*, suggesting that the model overfits the most on that particular word. We hypothesize that, for some reason, the instances of this word are more noisy than instances of other words. Because disagreements in our dataset have been manually resolved, we think that latent variables are a more likely explanation for the noise than mislabelings. In other words, we believe that for some reason skip-gram contexts are less informative of the senses of the word *lak* than of the other words.

Another interesting observation is that for some words the accuracy rises above that of a model trained on the entire training set of 400 instances, after which it drops and eventually the two accuracy curves converge. This effect is most prominent for *vatra* and *brusiti*, and somewhat less for *okvir* and *lak*. A similar effect has been observed by Chen et al. (2006) on some English verbs, suggesting that the effect can be traced down to model starting to overfit at some point. We think that this hypothesis is plausible, as it is also confirmed by the fact that we observe no drop in the training error. Moreover, we hypothesize that the drop in accuracy is due to the sampling of a sequence of noisy examples from the training set. By the same token as before, we tend to exclude mislabelings as the cause of the noise, but rather attribute the noise to non-informative contexts. The existence of such "bad examples" was hypothesized by Chen et al. (2006), who suggest that that adequate feature selection could solve the problem. We leave a detailed investigation for future work.

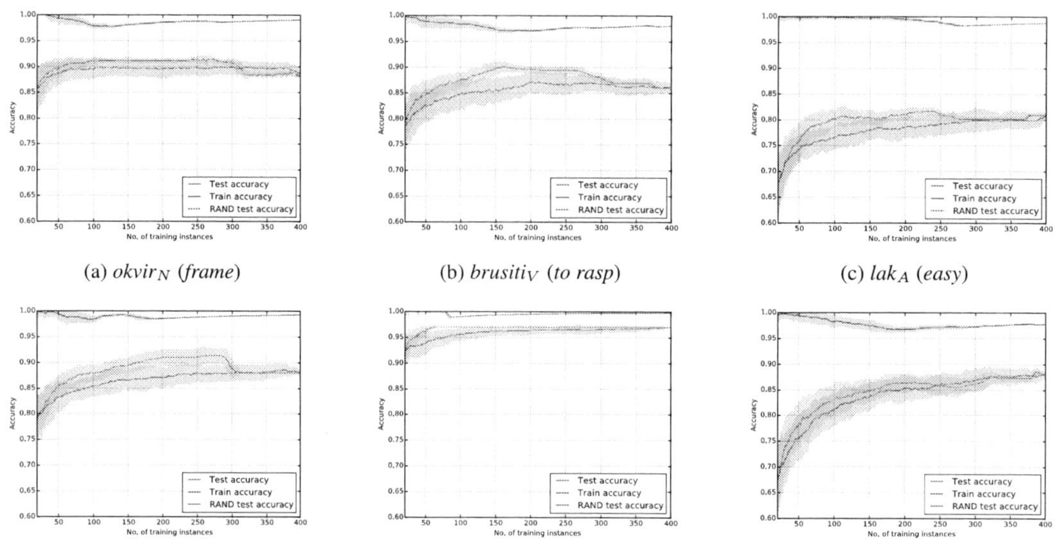

(a) $okvir_N$ *(frame)* (b) $brusiti_V$ *(to rasp)* (c) lak_A *(easy)*

(d) $vatra_N$ *(fire)* (e) $odlikovati_V$ *(to award)* (f) $prljav_A$ *(dirty)*

Figure 2: Learning curves for words from the lexical sample.

6 Conclusion

We have explored the use of active learning (AL) in Croatian word sense disambiguation (WSD). We manually compiled a sense-annotated dataset of six polysemous words. On this dataset, we have shown that by using uncertainty-based sampling we can reach a 99% of accuracy of a fully supervised model at the cost of annotating only 100 instances. On some words, the AL WSD even outperforms a fully supervised model.

Our main priority for future work is to extend our lexical sample. Having a more representative dataset at our disposal, we plan to study how AL WSD performance relates to the linguistic properties of polysemous words, and how these can be exploited to improve the sampling of instances. We also plan to investigate the issues of class imbalance, stopping criteria, and other uncertainty sampling methods.

Having in mind our ultimate goal of creating a cost-effective WSD for Croatian, another interesting direction for future work is to study AL WSD in a crowdsourcing (noisy multi-annotator) environment.

Acknowledgments

We are grateful to the ten annotators for their hard work, as well as to the three anonymous reviewers for their insightful comments and suggestions.

References

Steven Abney. 2007. *Semisupervised learning for computational linguistics*. CRC Press.

Nikola Bakarić, Jasmina Njavro, and Nikola Ljubešić. 2007. What makes sense? Searching for strong WSD predictors in Croatian. In *INFuture2007: Digital Information and Heritage*, pages 321–326.

Dominik Baś, Bartosz Broda, and Maciej Piasecki. 2008. Towards word sense disambiguation of Polish. In *Proceedings of IMCSIT*, pages 73–78, Wisla, Poland.

Bartosz Broda and Maciej Piasecki. 2009. Semi-supervised word sense disambiguation based on weakly controlled sense induction. In *Proceedings of IMCSIT*, pages 17–24, Mragowo, Poland.

Marine Carpuat and Dekai Wu. 2007. Improving statistical machine translation using word sense disambiguation. In *Proceedings of EMNLP-CoNLL*, volume 7, pages 61–72, Prague, Czech Republic.

Chih-Chung Chang and Chih-Jen Lin. 2011. LIBSVM: A library for support vector machines. *ACM Transactions on Intelligent Systems and Technology*, 2:27:1–27:27. Software available at `http://www.csie.ntu.edu.tw/~cjlin/libsvm`.

Jinying Chen, Andrew Schein, Lyle Ungar, and Martha Palmer. 2006. An empirical study of the behavior of active learning for word sense disambiguation. In *Proceedings of HLT-NAACL*, pages 120–127, New York, USA.

Timothy Chklovski and Rada Mihalcea. 2002. Building a sense tagged corpus with Open Mind Word

Expert. In *Proceedings of the ACL-02 Workshop on Word Sense Disambiguation: Recent Successes and Future Directions*, volume 8, pages 116–122, Philadelphia, USA.

Massimiliano Ciaramita and Yasemin Altun. 2006. Broad-coverage sense disambiguation and information extraction with a supersense sequence tagger. In *Proceedings of EMNLP*, pages 594–602, Sydney, Australia.

Philip Edmonds and Scott Cotton. 2001. Senseval-2: overview. In *Proceedings of SensEval-2*, pages 1–5, Toulouse, France.

Philip Edmonds and Adam Kilgarriff. 2002. Introduction to the special issue on evaluating word sense disambiguation systems. *Natural Language Engineering*, 8(04):279–291.

Philip Edmonds. 2000. Designing a task for Senseval-2.

Hany Hassan, Ahmed Hassan, and Sara Noeman. 2006. Graph based semi-supervised approach for information extraction. In *Proceedings of TextGraphs-1*, pages 9–16, New York, USA.

Nancy Ide, Tomaž Erjavec, and Dan Tufis. 2002. Sense discrimination with parallel corpora. In *Proceedings of the ACL-02 Workshop on Word Sense Disambiguation: Recent Successes and Future Directions*, volume 8, pages 61–66, Philadelphia, USA.

Mladen Karan, Jan Šnajder, and Bojana Dalbelo Bašić. 2012. Distributional semantics approach to detecting synonyms in Croatian language. *Information Society*, pages 111–116.

J Richard Landis and Gary G Koch. 1977. An application of hierarchical kappa-type statistics in the assessment of majority agreement among multiple observers. *Biometrics*, pages 363–374.

David D Lewis and William A Gale. 1994. A sequential algorithm for training text classifiers. In *Proceedings of ACM SIGIR*, pages 3–12, Dublin, Ireland.

Hang Li and Cong Li. 2004. Word translation disambiguation using bilingual bootstrapping. *Computational Linguistics*, 30(1):1–22.

Nikola Ljubešić and Filip Klubička. 2014. {bs,hr,sr}WaC – web corpora of Bosnian, Croatian and Serbian. In *Proceedings of WaC*, pages 29–35, Gothenburg, Sweden.

Olga Lyashevskaya, Olga Mitrofanova, Maria Grachkova, Sergey Romanov, Anastasia Shimorina, and Alexandra Shurygina. 2011. Automatic word sense disambiguation and construction identification based on corpus multilevel annotation. In *Text, Speech and Dialogue*, pages 80–90.

Katja Markert and Malvina Nissim. 2007. Semeval-2007 task 08: Metonymy resolution at semeval-2007. In *Proceedings of SemEval-2007*, pages 36–41, Prague, Czech Republic.

Diana McCarthy, Rob Koeling, Julie Weeds, and John Carroll. 2004. Finding predominant word senses in untagged text. In *Proceedings of ACL*, pages 279–286, Barcelona, Spain.

Rada Mihalcea, Timothy Anatolievich Chklovski, and Adam Kilgarriff. 2004. The Senseval-3 English lexical sample task. In *Proceedings of SensEval-3*.

Rada Mihalcea. 2004. Co-training and self-training for word sense disambiguation. In *Proceedings of CoNLL*, pages 33–40, Boston, USA.

Tomas Mikolov, Ilya Sutskever, Kai Chen, Greg S Corrado, and Jeff Dean. 2013. Distributed representations of words and phrases and their compositionality. In *Proceedings of NIPS*, pages 3111–3119, Nevada, USA.

Roberto Navigli. 2009. Word sense disambiguation: A survey. *ACM Computing Surveys (CSUR)*, 41(2):10.

Hwee Tou Ng. 1997. Getting serious about word sense disambiguation. In *Proceedings of the ACL SIGLEX Workshop on Tagging Text with Lexical Semantics: Why, What, and How*, pages 1–7, Washington, D.C., USA.

Zheng-Yu Niu, Dong-Hong Ji, and Chew Lim Tan. 2005. Word sense disambiguation using label propagation based semi-supervised learning. In *Proceedings of ACL*, pages 395–402, Michigan, USA.

Fredrik Olsson. 2009. A literature survey of active machine learning in the context of natural language processing. Technical report, Swedish Institute of Computer Science, Kista, Sweden.

Martha Palmer, Christiane Fellbaum, Scott Cotton, Lauren Delfs, and Hoa Trang Dang. 2001. English tasks: All-words and verb lexical sample. In *Proceedings of SenseEval-2*, pages 21–24, Toulouse, France.

Seong-Bae Park, Byoung-Tak Zhang, and Yung Taek Kim. 2000. Word sense disambiguation by learning from unlabeled data. In *Proceedings of ACL*, pages 547–554, Hong Kong, China.

John C Platt. 1999. Probabilistic outputs for support vector machines and comparisons to regularized likelihood methods. *Advances in Large Margin Classifiers*, 10(3):61–74.

Sameer S Pradhan, Edward Loper, Dmitriy Dligach, and Martha Palmer. 2007. Semeval-2007 task 17: English lexical sample, SRL and all words. In *Proceedings of SemEval-2007*, pages 87–92, Prague, Czech Republic.

Ida Raffaelli, Marko Tadić, Božo Bekavac, and Željko Agić. 2008. Building Croatian wordnet. In *Proceedings of GWC*, pages 349–360, Szeged, Hungary.

Burr Settles. 2010. Active learning literature survey. *University of Wisconsin, Madison*, 52(55-66):11.

Benjamin Snyder and Martha Palmer. 2004. The English all-words task. In *Proceedings of Senseval-3*, pages 41–43, Barcelona, Spain.

Christopher Stokoe, Michael P Oakes, and John Tait. 2003. Word sense disambiguation in information retrieval revisited. In *Proceedings of ACM SIGIR*, pages 159–166, Toronto, Canada.

Dan Tufiş, Radu Ion, and Nancy Ide. 2004. Fine-grained word sense disambiguation based on parallel corpora, word alignment, word clustering and aligned wordnets. In *Proceedings of COLING*, pages 1312–1318, Geneva, Switzerland.

Huizhen Wang, Jingbo Zhu, and Eduard Hovy. 2008. Learning a stopping criterion for active learning for word sense disambiguation and text classification. In *Proceedings of IJCNLP*, pages 366–372, Hyderabad, India.

Jingbo Zhu and Eduard H Hovy. 2007. Active learning for word sense disambiguation with methods for addressing the class imbalance problem. In *Proceedings of EMNLP-CoNLL*, volume 7, pages 783–790, Prague, Czech Republic.

Jingbo Zhu, Huizhen Wang, and Eduard Hovy. 2008a. Multi-criteria-based strategy to stop active learning for data annotation. In *Proceedings of COLING*, volume 1, pages 1129–1136, Manchester, UK.

Jingbo Zhu, Huizhen Wang, Tianshun Yao, and Benjamin K Tsou. 2008b. Active learning with sampling by uncertainty and density for word sense disambiguation and text classification. In *Proceedings of COLING*, volume 1, pages 1137–1144, Manchester, UK.

Automatic Classification of WordNet Morphosemantic Relations

Svetlozara Leseva, Maria Todorova, Tsvetana Dimitrova, Borislav Rizov, Ivelina Stoyanova, Svetla Koeva
Department of Computational Linguistics,
Institute for Bulgarian Language, Bulgarian Academy of Sciences

Abstract

This paper presents work in progress on a machine learning method for classification of morphosemantic relations between verb and noun synsets. The training data comprises 5,584 verb–noun synset pairs from the Bulgarian WordNet, where the morphosemantic relations were automatically transferred from the Princeton WordNet morphosemantic database. The machine learning is based on 4 features (verb and noun endings and their respective semantic primes). We apply a supervised machine learning method based on a decision tree algorithm implemented in Python and NLTK. The overall performance of the method reached F_1-score of 0.936. Our future work focuses on automatic identification of morphosemantically related synsets and on improving the classification.

1 Introduction

Following the observations that for languages with rich derivational morphology wordnets can recover vast amount of semantic information (Bilgin et al., 2004; Pala and Hlaváčková, 2007; Koeva et al., 2008; Barbu Mititelu, 2013), in recent years one of the main lines of research on wordnets has been focused on deciphering semantic information from derivational morphology and encoding it in and across wordnets. This paper investigates a machine learning method for classification of morphosemantic relations already identified between verb and noun synset pairs.

The morphosemantic relations as defined within the Princeton WordNet (PWN) (Agent, Undergoer, Instrument, Event, etc.) link verb–noun pairs of synsets containing derivationally related literals (Fellbaum et al., 2009). As semantic and morphosemantic relations refer to concepts, they are universal, and such a relation must hold between the relevant concepts in any language, regardless of whether it is morphologically expressed or not.

All verb and noun synsets in the PWN have been classified into semantic primes, such as person, animal, cognition, change, etc. (Miller et al., 1990), and corresponding labels, such as noun.person, noun.animal, noun.cognition, verb.cognition, verb.change have been assigned to them. Like the morphosemantic relations, the semantic primes are language independent. Moreover, there is a very strong relationship between the semantic primes of morphosemantically related synsets and the morphosemantic relation existing between them. Additional information that may be used to classify a morphosemantic relation comes from the semantics of derivational affixes.

We use the semantic primes and the derivational affixes of Bulgarian verb-noun pairs which are derivationally and morphosemantically linked in the Bulgarian WordNet (BulNet) (Koeva, 2008) as features in a machine learning method for an automatic classification of morphosemantic relations.

2 Related Work

Morphological descriptions in general lexical-semantic resources, such as wordnets (Fellbaum, 1999), Jeux de Mots (Lafourcade and Joubert, 2013) or Wolf (Sagot and Fišer, 2008) have been very popular in recent years.

The expression of morphosemantic relations through derivational means has been investigated in the wordnets of Turkish (Bilgin et al., 2004), Czech (Pala and Hlaváčková, 2007), Polish (Piasecki et al., 2012a; Piasecki et al., 2012b), Bulgarian (Koeva, 2008; Dimitrova et al., 2014), Serbian (Koeva et al., 2008), Romanian (Barbu Mititelu, 2012), among others. The work on the generation and/or identification of derivatives in a wordnet has been applied for wordnet expansion with new relations and synsets, and/or for

Proceedings of the 5th Workshop on Balto-Slavic Natural Language Processing, pages 59–64,
Hissar, Bulgaria, 10–11 September 2015.

the transfer of these relations and synsets to other wordnets (Bilgin et al., 2004; Koeva et al., 2008; Piasecki et al., 2012a).

The proposal in this paper draws also on research by Stoyanova et al. (2013) and Leseva et al. (2014), who suggest approaches to filtering morphosemantic relations assigned automatically to derivationally related synsets.

3 Linguistic Motivation

In the context of wordnets, morphosemantic relations hold between synsets containing literals that are derivationally related. In the wordnet structure these relations express knowledge additional to that conveyed by semantic relations, such as synonymy, hypernymy, etc. This paper uses the inventory of morphosemantic relations from the Princeton WordNet morphosemantic database[1] which includes 17,740 links connecting 14,877 unique synset pairs by means of morphosemantic relations.

The Princeton WordNet specifies 14 types of morphosemantic relations between verbs and nouns many of which may be related to semantic roles such as agent, instrument, location, etc., though the correspondence is not always straightforward (e.g., By-means-of). The relations are: Agent, By-means-of (inanimate Agents or Causes but also Means and possibly other relations), Instrument, Material, Body-part, Uses (intended purpose), Vehicle (means of transportation), Location, Result, State, Undergoer, Destination, Property, and Event (linking a verb to a deverbal noun denoting the same event). These relations have been assigned between pairs of verb and noun synsets containing at least one derivationally related verb–noun pair of literals. For example, the noun *teacher*:2 ('a person whose occupation is teaching') is the Agent of *teach*:2 ('impart skills or knowledge to'), the noun *machine*:4 ('any mechanical or electrical device that transmits or modifies energy to perform or assist in the performance of human tasks') is the Instrument of the verb *machine*:2 ('turn, shape, mold, or otherwise finish by machinery').

A morphosemantic relation points to two types of linguistic information: (i) a (possibly) language-dependent derivational means through which literals from the respective synsets are related, and (ii) largely language-independent semantic relation of a particular type. Currently, not all pairs of verb and noun synsets containing derivationally related literals in the PWN 3.0 have been assigned a morphosemantic relation – only 7,905 out of 11,751 noun synsets derivationally related to a verb synset and 7,962 out of 8,934 verb synsets derivationally related to a noun synset have a morphosemantic relation. Moreover, in the cases where derivation is used along with other types of word formation (e.g., compounding), the synsets are not related via a derivational relation, e.g., *bookbinder*:1 'a worker whose trade is binding books' has not been linked neither derivationally, nor by means of a morphosemantic relation to *bind*:8. Finally, as the linguistic generalisations behind the morphosemantic relations have been made on the basis of the English derivational morphology, the proposed set of types and instances of relations is not exhaustive for other languages. At the same time these relations are valid in other languages, even though they might not be morphologically expressed. These considerations suggest directions for research into morphosemantic relations.

As reported by Leseva et al. (2014) for Bulgarian, the derivational patterns associated with the morphosemantic relations exhibit considerable polysemy. For example, out of 45 derivational patterns associated with the Agent relation, only 13 are monosemous. The combination of the derivational suffix and the semantic prime of the noun can be a very strong indicator for some relations. For instance, a noun with the suffix *-tel* and the semantic prime noun.person (as in *uchitel* 'teacher') is an Agent, while a noun.artifact with the suffix *-tel* (as in *dvigatel* 'engine, motor, machine') is an Instrument. Thus, even though many suffixes are ambiguous, in many cases the ambiguity can be resolved by the semantic primes. In the PWN 3.0, there are 1,142 combinations of verb–noun semantic primes within the 14,877 morphosemantically linked verb–noun synset pairs. Some of the combinations are very indicative of the morphosemantic relation, e.g., verb.contact – noun.person: Agent – 313, Undergoer – 6; verb.change – noun.substance: Result – 51; Event – 1.

4 Training Data for Machine Learning

The PWN morphosemantic relations have been transferred onto the corresponding synset pairs in

[1] http://wordnetcode.princeton.edu/standoff-files/morphosemantic-links.xls

the Bulgarian WordNet (Koeva et al., 2010). An algorithm for recognising derivationally related pairs of literals, which uses string similarity and heuristics, has been applied on the mophosemantically related synset pairs in the Bulgarian WordNet. Similarity is established if at least one of the following conditions is met: i) one of the literals is a substring of the other; ii) the two literals have a common beginning (estimated to be at least half the length of the shorter literal); iii) the two literals have a Levenshtein distance smaller than a certain threshold. Verb–noun literal pairs found to be similar have been assigned a derivational relation – prefix, suffix, or conversion (Dimitrova et al., 2014). The derivational relations have been validated manually, resulting in 6,135 relations between 5,584 unique synset pairs.

In order to improve the consistency of the dataset and to reduce noise, we have performed certain procedures on the wordnet structure: i) manual inspection and disambiguation of morphosemantic relations in case of multiple relations assigned to a synset pair; ii) validation of the consistency of the semantic primes of nouns and verbs belonging to the same natural class and the semantic primes' shift in the hypernym–hyponyms paths; iii) consistency check of the type of the assigned morphosemantic relation against the semantic primes.

4.1 Disambiguation of Morphosemantic Relations

We have identified 450 cases of multiple relations assigned between pairs of synsets, which represent 50 different combinations of two (rarely three) relations. We assume that two unique concepts are linked by a unique semantic relation, thus we keep only one relation per pair of synsets. We have distinguished several cases of multiple relation assignment, which served as a point of departure when deciding which of the relations must be preserved.

(I) One of the relations excludes the other on semantic and (frequently) syntactic grounds. Consider the assignments: <Agent, Destination>, <Agent, Undergoer>. Except in a reflexive interpretation, an entity cannot be an Agent (the doer), on the one hand, and a Destination (recipient) or an Undergoer (patient or theme), on the other. The type of relation is signalled by the synset gloss and usually by the affix. In other cases, such as <Agent, Event>, <Agent, Instrument>, the choice of relation depends on the semantic prime, e.g., a noun with the prime noun.artifact or noun.act cannot be an Agent, and vice versa–a noun.person cannot be an Instrument or an Event.

(II) One of the relations implies the other, e.g., <Instrument, Uses>, as an Instrument is used for a certain purpose. The more informative relation (in this case Instrument) has been preferred.

(III) There is no strict distinction between the relations, e.g., <Result, Event>, <Result, State>, <State, Event>, <Property, State>. In such cases, the choices are motivated on the basis of semantic information from the synsets, such as the gloss, the literals or the semantic primes. Definitions are very helpful as often they give additional information which points to the type of morphosemantic relation, e.g., 'the act of...', 'a state of...', etc. especially where the semantic prime is more specific. Certain combinations of semantic primes have been empirically established to strongly suggest the type of relation, e.g., noun.state–verb.change points to Result, noun.state–verb.state – to State. The primes noun.act and noun.event on their own have been found to be very indicative of Events. These generalisations are made after inspecting the triples noun.prime–morphosemantic relation–verb.prime.

(IV) Where other indications are lacking, we have taken into account which of the relations is more typical for a given semantic prime and/or for the synsets in the local tree (hypernyms, hyponyms, sisters).

4.2 Validation of Semantic Primes

At certain nodes in some hypernym–hyponym paths the semantic prime changes so that the hyponyms of these nodes have a different semantic prime. This may affect the homogeneity of the prime–relation correspondences. For instance, half of the Body-part relations involve the prime noun.body, and the rest – noun.animal or noun.plant. The respective nouns denote body parts or organs of animals or plants and are consistent with the definition of the prime noun.body.

We have performed a series of consistency checks on the semantic primes in chains of the type $A > B > C_1, \ldots, C_n$ where A is the immediate hypernym of B, and B is the immediate hypernym of $C_1, \ldots, C_n$. Five types of inconsistencies were discovered: i) the leaves (terminal hyponyms) have a different semantic prime from their immediate hypernym (the majority of the instances, 1,175 out of 1,628 for the nouns, 1,043 out of 1,607 for the verbs); ii) the non-terminal node B has a different semantic prime from A, and $C_1, \ldots, C_n$ have the prime of B (382 cases for nouns, 374 for verbs); iii) some Cs have the semantic prime of A, others – of B (10 cases for nouns, 43 for verbs); iv) some Cs have the semantic prime of A, some – of B, and others – a third (different) one (43 cases for nouns, 133 for verbs); v) A and $C_1, \ldots, C_n$ have the same semantic prime and B has a different one (7 cases for nouns, 14 cases for verbs).

All the cases have been manually inspected. The majority of the shifts in the semantic primes reflect specificities of the hypernym–hyponym paths, e.g., solid:18 (noun.substance) > food:3; solid food:1 (noun.food). Cases of systematic inconsistency include noun.animal or noun.plant instead of noun.body; noun.animal or noun.plant instead of noun.substance, and so forth. We have decided to keep the assigned primes and to consider assigning the primes inherited from the hypernyms in addition to the original primes.

4.3 Cross-check of Semantic Primes with Morphosemantic Relations

We have looked at the correspondences between the type of morphosemantic relations and the semantic primes of the nouns since their correlation is stronger compared to the semantic primes of the verbs. Two types of validation for consistency were carried out: i) given a noun semantic prime, which morphosemantic relations are found for the synsets of this prime and what is their frequency distribution (i.e., to what extent are they typical for a given prime); ii) given a morphosemantic relation, which noun semantic primes are found for the synsets which bear this relation and what is their frequency distribution. These checks enabled us to establish clearer criteria for the relation – semantic prime label correspondences and to reduce noise in the data. For example, the nouns linked via the relation Agent belong to 17 semantic primes, but some of them are unsuitable, such as: noun.act, e.g., *scamper:1; scramble:2; scurry:1* ('rushing about hastily in an undignified way') – an Agent of *scurry:2; scamper:2; skitter:4; scuttle:1* ('to move about or proceed hurriedly'); noun.feeling, e.g., *temper:9; mood:1; humor:7; humour:7* ('a characteristic (habitual or relatively temporary) state of feeling') – an Agent of *humor:1; humour:1* ('put into a good mood'); noun.food *dinner:1* ('the main meal of the day served in the evening or at midday') – an Agent for *dine* ('have supper; eat dinner'). The unsuitable relations have been discarded based on the nature of the relationship between the synsets, taking into account the semantic prime of the noun.

As a result of this type of validation, we have been able to reduce the nominal semantic primes associated with a morphosemantic relation, in some cases significantly: Agent from 17 to 4 (noun.person, noun.animal, noun.plant, noun.group); Instrument – from 9 to 5 (noun.artifact, noun.cognition, noun.object, noun.substance, noun.communication); Material – from 6 to 4 (noun.artifact, noun.body, noun.food, noun.substance); State – from 10 to 5 (noun.artifact, noun.body, noun.substance, noun.food); Body-part – from 4 to 3 (noun.body, noun.animal, noun.plant) but noun.body subsumes the other two; Destination is associated primarily with noun.person (i.e., Recipients), to the exception of noun.artifact (1 relation) and noun.group (2 relations); Vehicle is associated only with noun.artifact. The other 7 relations – Event, Result, Attribute, By-means-of, Uses, Location, Undergoer – show greater diversity of semantic primes and few of them could be discarded.

5 Machine Learning Task

We propose a machine learning method for automatic classification of morphosemantic relations for verb–noun synset pairs already identified as morphosemantically and derivationally related. The training is performed on a set of 5,584 labeled data instances: verb–noun synset pairs from BulNet with assigned relations (see 4).

Each data instance is represented by a combination of 4 features for the machine learning: i) verb ending (with 172 values), ii) noun ending (with 294 values), iii) verb synset semantic prime (with 15 values), and iv) noun synset semantic prime (with 25 values).

The endings are the substrings of symbols from the end of the word backwards which minimally differentiate a noun and a verb, i.e., *-sha* and *-satel* for *pisha* 'write' and *pisatel* 'writer', respectively; *--ya* and *-ach* for *gotvya* 'to cook' and *gotvach* '(a) cook', respectively; etc. The endings may include a suffix or an inflection and part of the word's base, e.g., in *pisha – pisatel*, *-sha – -satel*: *-sh-* is a root consonant and *-a* – the inflection; *-s-* is a root consonant, *-a-* is a connecting vowel, and *-tel* is the noun suffix.

This is a basic classification task which uses the set of 14 morphosemantic relations in the PWN 3.0. We apply a supervised machine learning method based on a decision tree algorithm implemented in Python and NLTK.[2] The decision tree classifier is considered suitable for the task because each pair of verb–noun synsets is assigned a single relation. Also, it performs well on large datasets in reasonable time. Moreover, we empirically confirmed that this algorithm outperformed SVM and Naive Bayes on the particular dataset.

6 Results

The evaluation is based on 10-fold cross-validation. The overall F_1 score of the morphosemantic relations classifier based on machine learning is 0.936. Table 1 shows the precision, recall and F_1 score of the method's performance across different types of morphosemantic relations.

Relation	Total	Prec	Recall	F_1
has_vehicle	3	1.000	1.000	1.000
has_agent	748	0.997	0.996	0.997
has_location	78	0.987	0.987	0.987
has_event	3,580	0.984	0.947	0.966
has_instrument	90	0.978	0.889	0.933
has_body_part_actor	5	1.000	0.833	0.917
involves_property	84	0.750	0.969	0.860
has_destination	5	1.000	0.714	0.857
has_undergoer	164	0.720	0.922	0.821
has_state	189	0.695	0.821	0.837
has_uses	123	0.691	0.850	0.771
has_result	272	0.695	0.844	0.769
by_means_of	239	0.715	0.803	0.759
has_material	10	0.000	0.000	0.000

Table 1: Evaluation of the method's performance across different morphosematic relations.

The experiment shows that the combination of the pair of semantic primes and the verb and noun endings is a relatively reliable predictor of the type of morphosemantic relation to be assigned with F_1 score ranging between 0.759 and 0.997 depending on the relation (results for relations with a low frequency in the training data are unreliable).

The analysis of the errors helped us identify the clearly defined and consistent relations (such as has_agent, has_location), as well as those that are broadly defined and thus harder to identify both by the machine learning algorithm and by human experts (has_uses, has_result, by_means_of).

7 Conclusion and Future Work

Our current research is focused on testing the performance of the method in a controlled setting on the set of derivationally related synsets in the PWN which have not been assigned a morphosemantic relation yet. In such a way we will expand the dataset and enhance the density of synset relations in BulNet. More detailed feature engineering with expert evaluation based on various features will also be tested.

The main task for our future work is to develop methods for automatic assignment of morphosemantic relations to synsets that are derivationally related but are not connected in the respective wordnet. The major challenge is given a set of derivationally related synsets in the entire wordnet, to distinguish those literal pairs (and respectively – synsets) that are semantically related from those that formally coincide.

An envisaged direction of research along these lines is to employ WordNet-based similarity measures[3] to evaluate similarity between: a) verb and noun glosses from the semantically disambiguated corpus of glosses of the Princeton WordNet;[4] b) examples of the usage of the verbs and nouns from semantically anotated corpora such as the SemCor[5] and BulSemCor (Koeva et al., 2010). The semantic similarity approach takes into account: a) the use of the verb in the noun's gloss, or vice-versa, which would mean that one is defined by means of the other; b) the presence of the verb's hypernym (on one or more steps) in the noun's gloss, or vice-versa; c) the occurrence of the verb and the noun in semantically related context; etc. Further, other components of the WordNet's structure and synset description can be applied to verify the type of the relation, including the structure of the gloss, the presence of other relations, etc.

Although our work is focused on Bulgarian and primarily uses BulNet, the results, i.e., the morphosemantic relations, are transferrable across languages and can be used to enhance wordnets for other languages with semantic content.

[2] http://www.nltk.org/_modules/nltk/classify/

[3] http://wn-similarity.sourceforge.net/

[4] http://wordnet.princeton.edu/glosstag.shtml

[5] http://www.gabormelli.com/RKB/SemCor_Corpus

References

Verginica Barbu Mititelu. 2012. Adding morpho-semantic relations to the Romanian Wordnet. In *Proceedings of the Eight International Conference on Language Resources and Evaluation (LREC 2012)*, pages 2596–2601.

Verginica Barbu Mititelu. 2013. Increasing the effectiveness of the Romanian Wordnet in NLP applications. *Computer Science Journal of Moldova*, 21(3):320–331.

Orhan Bilgin, Ozlem Cetinoglu, and Kemal Oflazer. 2004. Morphosemantic relations in and across Wordnets – a study based on Turkish. In *Proceedings of the Second Global Wordnet Conference (GWC 2004)*, pages 60–66.

Tsvetana Dimitrova, Ekaterina Tarpomanova, and Borislav Rizov. 2014. Coping with derivation in the Bulgarian WordNet. In *Proceedings of the Seventh Global Wordnet Conference (GWC 2014)*, pages 109–117.

Christiane Fellbaum, Anne Osherson, and Peter E. Clark. 2009. Putting semantics into WordNet's "morphosemantic" links. In *Proceedings of the Third Language and Technology Conference, Poznan, Poland. [Reprinted in: Responding to Information Society Challenges: New Advances in Human Language Technologies. Springer Lecture Notes in Informatics]*, volume 5603, pages 350–358.

Christiane Fellbaum, editor. 1999. *WordNet: an Electronic Lexical Database*. MIT Press, Cambridge, MA.

Svetla Koeva, Cvetana Krstev, and Dusko Vitas. 2008. Morpho-semantic relations in Wordnet – a case study for two Slavic languages. In *Proceedings of the Fourth Global WordNet Conference (GWC 2008)*, pages 239–254.

Svetla Koeva, Svetlozara Leseva, Ekaterina Tarpomanova, Borislav Rizov, Tsvetana Dimitrova, and Hristina Kukova. 2010. Bulgarian sense-annotated corpus – results and achievement. In *Proceedings of the 7th International Conference of Formal Approaches to South Slavic and Balkan Languages (FASSBL-7)*, pages 41–49.

Svetla Koeva. 2008. Derivational and morphosemantic relations in Bulgarian Wordnet. *Intelligent Information Systems*, pages 359–368.

Mathieu Lafourcade and Alain Joubert. 2013. Bénéfices et limites de l'acquisition lexicale dans l'expérience jeuxdemots. In *Ressources Lexicales: Contenu, construction, utilisation, valuation. Linguisticae Investigationes, Supplementa 30*, pages 187–216.

Svetlozara Leseva, Ivelina Stoyanova, Borislav Rizov, Maria Todorova, and Ekaterina Tarpomanova. 2014. Automatic semantic filtering of morphosemantic relations in WordNet. In *Proceedings of CLIB 2014, Sofia, Bulgaria*, pages 14–22.

George A. Miller, Richard Beckwith, Christiane. Fellbaum, Derek Gross, and Katherine Miller. 1990. Introduction to Wordnet: an on-line lexical database. *International journal of lexicography*, 3(4):235–244.

Karel Pala and Dana Hlaváčková. 2007. Derivational relations in Czech WordNet. In *Proceedings of the Workshop on Balto-Slavonic Natural Language Processing*, pages 75–81.

Maciej. Piasecki, Radoslaw Ramocki, and Marek Maziarz. 2012a. Automated generation of derivative relations in the Wordnet expansion perspective. In *Proceedings of the 6th Global Wordnet Conference (GWC 2012)*, pages 273–280.

Maciej Piasecki, Radoslaw Ramocki, and Pawel Minda. 2012b. Corpus-based semantic filtering in discovering derivational relations. In A. Ramsay and G. Agre, editors, *Applications – 15th International Conference, AIMSA 2012, Varna, Bulgaria, September 12-15, 2012. Proceedings. LNCS 7557*, pages 14–22. Springer.

Benoit Sagot and Darja Fišer. 2008. Building a free french WordNet from multilingual resources. In *Proceedings of the Ontolex 2008 Workshop, Marrakech, Morrocco*.

Ivelina Stoyanova, Svetla Koeva, and Svetlozara Leseva. 2013. Wordnet-based cross-language identification of semantic relations. In *Proceedings of the 4th Biennal International Workshop on Balto-Slavic Natural Language Processing*, pages 119–128.

Applying Multi-dimensional Analysis to a Russian Webcorpus: Searching for Evidence of Genres

Anisya Katinskaya
Russian State University for the Humanities
Moscow, Russia
a.katinsky@gmail.com

Serge Sharoff
Leeds University
Leeds, UK
s.sharoff@leeds.co.uk

Abstract

The paper presents an application of Multi-dimensional (MD) analysis initially developed for the analysis of register variation in English (Biber, 1988) to the investigation of a genre diverse corpus, which was built from modern texts of the Russian Web. The analysis is based on the idea that each linguistic feature has different frequencies in different registers, and statistically stable co-occurrence of linguistic features across texts can be used for automatic identification of texts with similar communicative functions. By using a software tool which counts a set of linguistic features in texts in Russian and by performing factor analysis in R, we identified six dimensions of variation. These dimensions show significant similarities with Biber's original dimensions of variation. We studied the distribution of texts in the space of the dimensions of our factors and investigated their link to 17 externally defined Functional Text Dimensions (Forsyth and Sharoff, 2014), which were assigned to each text of the corpus by a group of annotators. The results show that dimensions of linguistic feature variation can be used for better understanding of the genre structure of the Russian Web.

1 Introduction

Automatic genre classification is an important step in different kinds of text processing tasks and in scientific research of linguists working with corpus data. As Mikhail Bakhtin (1996) said about genres: "Specific function (scientific, technical, journalistic, official, and informal) and specific conditions of each communication field generate specific genres, i.e., thematic, compositional, and stylistic types of utterances". This idea has special importance for texts from the Web since this communication field is in the process of continuous change, so it is difficult to make a fixed classification of Web genres, so that the annotators normally disagree about the genre labels (Sharoff et al., 2010). For that reason, we will use the Functional Text Dimensions (FTDs) which allow determining the similarity of texts in terms of their functional characteristics (Forsyth and Sharoff, 2014).

Since Biber's work (Biber, 1988) the idea for classification via a link between genres and their linguistic categories has been implemented by numerous researchers (Nakamura, 1993; Michos et al., 1996; Sigley, 1997; Stamatatos et al., 2001; Finn et al., 2002; Finn and Kushmerick, 2003; Lee and Myaeng, 2004). Linguistic parameters of different genres for Russian have also been studied. Braslavski (2011) investigated genre analysis in the context of Web search. A small set of simple syntactic constructions was used to distinguish fiction, news and scientific texts in (Klyshinsky et al., 2013). These three types of texts were also investigated in the space of 11 low-level frequency parameters, e.g., type/token ratio or verb frequency, in (Yagunova and Pospelova, 2014).

Our idea is to implement the MD analysis for Russian and, firstly, to test whether this approach could be used for finding sets of linguistic features covering a wide range of web texts rather than just three genres. Secondly, unlike (Sharoff et al., 2010) and (Forsyth and Sharoff, 2014) these studies have not investigated the issue of inter-annotator reliability.

MD analysis has not been applied to Russian language before, but it ha been used to analyse texts in English (Biber, 1988; de Mönnink et al.,

Proceedings of the 5th Workshop on Balto-Slavic Natural Language Processing, pages 65–74,
Hissar, Bulgaria, 10–11 September 2015.

2003; Crossley and Louwerse, 2007; Daems et al., 2013), Nukulaelae Tuvaluan (Besnier, 1988), Somali (Biber and Hared, 1994), Korean (Kim and Biber, 1994), Spanish (Biber and Tracy-Ventura, 2007; Parodi, 2007), Gaelic (Lamb, 2008), Brazilian Portuguese (Berber Sardinha et al., 2014).

In spite of variation in the use of terms "genre" and "register" among researchers, this study refers to externally recognized text types, e.g., news or fiction, as "genres" (Lee, 2001).

In Section 2 we shortly describe the methodology of the MD approach. In Section 3 we describe the corpus we used, the principles how we chose a set of linguistic features and the software tool built for extracting these features from texts. In Section 4 we analyse the dimensions of linguistic feature variation resulting from factor analysis and briefly compare them to dimensions from other works. Section 5 shows the distribution the FTDs in the factor space. In Section 6 we analyse the results and discuss possible applications.

2 Short Overview of Multi-dimensional Analysis

The procedure of the MD analysis can be described in several methodological steps (Biber et al., 2007). Firstly, texts are collected as a corpus representing the variety of genres. Then a research is performed to define a set of linguistics features to be found in texts of the corpus along with functions of features.

The third step is to develop a computer program to automatically identify linguistic features. After tagging of the corpus and correcting results by the researcher, additional programs compute frequency counts of each linguistic feature in each text, and the counts are normalized.

The next step is to conduct the procedure of finding latent features (co-occurrence patterns) among the linguistic features using factor analysis of the obtained frequency counts. Each set of co-occurrence patterns is referred to as a factor. The factors are interpreted in terms of their functions as underlying dimensions of linguistic feature variation. Factor scores of each text are calculated with respect to each dimension of variation. Then mean factor scores for each genre are computed and compared to each other to analyse specific linguistic features of each genre.

3 Data acquisition

3.1 Description of the Corpus

The corpus used for the experiment consists of 618 texts (see Table 1). The texts were collected from Open Corpora (Bocharov et al., 2011), as well as from news portals (e.g., chaskor.ru, ru.wikinews.org, ria.ru, lenta.ru), Wikipedia and other online encyclopedias (e.g., krugosvet.ru), online magazines (e.g., vogue.ru, popmech.ru) and text collections (primarily fiction, e.g., lib.ru), blogs (e.g., vk.com, lifejournal.com, habrahabr.ru), forums (e.g., forum.hackersoft.ru, litforum.ru), scientific and popular scientific journals (e.g., cyberleninka.ru, sci-article.ru), promotional web-sites (e.g., mvideo.ru, avito.ru), legal resources (e.g., base.garant.ru, consultant.ru), and other online resources.

Number of texts: 618
Number of words: 741831
Number of sentences: 52031
Length of texts: 88 (min), 10848 (max), 573 (med.)
Number of texts < 200 words: 133
Number of texts > 200 words: 482

Table 1: Annotated corpus used in study.

Noticeable differences in the length of texts are mostly determined by their genre characteristics: it is difficult to find a very long advertisement or a joke and a very short scientific paper or a law.

Despite the fact that we could have used a big collection of texts from the Web, at this stage we decided to settle on a manually built and quite small corpus for several reasons. Firstly, even in texts obtained from the same source, e.g., news or blog posts, we can often find considerable variation in subgenres. For instance, one news text from chaskor.ru expresses the author's attitude to the topic, whereas the second one is relatively neutral, so these two texts from the same news portal differ in their FTD A17 (evaluation).[1]

Secondly, we tried to obtain maximal variety of Web genres. Thirdly, annotation of texts on 17 parameters is very labour-intensive, while we wanted to ensure a reasonable level of inter-annotator agreement. A significant part of the corpus was annotated by 11 annotators with three annotations per text. Then the full corpus annotation has been revised by 2 annotators.

[1] http://goo.gl/XZdg1t and http://goo.gl/wMkuCL

Class	Main FTDs	Num of texts	Main interpretation
C1	A1, A13	21	Argumentative texts
C2	A11	101	Personal blogs
C3	A8	79	News reports
C4	A9	76	Legal texts
C5	A12	66	Advertisement
C6	A14	59	Scientific texts
C7	A16 (-A14)	186	Encyclopedic texts
C8	A7	33	Instructional texts
C9	A4, A16	10	Fictional texts

Table 2: Classes of the FTDs.

The annotated texts were clustered with scores of 17 FTDs as predictors. Clustering was performed by a variant of kNN, which had additional constraints to limit the size of small clusters; the method is fully described in (Lagutin et al., 2015). After manual analysis of the clustering results, nine stable classes (C1-C9) were revealed and interpreted as reliably annotated genres, which can also be described on the basis of their principal FTDs (see Table 2). In our paper below we will treat these classes as genres for illustrating dimensions of linguistic feature variation.

3.2 Linguistic Features

Sets of grammatical and lexico-grammatical linguistic features identified by Biber's tagger range from 60 to 120+ linguistic variables. The largest inventory (Berber Sardinha et al., 2014) comprises 190 features. For our purposes, we relied on the list presented in the Appendix 2 in (Biber et al., 2007) and the description of features in the manual of Multidimensional Analysis Tagger (Nini, 2014) that replicates Biber's tagger, while adapting the English features to reflect Russian grammar.

There are several reasons why we have chosen a relatively short list of features. Firstly, necessary features should be accessible for extraction from texts by the tools available to us (morphological tagger and our program, which we will describe further). For instance, it is very difficult to specify the difference between phrasal coordination (e.g., coordination of extended noun phrases) and independent clause coordination, using only POS tags and a small window (from 1 to 10 words) for shallow parsing. We plan to add a syntactic module to the next version of the feature tagger.

Secondly, each feature reflected the Russian grammar. For example, researchers disagree with respect to the existence of proforms of verbal phrases in Russian. Preposition stranding (when a preposition with an object occurs somewhere other than adjacent to its object, e.g., *the thing I was thinking of*) does not exist in Russian; therefore, we did not include such linguistic features to the list. The reflexive pronouns in Russian do exist, but their forms are different from the reflexive pronouns in English, which derive from personal pronouns and can be added to the corresponding features as it was done in MAT v.1.2. (*myself* as the first person pronoun, *itself* as the third person pronoun, and so on). For this reason, the Russian reflexive pronouns are considered as an independent linguistic feature.

Under nominalizations we mean verbal nouns like *возрождение*, 'revival', or *вход*, 'entrance'. A feature called 'wh-relative' means relative clause with a wh-element (e.g., *который*, 'which') that is fronted to the beginning of the clause. 'Wh-question' marks interrogative sentences with a wh-element at the left edge (e.g., *кто*, 'who'). A feature 'that-complement' means a complement clause with the complementizer *что* or *чтобы* ('that') at the left edge. More details see in (Bailyn, 2012).

The third reason is that we want to test our hypothesis about appropriateness of the Multi-dimensional approach for the task of automatic genre classification of texts of the Russian Web. The list of features can be extended in the future.

3.3 MD Analysis for Russian

Biber's computational tools have been used to tag lexical, grammatical, and syntactical features and to count their frequencies in each analysed text. Using large-scale dictionaries and context-dependent disambiguation algorithms, the tagger marks word classes and syntactic information. The description of the early version of the tagger is presented in (Biber, 1988), computational methods are outlined in (Biber, 1993a; Biber et al., 2007).

We have developed a program in Python, which uses a morphologically parsed corpus as an input.[2]

[2] https://github.com/Askinkaty/MDRus_analyser

Factors	PA1	PA2	PA3	PA4	PA5	PA6
PA1	1.00	-0.01	-0.16	0.30	0.49	0.17
PA2	-0.01	1.00	-0.28	0.13	0.17	-0.03
PA3	-0.16	-0.28	1.00	-0.53	-0.43	-0.22
PA4	0.3	0.13	-0.53	1.00	0.46	0.48
PA5	0.49	0.17	-0.43	0.46	1.00	0.20
PA6	0.17	-0.03	-0.22	0.48	0.20	1.00

Table 3: Inter-factor correlation.

	PA4	PA1	PA2	PA3	PA5	PA6
Proportion Variance	0.08	0.09	0.06	0.06	0.05	0.04
Cumulative Variance	0.08	0.17	0.23	0.29	0.34	0.38
Proportion Explained	0.22	0.22	0.15	0.15	0.14	0.11
Cumulative Proportion	0.22	0.45	0.60	0.75	0.89	1.00

Table 4: Output of the factor analysis.

RFTagger (Schmid and Laws, 2008) was used to process the corpus with the accuracy rate close to accuracy of the tools described in (Sharoff and Nivre, 2011), which is near 95-97%.[3] For the lexical features we used dictionaries derived from the Russian National Corpus.[4]

Then we can run our feature analyser for each text to identify and count linguistic variables. We have developed a processing algorithm for each feature, considering the requirements of Russian grammar and possible ambiguity, which we try to resolve by relatively simple methods such as specifying contextual conditions and exceptions. For example, we have to identify time adverbs *весной* (‘in spring’) or *порой* (‘at times’), which might be confused with nouns. In almost every case RFTagger processes them as nouns. Therefore, we should specify the context in which these words cannot be used as adverbs (e.g., if one of these words agrees with an adjective or a pronoun, it is likely to be a noun).

All processing rules were tested on wider outputs obtained from the General Internet Corpus of Russian (GICR) (Piperski et al., 2013). Because we work with texts from the Web, we took into account some possible mistakes. For instance, people often make mistakes with conjunctions like *вследствие того что* (‘because of’), *ввиду того что* (‘in view of that’) and miss commas or white spaces between words in these complex conjunctions. For our practical purposes, we have attempted a unified processing of the most common cases of this sort.

Unlike Biber, we did not edit the results of feature extraction because it is labour-intensive and not consistent with the idea of applying the method to a large-scale corpus in the next step. Accuracy of the most complicated rules (e.g., detection of proforms of noun phrases) is around 67-85%, simple rules have much higher accuracy, mostly above 95%.

Counted frequencies of all features in each text (except for word length, sentence length, and type/token ratio) are divided by the number of words in the texts. As an output of the program we get a matrix of 618 to 40 including the frequencies of 40 linguistic variables for each text.

4 Searching for Dimensions of Variation

4.1 Factor Analysis

Factor analysis is an important part of the MD analysis. It is a useful tool for investigating the underlying structure of complex phenomena and for reducing data to a smaller set of latent variables called factors. Each of the observed variables is assumed to depend on a linear combination of factors, and the coefficients (the strength of relation to a factor) are known as factor loadings. For the justification of factor analysis for genre research we refer the reader to (Biber, 1988).

[3] http://www.cis.uni-muenchen.de/~schmid/tools/RFTagger/
[4] http://www.ruscorpora.ru

Linguistic features, which are observed variables in our study, are supposed to co-occur in different texts. We are interested in systematic patterns among this co-occurrence. Patterns of variation reflect an underlying system of factors, with which variables have strong association. A rotated factor analysis was performed in R with Promax rotation since we assume possible correlation among factors (Kabakoff, 2011).

The inter-factor correlation ranges from -0.53 to 0.49, see Table 3. Other output of the factor analysis is presented in Table 4.

Table 5 presents linguistic features with factor loadings over 0.3 or below -0.3 correlating with corresponding factors. Features with lower loadings cannot be considered as informative for interpretation of factors. Large loading means stronger correlation between a feature and a factor. Only three features have been excluded (verbal adverb, concessive subordinate clauses, and pied-piping, which for Russian is interpreted as a preposition moved to the front of its relative clause) due to low factor loadings. Six dimensions of feature variation were selected as optimal for our data. Dimensions 3 and 5 are relatively small: each of them includes only three features.

The factor structure is very stable and does not change significantly if different models (maximum likelihood, iterated principal axis, etc.) or different types of rotation are used.

4.2 Interpretation of Dimensions of Variation

Each factor combines linguistic features that serve related communicative functions. It is also important that a feature can have positive or negative loading in a factor; therefore, features with opposite loadings have a complementary distribution. In our case, only three factors have so called negative features, i.e., features with negative loadings. For convenience, we will call the obtained factors as dimensions and rename PA4, PA1, PA2, PA3, PA5, and PA6 to D1, D2, D3, D4, D5, and D6 correspondingly.

The positive features of Dimension 1 (D1) are 1st person pronouns, 2nd person pronouns, exclamation, and wh-questions what can be associated with interactivity and indicates dialogue. A possible interpretation of place adverbs in D1 is proposed in (Biber, 1988), according to which place and time adverbs are 'reflecting the description of other people in particular places and times'. Nouns, long words, prepositional phrases, and attributive adjectives mostly relate to the informational purpose (high frequency of nouns and modifiers of noun phrases usually signs high informational saturation). It follows that D1 is very close to the 'Informational vs. Involved' dimension in (Biber, 1993b) since it also includes such features as nouns, word length, prepositional phrases, attributive adjectives vs. 1st and 2nd personal pronouns and wh-questions.

Dimension 1: interactive/informative POSITIVE FEATURES: 1th person pronoun, 2nd person pronoun, place adverb, exclamation, wh-question NEGATIVE FEATURES: word length, nouns, attributive adjective, all prepositional phrases (total PP)
Dimension 2: presentation of personal view of subject/impersonal POSITIVE FEATURES: pro-form of noun phrase (pro-form of NP), negation, mental verb, that-complement, speech verb, wh-relative, 3rd person pronoun, indefinite pronoun, predicative adjective, pro-form of adjective phrase (pro-adjective), reflexive pronoun, causative subordinate clause
Dimension 3: narrative/non-narrative POSITIVE FEATURES: past tense, perfect aspect NEGATIVE FEATURES: present tense
Dimension 4 : abstract/non-abstract POSITIVE FEATURES: passive participle clause, agentless passive, nominalization, passive with agent, active participle clause, type/token ratio NEGATIVE FEATURES: sentence length
Dimension 5 POSITIVE FEATURES: all adverbs, time adverb, indefinite pronoun
Dimension 6: directive/ non-directive/ POSITIVE FEATURES: infinitive, conditional subordinate clause, imperative mood, purpose subordinate clause

Table 5: Result of the factor analysis (factorial structure).

Dimension 2 (D2) combines features that can be interpreted as a report of speech of others (3th person pronouns, speech verbs) and features that can be used to frame a personal attitude towards some topic (mental verbs, that-complements, reflexive pronouns). Some features have a referential meaning: wh-relatives (elaborated reference), pro-forms of noun phrases, pro-adjectives, and indefinite pronouns, which can be interpreted as generalized reference in a shared context of communication between the author and the reader. D2 is somewhat similar to the dimension in (Grieve et al., 2010) called Thematic Variation Dimension and also similar in several features to the argumentative Dimension 2 in (Berber Sardinha et al., 2014). We will interpret D2 as the dimension presenting an informal personal argumentation or personal opinion on something like other's words or a context that is well known to the reader.

Two positive (past tense and perfect aspect) and one negative (present tense) features allow interpreting of Dimension 3 (D3) as narrative vs. non-narrative. A similar dimension in (Biber, 2004) has the label called 'Narrative-focused discourse'.

Dimension 4 (D4) includes a set of features like agentless passive, passive with an agent, many non-repeating words, and nominalizations and can be interpreted as presenting an abstract style of writing. It also correlates with high frequency of active and passive participle clauses. The negative correlation of this dimension with the average sentence length is unexpected. D4 is almost similar to the dimension called 'Abstract vs. Non-Abstract style' in (Biber, 1993b).

It is more difficult to interpret Dimension 5 (D5), which includes only the total number of adverbs, time adverbs (both usually narrative features), and indefinite pronouns. In the next section we will investigate which kind of texts is characterized by D5. This dimension is stable in the space of 40 features. However, having run the analysis with 63 linguistic features (it has not been fully tested at the time of writing), we got that adverbs and indefinite pronouns do not form a separate dimension and correlate with other dimensions along with place adverbs.

The features of Dimension 6 (D6) (infinitives, conditional subordinate clauses, imperative mood, purpose subordinate clauses) reflect the directive function. Purpose subordinate clauses mostly refer not to how some action can be performed but for what purpose. This dimension can be compared to Biber's dimension named 'Overt expression of persuasion' including infinitives, conditional subordination, and different modals (Biber, 1993b).

5 Distribution of Classes of the FTDs in the Space of Dimensions

It is interesting to see how the classes of the FTDs, which we interpret as genres in this study, relate to the six dimensions of feature variation. For this purpose, we counted dimension scores of each class by summation of dimension scores of texts having a value 2 on the corresponding FTD (or FTDs), see Table 2.

Class	D1	D2	D3	D4	D5	D6
C1	3.2	7.7	0.6	-4.1	4.4	2.8
C2	13.7	12.3	3.5	-12.9	12.0	7.7
C3	-4.0	-1.8	2.5	0.4	-1.9	-1.8
C4	-16.8	-15.7	-6.2	17.9	-15.8	-8.5
C5	-4.6	-8.1	-2.8	4.5	-4.8	-2.1
C6	-5.6	-6.0	-3.2	7.0	-5.8	-5.7
C7	-6.5	-7.8	-1.7	6.1	-5.6	-4.5
C8	6.0	-2.4	1.5	-3.5	3.0	9.0
C9	24.8	12.3	9.5	-19.5	13.4	9.8

Table 6: Medians of dimension scores for C1-C9.

Medians of the dimension scores of the classes are presented in Table 6. The difference between scores is statistically significant with $p\text{-value} < 0.05$.

Clusters C1 and C2 are quite close to each other; however, all average factor scores of C2 are considerably stronger than average factor scores of C1. The first class is a class of argumentative texts. Samples from C1 mostly include political articles, blog posts about social situation, and religious texts. Most of the texts are non-informative, slightly interactive, non-narrative, non-abstract, and slightly directive (religious texts are very directive). C1 has one main dimension D2, which means expressing a personal point of view on a particular subject and on positions of other people.

C2 is a big class of different personal blogs. These blogs are non-abstract, highly interactive, and expressing personal positions about a subject. The class has a relatively high value on the narrative dimension D3 because it is heterogeneous to some extent and includes a set of narrative personal stories.

A number of reviews from C2 (blogs with personal reasons about something like a political situation, a tour, a concert, or a book) have especially high scores on the argumentative dimension D2. So, if we want to distinguish reviews from other types of blogs automatically, we should take this feature into account.

C3 is a class of news reports. The texts of this class appear to be informative (D1), not presenting personal thoughts about describing events, not sharing the same context with readers (D2), narrative (D3), mostly neutral on 'abstract vs. non-abstract style' (D4), and non-directive (D6).

All legal texts belong to C4. This class is characterized by the highest value of D4, and other dimension values are low. The texts are very abstract, very informative, non-narrative, non-directive, and not presenting any personal positions about subjects. C4 is the most informative class in the set; its texts are characterized by long words, a large number of noun phrases, and its modifiers.

C5, the class of advertisements, has a large standard deviation for D1, D2 and D4-D6. The analysis of the texts which factor scores are far from the means of the dimensions indicated above showed that C5 includes very different sets of advertisements. It has an impact on the resulting dimension scores of the class. Most of advertising texts are informative, not showing personal argumentation about anything, and not highly directive; however, in the corpus we have several advertisements on dating sites which have appeal to potential partners and strong motivation to write a respond. As opposed to these addressee and personal focused texts, another set of advertisements is highly abstract because it describes technically complicated products (cameras, automobiles, synthesizers, etc.). It is unusual for advertisements in our corpus and more typical for scientific texts. So, we could see that values of dimensions scores could help us to find different subgenres in the genres of advertisement in the present corpus.

The type of texts related to a field of Science and Technology is included in the class C6. All the texts of the class are informative, non-narrative, non-directive, abstract, and not presenting a personal position. It is relevant for the scientific articles presented in the corpus.

C7 (encyclopedic texts) and C8 (instructive texts) have large standard deviations for D1, D2, D4, and D5. C7 includes texts which are highly informative and abstract, but also it contains a set of texts which do define some topics but not encyclopedic at all (interactive, non-abstract, and presenting a personal argumentation), e.g., a description of an episode from The Simpsons, a movie review or an obituary. We suppose that the problem with C7 can be solved by adding to the corpus more variety of texts defining some topic, especially texts not written by academic language. On the other hand, it might be reasonable to suppose that we had some errors in the annotation on the FTD 16 (defining a topic).

The main characteristic of C8 is high values of D6, which has a directive meaning. Looking at the samples from the class, we can understand that large values of a standard deviation are due to the fact that C8 consists of two sets of different instructions. The first small set consists of technical instructions, user's guides, and recipes; they all are informative, non-interactive, and abstract. The second big set includes highly interactive and non-abstract texts with some kind of informal communication with the reader, for example, a blog post advising on how to quit smoking. This spread of dimension values shows two different types (or subgenres) of instructions in our corpus.

Fiction texts of C9 are highly interactive, presenting personal attitude and argumentation, highly narrative, non-abstract, and directive. We undoubtedly should extend the corpus for further research because it contains only 10 fictional texts although they are quite long. Even though it is difficult to analyse the class C9, it shows the highest values on D3 (narrative vs. non-narrative). C9 is also highly marked on D2 which once again shows the close proximity of D2 to a personal side of discourse. Only C9 has as high values on D6 as C8. Analysis of the samples of C9 showed that it is mostly due to specific features of fictional texts in our corpus (high frequency of infinitives, purpose and conditional subordinate clauses).

Concerning D5, which includes only such features as total adverbs, time adverbs, and indefinite pronouns, we have a hypothesis that this dimension is a part of some other dimension, which might be or might be not presented in our current set. After analysing the medians of the scores on D5, we can suppose that D5 is close to D1 or D2. High positive scores on D5 mark mostly personal blogs and fictional texts. Negative scores are typical for legal texts, scientific, encyclopedic texts, and adverts. All texts labeled by the highest values of D5 are personal blog stories, so we assume that D5 is a part of D2. D5 is also very similar to the negative pole of the dimension called 'Elaborated vs. Situated reference' in (Biber, 1993b) including such features as place, time and other adverbs.

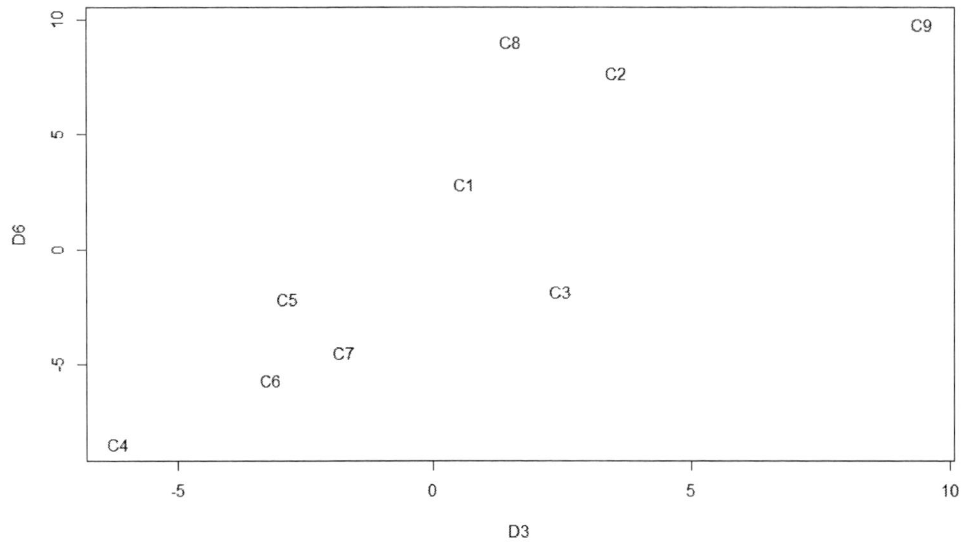

Figure 1: Distribution of 9 classes of the FDTs in D3 (narrative vs. non-narrative) and D6 (directive vs. non-directive).

Figure 3 presents an illustration how the classes are located in the space of D3 (narrative vs. non-narrative) and D6 (directive vs. non-directive).

6 Conclusions and Further Research

We have investigated variations in the linguistic properties of texts from the Russian Web by applying Biber's Multi-dimensional analysis to a Web corpus and have successfully used a much bigger Web corpus (GICR) to build a linguistic tagger.

By using factor analysis, we found six dimensions around which all functionally similar linguistic features are grouped for the presented corpus, and which were interpreted from the point of view of their functions. The dimensions obtained in this study are very similar to (Biber, 1993b) except for D2, which combines features usually found in several other dimensions such as 'Involved' (e.g., mental verbs or negation), 'Elaborated reference' (e.g., relative clauses), and 'Narrative' (e.g., 3rd personal pronouns, speech verbs). A larger corpus might provide a better match to the classical features.

Russian is not fundamentally different from English with respect to implementation of MD analysis; many features can be mapped, even though more morphological and syntactical features need to be processed.

The results of the MD analysis show that the classes of the FTDs (close to traditional genres) and the dimensions of language variation in Russian have evident connection. Every class has its own place in the multidimensional space of linguistic features. Deviations in dimension values for each text in each cluster allow us to find errors in annotation or functional groups of texts within a cluster (e.g., technical instructions vs. advice in C8). This shows that the MD approach can be used for finding text features specific for different genres and also for detecting fine-grained differences between subgenres.

The FTDs are not genres, but we assume that different genres in big corpora can be described by sets of different FTDs, so we should be able to identify them in texts. Our analysis shows that every major FTD describing a genre corresponds to a set of linguistic features. This could be used for the purpose of the automatic genre classification (the results of the first experiments with classification see in Lagutin et al., 2015).

In further research we intend to examine the FTDs in the space of an extended set of linguistic features, to experiment with a bigger corpus and to add discourse structure features.

Acknowledgements

This study has been supported by a joint project with Skoltech and Moscow State University, 'Brains, minds and machines' (Joint Lab. Agr. - No 081-R 1.10.2013).

References

John F. Bailyn. 2012. *The Syntax of Russian.* Cambridge: CUP, pages 84–109.

Mikhail Bakhtin. 1996. The problems of speech genres [Problemy rechevykh zhanrov]. *Russian dictionaries [Risskie slovari]. Collected writings.* Moscow, pages 159–206.

Tony Berber Sardinha, Carlos Kauffmann, and Cristina Mayer Acunzo. 2014. A multi-dimensional analysis of register variation in Brazilian Portuguese. *Corpora*, volume 9(2), pages 239–271.

Niko Besnier. 1988. The linguistic relationships of spoken and written Nukulaelae registers. *Language,* volume 64(4), pages 707–736.

Douglas Biber. 1986. Spoken and written textual dimensions in English: resolving the contradictory findings. *Language*, volume 62, pages 384–414.

Douglas Biber. 1988. *Variation across Speech and Writing.* Cambridge: CUP.

Douglas Biber. 1993a. Using register-diversified corpora for general language studies. *Computational Linguistics*, volume 19, pages 219–241.

Douglas Biber. 1993b. The multi-dimensional approach to linguistic analyses of genre variation: an overview of methodology and findings. *Computers and the Humanities,* volume 26, pages 331–345.

Douglas Biber. 2004. Conversation text types: a multi-dimensional analysis. In Gérald Purnelle, Cédrick Fairon, and Anne Dister (eds.) *Le poids des mots: Proc. of the 7th International Conference on the Statistical Analysis of Textual Data*, Louvain: Presses universitaires de Louvain, p.15–34.

Douglas Biber and Mohamed Hared. 1994. Linguistic correlates of the transition to literacy in Somali: language adaptation in six press registers. In Douglas Biber and Edward Finegan (eds.) *Sociolinguistic Perspectives on Register*, Oxford, pages 182–216.

Douglas Biber and Nicole Tracy-Ventura. 2007. Dimensions of register variation in Spanish. In Giovanni Parodi (ed.) *Working with Spanish Corpora,* London: Continuum, pages 54–89.

Douglas Biber, Ulla Connor, and Thomas A. Upton. 2007. *Discourse on the Move: Using Corpus Analysis to Describe Discourse Structure,* Amsterdam – Philadelphia, pages 261–271.

Victor Bocharov, Svetlana Bichineva, Dmitry Granovsky, et al. 2011. Quality assurance tools in the OpenCorpora project. *Proc. Dialogue, Russian International Conference on Computational Linguistics,* Bekasovo, pages 101–110.

Pavel Braslavski. 2011. Marrying relevance and genre rankings: an exploratory study. *Genres on the Web Computational Models and Empirical Studies. Text, Speech and Language Technology,* volume 42, pages 191–208.

Scott A. Crossley and Max Louwerse. 2007. Multi-dimensional register classification using bi-grams. *International Journal of Corpus Linguistics,* volume 12(4), pages 453–478.

Jocelyne Daems, Dirk Speelman, and Tom Ruette. 2013. Register analysis in blogs: correlation between professional sector and functional dimensions. *Leuven Working Papers in Linguistics,* volume 2(1), pages 1–27.

Jesse Egbert, Douglas Biber, and Mark Davies. 2015. Developing a bottom-up, user-based method of web register classification. *Journal of the Association for Information Science and Technology,* pages 1–15.

Aidan Finn, Nicholas Kushmerich, and Barry Smyth. 2003. Learning to classify documents according to genre. *IJCAI-2003 Workshop on Computational Approaches to Text Style and Synthesis*, Acapulco, pages 35–45.

Richard S. Forsyth and Serge Sharoff. 2014. Document dissimilarity within and across languages: a benchmarking study. *Literary and Linguistic Computing,* volume 29, pages 6–22.

Jack Grieve, Douglas Biber, Eric Friginal, and Tatiana Nekrasova. 2010. Variations among blogs: a multi-dimensional analysis. In Alexander Mehler, Serge Sharoff, and Marina Santini (eds.) *Genres on the Web: Computational Models and Empirical Studies*, Berlin – New York: Springer, pages 303–323.

Robert Kabakoff. 2011. *R in Action. Data Analysis and Graphics with R.* New York, pages 347–348.

YouJin Kim and Douglas Biber. 1994. A corpus-based analysis of register variation in Korean. In Douglas Biber and Eric Finegan (eds.) *Sociolinguistic Perspectives on Register*, Oxford, pages 157–181.

Eduard Klyshinsky, Natalia Kochetkova, Oksana Mansurova, Elena Iagounova, Vadim Maximov, and Olesia Karpik. 2013. Development of Russian subcategorization frames and its properties investigation. *Keldysh Institute preprints,* Moscow, no. 41, pages 1–23.

Mikhail Lagutin, Anisya Katinskaya, Vladimir Selegey, Serge Sharoff, and Alexey Sorokin. 2015. Automatic classification of web texts using Functional Text Dimensions. *Proc. Dialogue, Russian International Conference on Computational Linguistics,* Bekasovo, volume 1, pages 398–414.

William Lamb. 2008. *Scottish Gaelic Speech and Writing: Register Variation in an Endangered Language.* Belfast: Cló Ollscoil na Banríona.

David Lee. 2001. Genres, registers, text types, domains, and styles: clarifying the concepts and navigating a path through the BNC jungle. *Language Learning and Technology*, volume 5(3), pages 37–72.

Yong-Bae Lee and Sung Hyon Myaeng. 2004. Automatic identification of text genres and their roles in subject-based categorization. *Proc. of the 37th Hawaii International Conference on System Science (HICSS '04)*, pages 1–10.

Stephanos E. Michos, Efstathios Stamatatos, Nikos Fakotakis, and Georgios Kokkinakis. 1996. An empirical text categorizing computational model based on stylistic aspects. *Proc. of the 8 the International Conference on Tools with Artificial Intelligence (TAI'96),* pages 71–77.

Inge de Mönnink, Niek Brom, and Nelleke Oostdijk. 2003. Using the MF/MD method for automatic text classification. In Sylviane Granger and Stephanie Petch Tyson (eds.) *Extending the Scope of Corpus-based Research: New Applications, New Challenges*, Amsterdam, pages 15–25.

Junsaku Nakamura. 1993. Statistical methods and large corpora – a new tool for describing text type. In Mona Baker, Gill Francis, and Elena Tognini-Bonelli (eds.) *Text and technology*, Philadelphia – Amsterdam, pages 291–312.

Andrea Nini. 2014. *Multidimensional Analysis Tagger 1.2, Manual.* Available: http://sites.google.com/site/multidimensionaltagger

Giovanni Parodi. 2007. Variation across registers in Spanish: exploring the El Grial PUCV corpus. In Giovanni Parodi (ed.) *Working with Spanish Corpora*, London: Continuum, pages 11–53.

Alexander Piperski, Vladimir Belikov, Nikolay Kopylov, Vladimir Selegey, and Serge Sharoff. 2013. Big and diverse is beautiful: a large corpus of Russian to study linguistic variation. *Proc. 8th Web as Corpus Workshop (WAC-8),* pages 24–29.

Alexey Sorokin, Anisya Katinskaya, and Serge Sharoff. 2014. Associating symptoms with syndromes: reliable genre annotation for a large Russian webcorpus. *Proc. Dialogue, Russian International Conference on Computational Linguistics,* Bekasovo, pages 646–659.

Helmut Schmid and Florian Laws. 2008. Estimation of conditional probabilities with decision trees and an application to fine-grained POS tagging. *Proc. of the 22nd International Conference on Computational Linguistics (COLING'08)*, Manchester, volume 1, pages 777–784.

Serge Sharoff. 2010. In the garden and in the jungle: comparing genres in the BNC and the internet. In Alexander Mehler, Serge Sharoff, and Marina Santini (eds.) *Genres on the Web: Computational Models and Empirical Studies*, Berlin – New York: Springer, pages 149–166.

Serge Sharoff and Joakim Nivre. 2011. The proper place of men and machines in language technology: processing Russian without any linguistic knowledge. *Proc. Dialogue, Russian International Conference on Computational Linguistics*, Bekasovo, pages 591–604.

Efstathios Stamatatos, Nikos Fakotakis, and Georgios Kokkinakis. 2001. Automatic text categorization in terms of genre and author. *Computational Linguistics,* volume 26(4), pages 471–495.

Robert Sigley. 1997. Text categories and where you can stick them: a crude formality index. *International Journal of Corpus Linguistics*, volume 2(2), pages 199–237.

Elena Yagunova and Anna Pospelova. 2014. Opyt primeneniya stilevyh i zhanrovyh harakteristik dlya opisaniya stilevyh osobennostej kollekcij tekstov. *Novye informacionnye tekhnologii v avtomatizirovannyh sistemah,* no. 17, pages 347–356.

Remarkable Similarity of Clausal Coordinate Ellipsis in Russian Compared to Dutch, Estonian, German, and Hungarian

Karin Harbusch and **Denis Krusko**
Computer Science Department
University of Koblenz–Landau, Koblenz, Germany
harbusch, kruskod@uni-koblenz.de

Abstract

Elliptical constructions can help to avoid repetition of identical constituents during natural-language generation. From grammar books, it is not easy to extract executable rules for ellipsis—in our case in Russian. Therefore we follow a different strategy. We test the accuracy of a rule set that has been evaluated for the two Germanic languages, Dutch and German, and the two Finno-Ugric languages, Estonian and Hungarian. For a Russian test corpus of about 100 syntactically annotated coordinated sentences that systematically vary the conditions of rule application, our Java program can automatically produce all elliptical variants. Over- and undergeneration in the resulting lists have been tested in two experiments with native speakers. Basically, the rules work very well for Russian. Within the four target languages, Russian works best with the Estonian amendments. Here we report two slight deviations partially known from the linguistic literature.

1 Introduction

In natural-language generation, ellipsis can help to avoid repetition of identical constituents. For instance, the conceptual structure 'eat(Peter, apples) & eat(Mary, apples)' where 'eat' and 'apples' occur two times can be formulated as *Peter eats apples and Mary too*, a case of Stripping. However, many other paraphrases can be produced such as the aggregation into one sentence with NP-coordination (*Peter and Mary eat apples*)—a case of reduction we do not address in the following as it works on the conceptual structure whereas we only deal with syntactic structures as input.

Ellipsis occurs frequently in written and spoken language. In the following, we study four types of clausal coordinate ellipsis (CCE): (1) Gapping (including Long Distance Gapping (LDG), Subgapping and Stripping), (2) Forward Conjunction Reduction (FCR), (3) Backward Conjunction Reduction (BCR), and (4) Subject Gap with Finite/Fronted Verb (SGF). In German written text, clausal coordination, i.e., the two conjuncts comprise verbal constructions (not necessarily finite), occurs in 14 and ellipsis in at least one of the two conjuncts in 7 percent of the investigated corpus (cf. Harbusch & Kempen, 2007). All these types of clausal coordinate ellipsis also emerge in spontaneous speech in German (cf. Harbusch & Kempen, 2009a). This observation is in line with English corpus studies (see, e.g., Greenbaum & Nelson, 1999) and Dutch (Harbusch, 2011).

For recent theoretical treatments of CCE in various linguistic frameworks see, e.g., Schwabe & Zhang, 2000; Frank, 2002; Beaver & Sag, 2004; te Velde, 2006; Haspelmath, 2007; Johnson, 2009; Kempen, 2009; Van Craenenbroeck & Merchant, 2013; Griffiths & Lipták, 2014. For Russian as target language, see, e.g., Kazenin, 2006 or Gribanova, 2013. Parsing elliptical constructions is a difficult problem partially due to the fact that both conjuncts may be grammatically incorrect when viewed in isolation (see, e.g., Kobele, 2012). In a natural-language generation-system, CCE is only one realization option (cf. Shaw 1998) out of many (e.g., Pronominalization also avoids repeating the same NP). The implemented CCE-generation component ELLEIPO, which embodies the CCE rule set we present below, can serve as a post-editing component for NLG systems that provide a syntactic structure annotated with co-referentiality tags (cf. Harbusch & Kempen, 2009b). ELLEIPO takes these non-elliptical (redundant) structures as input and provides all reduced to CCE options as output. ELLEIPO was originally developed for Dutch and German (see Harbusch & Kempen, 2006), but the implemented

Proceedings of the 5th Workshop on Balto-Slavic Natural Language Processing, pages 75–80,
Hissar, Bulgaria, 10–11 September 2015.

set of CCE rules was designed in a language-independent manner. This makes it possible to discover CCE rules in a new target language. For the Finno-Ugric language Estonian, Harbusch, Koit & Õim (2009) report high accuracy of the rule set, which suggests that the entire process is language independent. However, Estonian is suspected to be strongly influenced by language contact with Germanic languages. Nevertheless, Hungarian, another Finno-Ugric language, yields equally good results (cf. Harbusch & Bátori, 2013).

In the present paper, we aim to further verify our claim that CCE can be generated by language-independent rules by testing ELLEIPO's rules for Russian. To this purpose, we built a test corpus of about 100 Russian syntactic structures of (unreduced) coordinated sentences in Russian varying the conditions for CCE-rule application. RUSSIAN-ELLEIPO produces all CCE reductions for the test corpus. In the first experiment, we let native speakers of Russian judge the quality of the output (*overgeneration* of the CCE rules). In the second, native speakers generated all reductions (inclusive Pronominalization etc.) for unreduced coordinated sentences in order to spot CCE realizations that ELLEIPO does not generate (*undergeneration*). In general, we observed a very high level of accuracy of the CCE rules.

The paper is organized as follows. In Section 2, we define the CCE phenomena ELLEIPO is able to generate. In Section 3, we describe the test corpus, and elaborate on ELLEIPO's output and on the user studies. In Section 4, we outline our results. In the final Section, we draw some conclusions and address future work.

2 Definition of the CCE Rules

We distinguish four types of CCE applicable to *binary and*-coordinations, and specify elision conditions on the first (*anterior*) and second (*posterior*) member of two conjoined clauses connected by the Russian equivalent *i*[1] of the coordinating conjunction *and* (cf. examples in Table 1).

The CCE rules of ELLEIPO are based on the psycholinguistically motivated definitions of CCE types proposed by Kempen (2009). They check the following conditions in syntactic trees whose inner nodes additionally provide 'referential identity features'.

[1]As in Russian, *a* 'but' is used for contrasts, we vary our examples in the Gapping test where contrast is mandatory.

GAPPING (g)	(1) Ûrij **živët** v Tambove i ego synov´â ~~**živut**~~$_g$ Ûrij live$_{3SG}$ in Tambov and his sons live$_{3PL}$ v Kaluge in Kaluga 'Ûrij **lives** in Tambov and his sons ~~**live**~~$_g$ in Kaluga.'
	(2) Ûrij **živët** v Tambove i v Kaluge ~~**živut**~~$_g$ Ûrij live$_{3SG}$ in Tambov and in Kaluga live$_{3PL}$ ego synov´â his sons 'Ûrij **lives** in Tambov and in Kaluga, his sons ~~**live**~~$_g$'
LDG ((g)$^+$g)	(3) **Segodnâ dolžen** Pëtr svoû mašinu myt´ i Today should Pëtr his car wash$_{INF}$ and ~~**segodnâ**~~$_{gg}$ ~~**dolžna**~~$_g$ Maša svoj velosiped ~~**myt´**~~$_{gg}$ today should Maša her bike wash$_{INF}$ 'Today Pëtr **should wash** his car and ~~**today**~~$_{gg}$ Maša ~~**should**~~$_g$ ~~**wash**~~$_{gg}$ her bike'
SUBGAP-PING (g)	(4) Ivan **hočet** spat´ a Pëtr ~~**hočet**~~$_g$ mečtat´ Ivan want$_{3SG}$ sleep$_{INF}$ but Pëtr want$_{3SG}$ dream$_{INF}$ 'Ivan **wants** to sleep but Pëtr ~~**wants**~~$_g$ to dream'
STRIP-PING (str)	(5) Â **splû** i ty ~~**spiš**~~$_{str}$ tože I sleep$_{1SG}$ and you sleep$_{2SG}$ too 'I **sleep** and you ~~**sleep**~~$_{str}$ too'
FCR (f)	(6) **Cvetaevu** lûblû **â** i ~~**Cvetaevu**~~$_f$ Cvetaeva$_{ACC}$ like$_{1SG}$ I and Cvetaeva$_{ACC}$ čitaû ~~**â**~~$_s$ často read$_{1SG}$ I often 'I like **Cvetaeva** and ~~**Cvetaeva**~~$_f$ read ~~**I**~~$_s$ often'
	(7) Maša slyšala, **[čto Pëtr]** popal v Mary hear$_{PST.SG.F}$ that Pëtr get$_{PST.SG.F}$ an avariû i [~~**čto Pëtr**~~]$_f$ mog umeret´ accident and that Pëtr can$_{PST_{SG}.M}$ die$_{INF}$ 'Mary heard **that Pëtr** had an accident and [~~**that Pëtr**~~]$_f$ could die'
BCR (b)	(8) Maša **pridët** do trëh ~~**časov**~~$_b$ Maša come$_{FUT.3SG}$ before three$_{ACC}$ o'clock a Katâ ~~**pridët**~~$_g$ posle četyrëh **čhasov** but Katâ come$_{FUT.3SG}$ after four$_{ACC}$ o'clock 'Maša **will come** before three ~~**o'clock**~~$_b$ and Katâ [~~**will come**~~]$_g$ after four **o'clock**'
SGF (s)	(9) V les hodil **ohotnik** Into forest$_{ACC.SG}$ go$_{PST.SG.M}$ the hunter i podstrelil ~~**ohotnik**~~$_s$ odnogo zajca and shot$_{PST.SG.M}$ the hunter one$_{ACC.M}$ hare 'Into the forest went **the hunter** and [~~**the hunter**~~]$_s$ shot a hare'

Table 1: CCE examples in Russian (using the *ISO 9* transliteration standard for better readability). Crossed-out text represents elisions. Subscripts indicate CCE type. Elided constituents and their overt counterparts are marked in bold font.

1. *Gapping* ignores word order (compare example (1) with the marked word order in (2). It only requires lemma-identity of the two Verbs in the two conjuncts & contrastiveness[2] of the remnants (non-elided constituents). For *lemma-identity* only the stems need to coincide. However, morphological properties such as Number or Person of a Verb may differ in the two conjuncts (e.g., in example (1), *živët* and *živut* are lemma-identical). The Gapping variant *Long-Distance Gapping (LDG)* recursively applies the general Gapping conditions top-down to corresponding Verb pairs in the structure, provided they are in the range of a so-called superclause[3] in both conjuncts. *Subgapping* works as LDG but a Nonfinite Verb structure happens to be not identical; this yields a Nonfinite clausal remnant in the second conjunct. *Stripping* is applied after any form of Gapping: during read-out of Gapping results it inspects whether there is no more than one non-Verb remnant; in that case read-out adds a language-specific stripping particle.

2. *Forward-Conjunction Reduction (FCR)* requires wordform-identity, i.e., in addition to lemma- and grammatical-function identity, identity of the morphological features is needed in the left-periphery of major clausal constituents, i.e., both clausal conjuncts should start with a wordform-identical sequence of FULL constituents.

3. *Backward-Conjunction Reduction (BCR)* is licensed by lemma-identity in the right-periphery, that is, both clausal conjuncts end with the same sequence of wordform and grammatical-function identical WORDS (e.g., in example (8), *o'clock* is such a sequence). Note that FCR and BCR are not complete mirror images because only BCR is allowed to disregarding major constituent boundaries.

4. *Subject Gap with Finite/Fronted Verb (SGF)* requires wordform-identical Subjects where the first conjunct starts with Verb/Modifier/Adjunct or where the first conjunct is a Conditional Subordinate Clause (Subject-Verb-Inversion) & FCR is applied if licensed.

3 Set-up of RUSSIAN-ELLEIPO

In order to use ELLEIPO for any new target language, the existing Java implementation of ELLEIPO has to be changed only minimally because the rule set works target-language independently. We added the Russian Conjunction and the Russian Stripping particle along with its position (leading or trailing) in the language-specific part of the existing Java code.

In order to test the accuracy in a new target language, an appropriate *test corpus* of ELLEIPO should contain structures that trigger ALL constraints in the rule set, i.e., lemma- and wordform-identity, contrastiveness, grammatical-function and word-order variation in the left- and right periphery. A blueprint of such a collection is ELLEIPO's test corpus of about 100 sentences for German and Dutch (see Harbusch & Kempen, 2006). All these sentences have been translated into Russian. In order to avoid biases, preserving the meaning was not essential but trying to keep the varying constraints active in the Russian syntactic trees, i.e., natural constructions in Russian have been set up (cf. clues for rule application/failure of all phenomena in Table 2; N.B. that several phenomena can occur in one test sentence). The large number of Gapping examples represents the great variety of word ordering to be ignored, contrastiveness to be obeyed, differing superclause-boundary violation-options (relevant for LDG and Subgapping), grammatical-function and lemma and wordform variation. The larger number of FCR tests compared to (the near mirror image) BCR results from more variation options for major constituents in the frontfield of a sentence compared to the limited word variation in the right periphery in BCR. For SGF, the range of options is also restricted.

Processing the Russian test corpus, ELLEIPO provides a condensed list of all reductions

[2] *Contrastiveness* constraints rule out elisions such as *I eat apples and you ~~eat~~ in the car*—which is comprehensible but not grammatical.

[3] A *superclause* is defined as a hierarchy of Finite or Nonfinite Clauses that—with the possible exception of the topmost clause—do not include a Subordinating Conjunction. In (3), the Subjects *Pëtr* and *Maša* each belong to a Main Clause headed by the Verb *dolžen* 'should' whereas *segodnâ* 'today' and *svoû mašinu/svoj velosiped* 'his car/her bike' belong to the Nonfinite Complement Clause headed by the Infinitive *myt´* 'wash'. Nevertheless, they form one superclause in each of the conjuncts. Example (7)—actually, a case of FCR where no superclause test is elicited—contains two superclauses in each conjunct, due to the Subordinating Conjunction *čto* 'that'.

CCE Rule	Number of inclusions
GAPPING	91
STRIPPING	17
FCR	72
BCR	25
SGF	17

Table 2: Phenomena in the Russian test corpus.

with/without subscripts—slightly more elaborate than indicated in Table 1. ELLEIPO adds unique numbers to each CCE token so that an elided constituent and its remnant directly correspond. For instance, ELLEIPO's output for example (3) spells out the sentence variant depicting Subgapping along with Backward-Conjunction Reduction (cf. subscript number #4 for BCR in **Segodnâ**$_{2\ 3}$ **dolžen**$_{1}$ Pëtr svoû mašinu **myt´**$_{4\text{-b}\ 2}$ i ~~**segodnâ**~~$_{2\text{-gg}\ 3\text{-f}}$ ~~**dolžna**~~$_{1\text{-g}}$ Maša svoj velosiped ~~**myt´**~~$_{2\text{-gg}}$—also notice subscript #3 licensing *segodnâ* for FCR). ELLEIPO's read-out component can spell out all possible combinations of elisions (with or without elaborate subscripts).

The complete lists of unreduced and reduced sentences form the text materials we presented to the participants in the two experiments that we carried out to calculate the accuracy of our CCE rules, specifically, the amount of *overgeneration* and *undergeneration* of the rule set in Russian. In experiment 1, we targeted overgeneration. We had native speakers judge the acceptability of the elliptical structures proposed by the CCE generator for the test corpus. In experiment 2, aiming to detect undergeneration, we tried to elicit yet undiscovered elision types for a standard corpus of unreduced test sentences (i.e., sentences without CCE). Obviously, the scope of the latter experiment is restricted, due to the limited number and variability of the sentences presented to the participants.

We used a rating scale specifying three levels of acceptability of a reduced sentence (*good, dubious, unacceptable*) in order to avoid overtaxing and exhausting the test subjects—in contrast to the very fine-grained method for grammaticality rating used by Keller (2000). In case of dubious acceptability, more details have been asked. Basically, a more fine-grained tendency for more/less acceptability as well as insights in misinterpretations have been traced. This type of comments was obtained in an *interview situation with a moderator*.[4] The moderator should be a linguist speaking the target language to bring up follow-up questions. Such digression does not spoil the study—compared to a standardized experiment as in Psychology. Another deviation from standardized testing (originally proposed for Usability (UX) Testing and verified with a meta-study on case studies by Nielsen (2012)) works very well here. Few test subjects—Jakob Nielsen suggests five in UX, although, user behavior varies more than in grammaticality rating—suffice to point out the majority of all problems.

In experiment 1, we let three native speakers of Russian evaluate ELLEIPO's output. The participants always saw unreduced sentences together with the reduced ones. This setup is necessary because it is known that, although some reductions are acceptable in themselves, they do not express the same meaning as its unreduced counterpart (cf. example (12) in next section). We counted a match as successful if at least one participant judged it acceptable.[5]

In experiment 2, we tried to identify *undergeneration* with the CCE rule set, i.e., judged acceptable by native speakers but failing to be produced by ELLEIPO. For this purpose we presented unreduced sentences only and let the participants freely produce any kind of reduction crossing their mind. In the list of answers we first identified Pronominalization, One-anaphora and other non-CCE forms of ellipsis as they do not count in our study (however, the participants cannot know this). Given the high amount of different linguistic constructions the participants produced, the motivation of the participants during the experiments can be judged to be high (so to speak playful in a positive sense). The experiment unveiled great similarities of Russian with Estonian and Hungarian which allow weaker word-ordering conditions for SGF and FCR (e.g., Ditransitive Verbs allow for non-peripheral elision of wordform and grammatical-function identical constituents).

[4]Further options are unmoderated tests conducted in an observation lab or (internet) questionnaires. The user studies for Estonian, Hungarian and Russian were conducted as face-to-face interviews to make test subjects try considerably harder (cf. Schulte-Mecklenbeck and Huber, 2003). Moreover, all kinds of misinterpretation can be discussed on the spot given that the moderator remains neutral in order to minimize unwelcome influence on the results of the test.

[5]This weak acceptability criterion was prompted by the fact that CCE acceptability ratings can give rise to wide inter-rater variability. In German, grammar books (and ELLEIPO) license BCR for constituents that are lemma-identical but not grammatical-function identical. However, many German native speakers rule out *Hilf* ***[~~dem Mann~~]***$_{DAT}$ *und reanimier* ***[den Mànn]***$_{ACC}$ 'Help and reanimate the man'.

4 Results

In experiment 1 (on overgeneration), 79 % of the sentences produced by ELLEIPO were judged acceptable. At a first glance this sounds meager. However, one should realize that if ELLEIPO wrongly applies a CCE rule, it does so for all sentences embodying the same trigger condition. Second experiment accomplished 97 % accuracy. The number of identified CCE tokens along with over- and undergeneration cases by type of CCE rules is shown in Figure 1. Note: the columns show absolute numbers, not percentages.

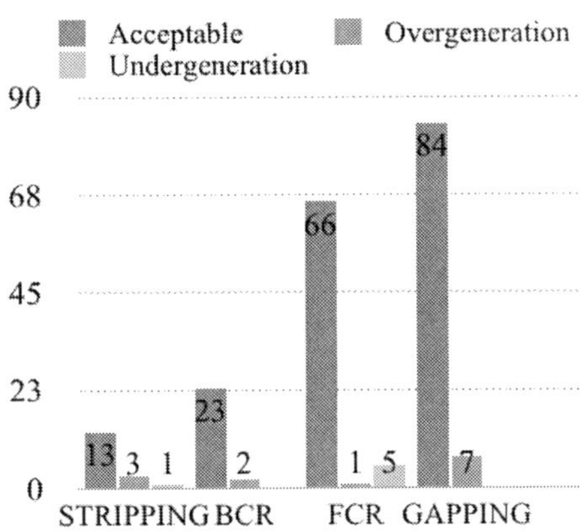

Figure 1: Numbers of cases revealing over- and undergeneration in the two experiments.

Comparison of our Russian data with those obtained in previous work for the two Finno-Ugric languages revealed interesting similarities. In Estonian and Hungarian, the left-periphery constraint is less strict compared to Dutch and German. In SGF, Estonian and Hungarian allow for more freedom in the frontfield whereas this is not possible in Dutch and German. In Russian, Arguments in the frontfield also license FCR (cf. example (10) with a Complement Clause in the frontfield).

(10) **Examen** **sdat´** hočet **on/student** i
The-exam$_{ACC}$ pass$_{INF}$ will he/student and

~~**examen**~~$_{f}$ ~~**sdat´**~~$_{f}$ možet ~~**on/student**~~$_{s}$ tože
the-exam$_{ACC}$ pass$_{INF}$ can he/student also
'The exam, he/the student wants to pass and he is also able to'

The typical superclause violation identified as acceptable in Hungarian for the subordinating conjunction *hogy* 'that' was not obtained in Russian (cf. example (11)). However, some informants indicate they might use it in colloquial spoken Russian.

(11) Maša **nadeetsâ** čto Pëtr **ujdet** i
Maša hope$_{3SG}$ that Pëtr leave$_{3SG}$ and

Katâ ~~**nadeetsâ**~~$_{g}$ that Jan ~~**ujdet**~~$_{gg}$
Katâ hope$_{3SG}$ that Jan leave$_{3SG}$
'Mary hopes that Peter leaves and Cathrine hopes that Jan leaves'

The acceptability judgments suggest two rule amendments that could help avoiding overgeneration and serious misunderstandings of the reduced sentences. In Long-Distance and Subgapping, exactly two constituents may remain in the second conjunct (see example (12) where the participants interpret the reduced sentence as 'you are in the bus'). Obviously, in Russian any inflected form of 'to be' is assumed to be left out for two remaining remnants instead of taking into account the Verbal constituents in the anterior conjunct. Notice, that we expected this reaction as this Russian-specific CCE phenomenon is discussed in the literature (see, e.g., Kazenin, 2006).

(12) * Â **[vižu Petra kotoryj spit]** v mašine i
I see$_{1SG}$ Pëtr$_{ACC}$ who sleep$_{3SG}$ in car$_{DAT}$ and

ty ~~**[vidеš´ Petra kotoryj spit]**~~$_{g}$ v avtobuse
you see$_{2SG}$ Pëtr$_{ACC}$ who sleep$_{3SG}$ in bus$_{DAT}$
'I see Pëtr that sleeps in the car and you in the bus'

Another remarkable difference that we could not trace in the linguistic literature is the fact that Russian speakers do not allow violation of *co-referentiality* of elided constituents (cf. example (13)). In this sentence, the constituents *svoj velosiped* 'his bike' cannot be elided by Gapping because the two constituents refer to two different referential objects (4 % of the reduced corpus sentences were rejected due to this fact).

(13) Maša slyšala, **čto** Ûrij **svoj velosiped pomyl**
Maša hear$_{PST.SG.F}$ that Ûrij his bike wash$_{PST.SG.M}$

i ~~**čto**~~$_{f}$ Pëtr **svoj velosiped pomyl**
and that Pëtr his bike wash$_{PST.SG.M}$
'Maša heard, that Ûrij and Pëtr washed their bikes'

5 Conclusions

We have identified remarkable similarity of the language-independent CCE rules in Russian compared to Dutch, Estonian, German, and Hungarian. Russian ellipsis reveals the highest similarity to Estonian if written text quality is considered.

As for future work, we plan to conduct a corpus study into Russian treebanks of spoken and written language in order to find additional subtle deviations that go beyond our studies (cf. Harbusch & Kempen, 2007).

Acknowledgements

We thank Gerard Kempen for helpful discussions on earlier versions of the paper, and three reviewers for constructive criticism.

References

John Beavers and Ivan A Sag. 2004. Coordinate ellipsis and apparent non-constituent coordination. In *Proceedings of the HPSG04 Conference*, pages 48–69.

Anette Frank. 2002. A (discourse) functional analysis of asymmetric coordination. In *Procs. of the LFG02 Conference*, pages 174–196.

Vera Gribanova. 2013. Verb-stranding verb phrase ellipsis and the structure of the Russian verbal complex. *Natural Language & Linguistic Theory*, 31(1):91–136.

James Griffiths and Anikó Lipták. 2014. Contrast and island sensitivity in clausal ellipsis. *Syntax*, 17(3):189–234.

Karin Harbusch and István Bátori. 2013. Clausal Coordinate Ellipsis (CCE) in Hungarian compared to cce in Dutch, German, and Estonian. In *Approaches to Hungarian: Volume 13: Papers from the 2011 Lund conference*, volume 13, page 45. John Benjamins Publishing.

Karin Harbusch and Gerard Kempen. 2006. Elleipo: A module that computes coordinative ellipsis for language generators that don't. In *Proceedings of the Eleventh Conference of the European Chapter of the Association for Computational Linguistics: Posters & Demonstrations*, pages 115–118. Association for Computational Linguistics.

Karin Harbusch and Gerard Kempen. 2009a. Clausal coordinate ellipsis and its varieties in spoken German: A study with the TüBa-D/S treebank of the Verbmobil corpus. In *Eighth International Workshop on Treebanks and Linguistic Theories*, pages 83–94. EDUCatt.

Karin Harbusch and Gerard Kempen. 2009b. Generating clausal coordinate ellipsis multilingually: A uniform approach based on postediting. In *Proceedings of the 12th European Workshop on Natural Language Generation*, pages 138–145. Association for Computational Linguistics.

Karin Harbusch, Mare Koit, and Haldur Õim. 2009. A comparison of clausal coordinate ellipsis in Estonian and German. In *Proceedings of the 12th Conference of the European Chapter of the Association for Computational Linguistics: Demonstrations Session*, pages 25–28. Association for Computational Linguistics.

Karin Harbusch. 2011. Incremental sentence production inhibits Clausal Coordinate Ellipsis: A treebank study into Dutch and German. *Schlangen, D. & Rieser, H. (Eds.). Dialogue and Discourse*, 2(1):313—-332.

Martin Haspelmath. 2007. Coordination. In *Language Typology and Linguistic Description*, volume 2, pages 1–51. Cambridge University Press, Cambridge, UK, 2 edition.

Kyle Johnson. 2009. Gapping is not (VP-) ellipsis. *Linguistic Inquiry*, 40(2):289–328.

Konstantin Kazenin. 2006. Polarity in Russian and the typology of predicate ellipsis. *Ms., Moscow State University*.

Frank Keller. 2000. *Gradience in grammar: Experimental and computational aspects of degrees of grammaticality*. Ph.D. thesis, University of Edinburgh, UK.

Gerard Kempen. 2009. Clausal coordination and coordinative ellipsis in a model of the speaker. *Linguistics*, 47(3):653–696.

Gregory M Kobele. 2012. Eliding the derivation: a minimalist formalization of ellipsis. In *Proceedings of the HPSG 2012 conference*.

Jakob Nielsen. 2012. How many test users in a usability study? Online article with date: June 4, 2012, see: http://www.nngroup.com/articles/how-many-test-users.

Michael Schulte-Mecklenbeck and Oswald Huber. 2003. Information search in the laboratory and on the web: With or without an experimenter. *Behavior Research Methods, Instruments, & Computers*, 35(2):227–235.

Kerstin Schwabe and Ning Zhang. 2000. *Ellipsis in conjunction*, volume 418. Max Niemeyer Verlag.

James Shaw. 1998. Segregatory coordination and ellipsis in text generation. In *Proceedings of the 17th international conference on Computational linguistics-Volume 2*, pages 1220–1226. Association for Computational Linguistics.

John R Te Velde. 2006. *Deriving coordinate symmetries: A phase-based approach integrating Select, Merge, Copy and Match*, volume 89. John Benjamins Publishing.

Jeroen Van Craenenbroeck and Jason Merchant, 2013. *Ellipsis phenomena*, pages 701–745. Cambridge University Press, Cambridge, in Marcel den Dikken (ed.), The Cambridge handbook of generative syntax edition.

Universalizing BulTreeBank: a Linguistic Tale about Glocalization

Petya Osenova
Linguistic Modeling Department
IICT-BAS
petya@bultreebank.org

Kiril Simov
Linguistic Modeling Department
IICT-BAS
kivs@bultreebank.org

Abstract

The paper presents the strategies and conversion principles of BulTreeBank into Universal Dependencies annotation scheme. The mappings are discussed from linguistic and technical point of view. The mapping from the original resource to the new one has been done on morphological and syntactic level. The first release of the treebank was issued in May 2015. It contains 125 000 tokens, which cover roughly half of the corpus data.

1 Introduction

The efforts within the NLP community towards universalized language datasets for getting comparable, objective and scalable results in parsing and other tasks are not so recent. Concerning syntax, some shared representations have been proposed and used at CoNLL contests on dependency parsing in 2006 (Buchholz and Marsi, 2006) and 2007 (Nivre et al., 2007). Another stream of sharing the same annotation framework was the adoption of the schemes of already existing treebanks. For example, a number of syntactic annotation works followed the style of Prague Dependency Treebank (Bejček et al., 2013) (i.e., Slovene (Džeroski et al., 2006), Croatian (Berovic et al., 2012), Tamil (Ramasamy and Žabokrtsky, 2012) etc.); many other treebanks followed the Penn Treebank style (i.e., Arabic (Maamouri et al., 2008), Chinese (Xue et al., 2005), etc.). An alternative way of pursuing a common annotation architecture is the pre-shared core deep grammar, such as the Matrix Grammar (Bender et al., 2002) in DELPH-IN initiative,[1] which helps to develop the language specific part further. However, all shared annotation schemes face the same challenges, namely what model might ensure maximum coverage of language specific phenomena and then, how to deal with the phenomena that are easy to universalize, and with those that are hard to incorporate.

The most recent initiatives which refer to Stanford typed dependencies (de Marneffe and Manning, 2008) and Universal Dependencies (de Marneffe et al., 2014) are not an exception to the above presented situation. They build on the existing treebanks and aim at universal parts-of-speech (POS) and dependency relations. With more and more languages coming on board, new issues are raised and considered. For that reason, the Universal Dependencies initiative has taken a dynamic approach. This means that there are regular releases of the treebanks in accordance to some current annotation model. Each release is frozen to its agreed annotation model. Then the model is enriched, changed, reconsidered, and the follow-up release takes into account the revised one. It seems that versioning is indeed the only fair way to tackle the diversity of language phenomena.

BulTreeBank did not participate in the first release of universalized treebanks (UD v1.0 (Nivre et al., 2015)). However, part of it was delivered in the second one – UD v1.1 (Agić et al., 2015) together with other 17 languages. Its size is 125 000 tokens, which constitute half of the data.

In this paper we present the strategies of converting BulTreeBank into Universal Dependency format with respect to morphology and syntax. The undertaken conversion steps and various linguistic issues are discussed in the context of manual/automated work and universal/specific language features.

The structure of the paper is as follows: Section 2 focuses on related work. Section 3 highlights the BulTreeBank resource in a nutshell. Section 4 outlines the universalizing principles of morphology and syntax. Section 5 describes the conversion procedure. Section 6 reports on some

[1] http://www.delph-in.net/matrix/

Proceedings of the 5th Workshop on Balto-Slavic Natural Language Processing, pages 81–89,
Hissar, Bulgaria, 10–11 September 2015.

preliminary results from training MATE Tools on the converted treebank. Section 7 concludes the paper.

2 Related Work

The Universal Dependency initiative evolved mainly from the Stanford Type Dependency efforts and Google attempts (Petrov et al., 2012) in universalizing parts-of-speech. However, it is also ideologically related to CoNLL contests (2006 and 2007).

The universalizing activities started with two main directions of research. The first can be illustrated by the work of Rosa et al. (2014) where 30 treebanks have been harmonized into a common Prague Dependency style, and then converted into Stanford Dependencies.[2] It does not handle language specific features. BulTreeBank was also among the harmonized treebanks. The second can be exemplified by the work of Sanguinetti and Bosco (2014) and Bosco and Sanguinetti (2014). The authors describe the conversion of the parallel treebank ParTUT (Italian, English, French) into Stanford dependencies. In the same context is the work of Lipenkova and Souček (2014) on Russian dependency treebank.

Later on came also work on the conversion of the treebanks into Universal Dependencies. These include the conversion of the Swedish treebank (Nivre, 2014) and the Finnish treebank (Pyysalo et al., 2015). The experiments with the converted Finnish treebank showed that the parsing results are better with the Universal Dependencies (UD).

3 BulTreeBank Resource in a Nutshell

The original BulTreeBank (Simov et al., 2004; Simov and Osenova, 2003) that has been used in the conversion to the universal format comprises 214,000 tokens, which form a little more than 15,000 sentences. Each token has been annotated with elaborate morphosyntactic information. The original XML format of the BulTreeBank is based on HPSG. The syntactic structure is presented through a set of constituents with head-dependant markings. The phrasal constituents contain two types of information: the domain of the constituent (*NP, VP* etc.) and the type of the phrase (head-complement (*NPC, VPC* etc.), head-subject (*VPS*), head-adjunct (*NPA, VPA* etc.). The treebank provides also functional nodes, such as clausal ones – *CLDA* (subordinate clause introduced by the auxiliary particle да to), *CLCHE* (subordinate clause introduced by the subordinator че that), etc.

Tracing back to the developments of BulTreeBank, its first 'glocalization' happened in 2006, when it was converted into the shared CoNLL dependency format – (Chanev et al., 2006), (Chanev et al., 2007). The rich structure was flattened to a set of 18 relations.[3] This part consists of 196 000 tokens, because the sentences with ellipses were not considered.

Alternative versions of BulTreeBank exist in two other popular formats: PennTreebank (Ghayoomi et al., 2014) and Stanford Dependencies (Rosa et al., 2014). The former was used for constituent parsing of Bulgarian, while the latter was part of a bigger endevour towards universalizing syntactic annotation schemes of many languages.

Now, BulTreeBank is part of the common efforts that evolved from the previous initiatives towards the creation of comparable syntactically annotated multilingual datasets. For the Universal Dependencies initiative we used the original BulTreeBank constituent-based format, because in the previous conversions to dependency format some important information was either lost, or underspecified.

4 Universalizing Morphology and Syntax

At this stage our conversion adheres fully to the universal annotation schemes. This means that we postponed the addition of language specific features for the next stage. The only language specific feature considered in this version is the morphologically marked count form – remnant of the old Slavic dual form within the category of Number. The morphological mapping includes parts-of-speech and their lexical as well as inflectional features. The syntactic mapping focuses on dependency relations.

In this section we do not aim at exhaustive description of the mappings, but rather at illustrating the varieties between the models.

4.1 Morphology

In morphology the following mapping cases occurred from the direction of the original tagset to

[2]This initiative as well as the Universal Dependencies stream build on the idea of interset, proposed by Zeman (2008).

[3]http://www.bultreebank.org/dpbtb/

the UD tagset: identical parts-of-speech, division of one POS into more parts-of-speech and changing the POS. It should be noted however that all the processes are interrelated.

1. **Direct Mapping.** The first case refers to subordinators and conjunctions, adjectives, prepositions.

2. **Division of one POS into more parts-of-speech.** The BulTreeBank original POS tagset[4] respects the morphological nature of the parts-of-speech, i.e., their origin. The UD tagset, however, is more syntactically oriented. It considers the syntactic function at the cost of parts-of-speech partitioning into several other groups. For example, in our original tagset the group of pronouns is homogeneous in spite of their differing functions. However, in UD this group is split into the groups DET, PRON and ADV. The category DET (determiner) is syntactic for Bulgarian, since the definite article is a phrasal affix and part of the word (масата 'table.DET' the table; високата маса 'tall.DEF table' the tall table). Thus, to this category belong the appropriate pronouns that are used attributively (definite, indefinite, collective, etc.). The pronouns that are used substantively, remain in the group PRON (pronoun). The pronouns that are used adverbially, are considered in the group ADV (adverb). Another division applies to nouns. The common ones map the group NOUN, while the proper nouns go to the specific group PROPN. Numerals also divide between the groups of ADJ, ADV and NUM. The verbs are divided into the groups VERB (main verbs, copulas and modals, participles that are part of verb forms), AUX (auxiliaries), ADJ (participles with attributive usages).

3. **Changing the POS**. One case of changing the original POS is the transition of the affirmative and negative particles to the group of INTJ (interjections). Also, all the pronouns that went to DET group, also changed their POS label.

Concerning the UD set of accompanying features, three of them were not specifically encoded in the original tagset: animacy, degree and passive forms. Concerning animacy, in Bulgarian the grammar-related dichotomy is more specific – Person vs. Non-Person. Thus, it is derivable from some explicit grammatical features, such as the case in some pronouns, the count form of the masculine nouns and the masculine form of the numerals. Concerning degree, the original tagset does not differentiate among positive, comparative and superlative forms. Concerning passive, active voice is considered a default, and passive form is handled at the syntactic level, since both ways of its formation are analytical (participial forms and se-forms).

4.2 Syntax

The transfer of the syntactic relations faces the following situations: direct transfer relations; non-direct relations; 'floating' relations and non-handled relations.

1. **Direct transfer relations.** Direct mappings are those that provide the necessary information on phrasal level. They include relations like *dobj*, *iobj*, *nsubj*, *csubj*, etc.[5] Also the distinction between the relations *aux* and *cop* is directly derived from the original annotation. The former being annotated lexically with V(erb) and the latter being annotated syntactically with a head-complement relation (VPC).

2. **Non-direct relations.** Indirect mappings are those that provide the necessary information in a more underspecified way. One example of such relations is the division of our original complement clauses (CLDA, CLCHE, etc.) into control (*xcomp*) and non-control ones (*ccomp*) within UD. Another example is the division of our head – adjunct nominal phrase (NPA) into several relations depending on the non-head sister: *nummod* (the non-head sister is numeral), *amod* (the non-head sister is adjective), *det* (the non-head sister is determiner). The division of complement clauses and head-adjunct nominal phrases into more specific structures is linguistically sound with respect to semantics. Our original style introduces preferences to generalization over structural analyses. In our opinion, these two approaches exhibit two different models

[4] http://www.bultreebank.org/TechRep/BTB-TR03.pdf

[5] The UD labels are given in footnote 6.

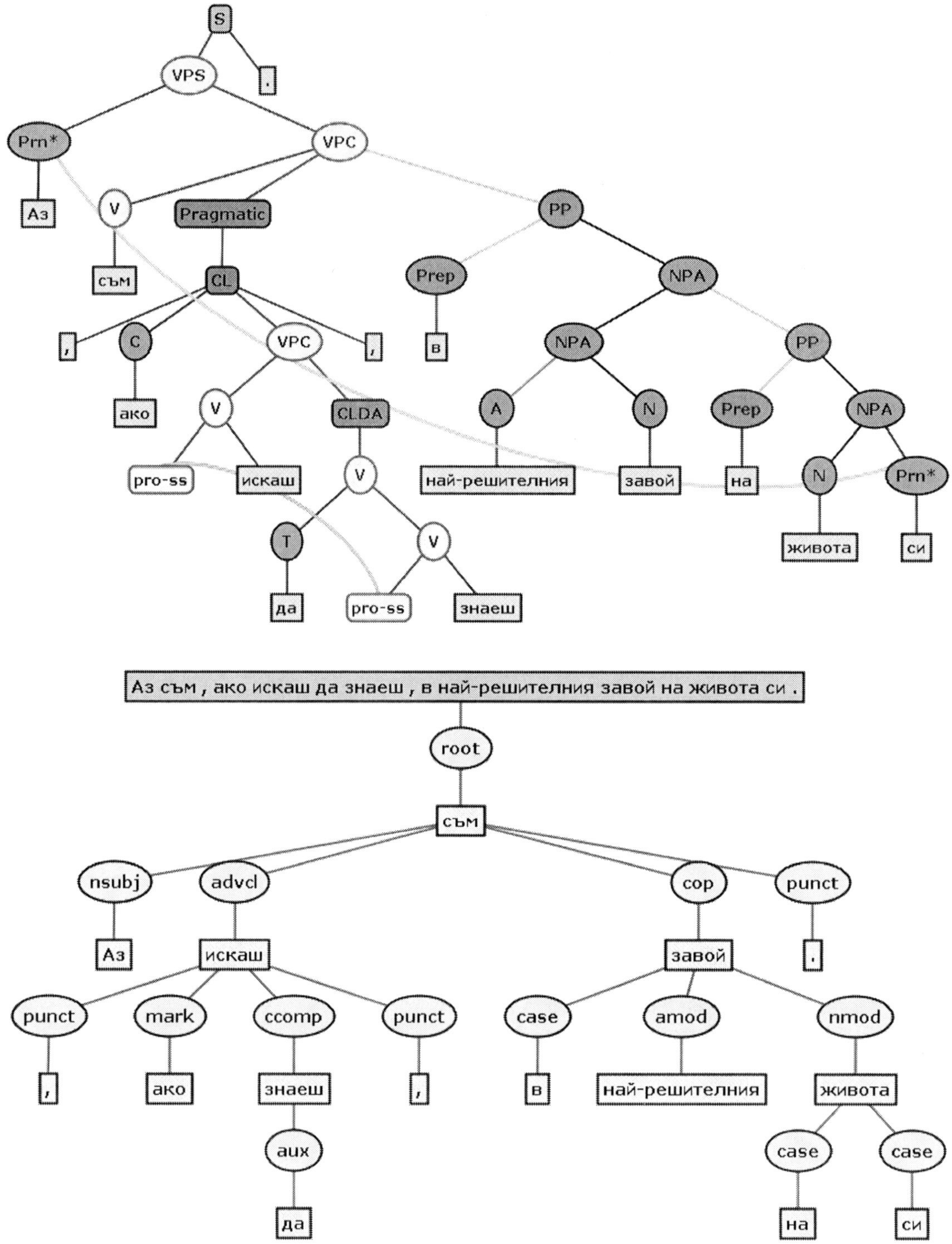

Figure 1: An HPSG-based tree and a Universal Dependency tree for the sentence: Аз съм, ако искаш да знаеш, в най-решителния завой на живота си. 'I am, if want.2PER.SG to know.2PER.SG, in most-crucial turn of life.DEF my.REFL' If you would like to know, I am in the most important turn of my life.

which might be useful for various tasks in NLP. Also, in the original treebank the passive constructions together with their participants were not marked explicitly. Hence, additional work was needed for annotating relations such as *nsubjpass* (nominal subject of a passive verb form) and *csubjpass* (clausal subject of a passive verb form). Thus, the specific auxiliary relation *auxpass* (relation between an auxiliary verb and the main verb form) is handled manually (see in Table 2 that at the moment only one such relation is available in the data).

3. **'Floating' relations.** There are mappings that have selected one alternative among several appropriate possibilities in the tagset. Such decisions might be temporary, since they are likely to be reconsidered in the future. Such a case is the encoding of the question particle ли 'li' in Bulgarian, which is used in yes – no questions. At the moment it is annotated with the relation *discourse*, but there are also other options, such as *aux*, *expl* or *mark*.

   Here also belongs the phenomenon of clitic doubling. In the original annotation we consider argument-like clitics at lexical level, while their counterparts (long pronoun forms or nouns) – at syntactic level. Here is an example: На него му се падна труден въпрос на изпита. 'To **him.LONG-PRON him.SHORT-PRON** REFL happened difficult question at exam.DEF' He got a difficult question at his exam.

   In UD, however, at the moment clitics receive two different relations depending on whether they are part of clitic doubling (then they are marked as *expl*) or not (then they are marked as *dobj* or *iobj*)).

4. **Non-handled relations.** We still have to analyze the elliptical phenomena in the remaining sentences of the treebank. Another thing to be reflected in the next release is the secondary predication, since this phenomenon requires also some co-reference information. Here is an example: Тя влезе тъжна в стаята. 'She entered **sad.FEM-SG** in room.DEF' She entered the room sad.

5 Conversion Procedure

Since in our original resource some multiword expressions were analyzed as one unit (especially those that matched one POS), for the UD scheme they had to be syntactically analyzed. In cases where it was not obvious what the head and dependencies are, the expressions were processed manually.

The parts-of-speech together with the relevant grammatical features were converted automatically through pre-defined mappings.

The syntactic relations required more work. Part of them were converted automatically, while part of them needed human intervention. For that reason all sentences with at least one unsolved mapping have been left for the next release.

In almost every constituent the head daughter could be determined unambiguously. However, more specific rules are needed in some combinations of constituents. For example, in *NP*s of type *NN* the head might be the first or the second noun depending on the semantics of the phrase. In such cases manual annotation of the head is necessary. Coordinations originally have been considered to be non-headed phrases, where the grammatical function overrides the syntactic labels. Thus, they also needed some special conversion treatment.

The procedure for the conversion of the BulTreeBank to Universal Dependencies is rule-based. The rules are of two kinds: (1) lexical head identifier moving up the constituent tree; and (2) relation assignment for a constituent node of the dependent child when all children of the parent node have lexical identifiers.

For example, let us have the following constituent, whose lexicalized example might be this one: твърде висок зелен стол. 'too tall green chair' [**NPA** [**APA** too tall] [**NPA** green chair]].

$$\texttt{NPA} \rightarrow \texttt{APA}_{id_1}\ \texttt{NPA}_{id_2}\ ,$$

where id_1 is a lexical head identifier for the adjectival phrase APA and id_2 is a lexical head identifier for the noun phrase NPA. Then we establish the relation amod from $\texttt{APA}_{id_1}$ to $\texttt{NPA}_{id_2}$ and the identifier for the child NPA is moved up, because the lexical head of the child NPA is the lexical head for the whole phrase. After the application of these two rules we have the constituent tree annotated with lexical identifiers and dependency relations in this way:

$$\texttt{NPA}_{id_2} \rightarrow \texttt{APA}_{id_1,amod}\ \texttt{NPA}_{id_2}\ .$$

Through the recursive application of such rules for the different types of phrases we annotated the whole constituent trees with lexical identifiers and universal dependency relations. When the root node receives an identifier, then the process stops and the constituent tree is converted to universal dependency tree.

In this way, we keep the original constituent annotation, while constructing the universal dependency annotation on top of it.

Some constructions like coordination, as mentioned above, require more complicated rules, since the necessary information was not directly encoded but it is trackable via the morphological annotation. However, the basic principle is the same.

Label	Num	Label	Num
A	9922	M	2436
APA	681	N	31513
APC	247	ND-Elip	27
Adv	5197	NPA	27664
AdvPA	381	NPC	67
AdvPC	52	Nomin	17
C	5407	PP	17478
CL	1479	Participle	3883
CLCHE	722	Prep	17286
CLDA	1965	Pron	9315
CLQ	166	Subst	497
CLR	1084	T	4817
CLZADA	147	V	22431
Conj	5465	VPA	8576
ConjArg	8958	VPC	11291
CoordP	4387	VPF	203
Gerund	15	VPS	9579
H	1037	Verbalised	4
I	25		

Table 1: Statistics over the HPSG Labels.

Table 1[6] summarizes the statistics of the syntactic labels in the original HPSG-based BulTreeBank, while Table 2[7] gives an overview of the converted BulTreeBank-UD. As it can be seen, direct comparisons cannot be made due to the fact that most often one original relation has been divided into more relations, or some UD relation combines material from two or more original ones. But even in such a setting, it can be observed that the most frequent type of relation is the one, in which a noun is connected to another noun via preposition (see relation PP in Table 1 and relations *case* and *nmod* in Table 2).

Label	Num	Label	Num
acl	1051	discourse	591
advcl	1258	dobj	5332
advmod	4437	expl	2790
amod	9528	iobj	2655
appos	38	mark	1410
aux	4839	mwe	671
auxpass	1	name	1110
case	18362	neg	1137
cc	3992	nmod	17293
ccomp	2428	nsubj	8506
conj	4573	nsubjpass	789
cop	1944	nummod	1460
csubj	368	punct	18013
csubjpass	16	root	9405
det	1586	vocative	6

Table 2: Statistics over the Universal Dependency Labels.

Additionally, in Fig. 1 an original treebank sentence is shown together with its UD conversion. Definitely, the new presentation flattens the tree,

[6] **A** – lexical adjective; **APA** – head-adjunct adjective phrase; **APC** – head-complement adjective phrase; **Adv** – lexical adverb; **AdvPA** – head-adjunct adverb phrase; **AdvPC** – head-complement adverb phrase; **C** – lexical conjunction; **CL** – clause that is outside the specific classes of clauses; **CLCHE** – clause introduced via "che" conjunction; **CLDA** – clause introduced via "da" verbal form; **CLQ** – interrogative clause; **CLR** – relative clause; **CLZADA** – adjuct clause for purpose; **Conj** – conjuction in a coordination phrase; **ConjArg** – argument of a coordination phrase; **CoordP** – coordination phrase; **Gerund** – lexical gerund form; **H** – lexical family name; **I** – lexical interjection; **M** – lexical numeral; **N** – lexical noun; **ND-Elip** – elliptical noun defined in the discourse; **NPA** – head-adjunct noun phrase; **NPC** – head-complement noun phrase; **Nomin** – nominalization of a phrase; **PP** – prepositional phrase; **Participle** – lexical participle; **Prep** – lexical preposition; **Pron** – lexical pronoun; **Subst** – substantive usage; **T** – lexical particle; **V** – lexical finite verb form; **VPA** – head-adjunct verb phrase; **VPC** – head-complement verb phrase; **VPF** – head-filler verb phrase; **VPS** – head-subject verb phrase; **Verbalised** – verbalization of a phrase.

[7] **acl** – clausal modifier of noun; **advcl** – adverbial clause modifier; **advmod** – adverbial modifier; **amod** – adjectival modifier; **appos** – appositional modifier; **aux** – auxiliary; **auxpass** – passive auxiliary; **case** – case marking; **cc** – coordinating conjunction; **ccomp** – clausal complement; **conj** – conjunct; **cop** – copula; **csubj** – clausal subject; **csubjpass** – clausal passive subject; **det** – determiner; **discourse** – discourse element; **dobj** – direct object; **expl** – expletive; **iobj** – indirect object; **mark** – marker; **mwe** – multi-word expression; **name** – name; **neg** – negation modifier; **nmod** – nominal modifier; **nsubj** – nominal subject; **nsubjpass** – passive nominal subject; **nummod** – numeric modifier; **punct** – punctuation; **root** – root; **vocative** – vocative

but it also adds more specific relations to it. It should be noted that the two lines in the HPSG-based tree in Fig. 1 connect the coreferences in the sentence (between the subject 'I' and the reflexive pronoun; and between the unexpressed subjects of the verbs 'want' and 'know').

6 Preliminary Experiments for POS Tagging and Dependency Parsing

We performed some preliminary experiments with the BulTreeBank-UD to train existing tools for POS tagging and Dependency Parsing. The 10-fold cross validation approach was used. We selected MATE tools[8] for the experiments, because they provide all the necessary components in one framework. The results are surprisingly good for the POS and Morphological tagging, while the dependency parsing performs somewhat sub-optimally. As background information it should be noted that the state-of-the-art results achieved in our previous work, with different data and different settings are as follows: in POS tagging (13 tags) – 99.30 % accuracy; in morphological tagging (680 tags) – 97.98 % accuracy (Georgiev et al., 2012), and in dependency parsing on BulTreeBank (ConLL-2006): LAS – 89.14 % and UAS – 92.45 % (Simova et al., 2014), using an ensemble model.

The current results are presented in Table 3 below:

Task	Accuracy	LAS	UAS
POS Tagging	96.89 %	–	–
Mor. Tagging	98.50 %	–	–
Dep. Parsing	–	83.50 %	88.08 %

Table 3: Evaluation. LAS = Labeled Accuracy Score, UAS = Unlabeled Accuracy Score.

However, we consider these results preliminary, because, as it was mentioned above, only part of the original treebank has been transformed into the universal representation and thus, only this part was used for the training. Additionally, many complex phenomena have not been represented within the current version yet.

It is worth noting that at the moment the original BulTreeBank tagset consists of 680 tags, while the UD one has 535 tags as combinations between POS and the respective grammatical features. This situation will change when more language specific features are added.

[8] http://code.google.com/p/mate-tools/

7 Conclusion

In this paper we describe the conversion of the original HPSG-based BulTreeBank into the Universal Dependencies format. The process included assigning Universal POS and Universal Morphological Features to the original annotations as well as conversion of the tree structures.

The conversion and the label assignments were done mainly automatically with a high level of certainty because the dependent elements in the original treebank were easy to track. At the same time, some phenomena will be detailed and handled in the next release of the treebank due to the need of human intervention in the language or annotation model specific cases.

The reported effort is part of a wider initiative that includes many languages and working groups. As such it faces similar challenges and shares similar perspectives. The main challenge is the proper handling of the language universal and language specific phenomena at a minimal linguistic and data model loss. The most important perspective is the ultimate goal of having comparable syntactically annotated resources for many languages that would serve better for various NLP tasks.

Acknowledgements

This research has received partial support by the EC's FP7 (FP7/2007 – 2013) project under grant agreement number 610516: "QTLeap: Quality Translation by Deep Language Engineering Approaches" and FP7 grant 316087 AComIn "Advanced Computing for Innovation", funded by the European Commission in 2012 – 2016.

We are grateful to the three anonymous reviewers, whose remarks, comments, suggestions and encouragement helped us to improve the initial variant of the paper. All errors remain our own responsibility.

References

Željko Agić, Maria Jesus Aranzabe, Aitziber Atutxa, Cristina Bosco, Jinho Choi, Marie-Catherine de Marneffe, Timothy Dozat, Richárd Farkas, Jennifer Foster, Filip Ginter, Iakes Goenaga, Koldo Gojenola, Yoav Goldberg, Jan Hajič, Anders Trærup Johannsen, Jenna Kanerva, Juha Kuokkala, Veronika Laippala, Alessandro Lenci,

Krister Lindén, Nikola Ljubešić, Teresa Lynn, Christopher Manning, Héctor Alonso Martínez, Ryan McDonald, Anna Missilä, Simonetta Montemagni, Joakim Nivre, Hanna Nurmi, Petya Osenova, Slav Petrov, Jussi Piitulainen, Barbara Plank, Prokopis Prokopidis, Sampo Pyysalo, Wolfgang Seeker, Mojgan Seraji, Natalia Silveira, Maria Simi, Kiril Simov, Aaron Smith, Reut Tsarfaty, Veronika Vincze, and Daniel Zeman. 2015. Universal Dependencies 1.1. LINDAT/CLARIN digital library at Institute of Formal and Applied Linguistics, Charles University in Prague.

Eduard Bejček, Eva Hajičová, Jan Hajič, Pavlína Jínová, Václava Kettnerová, Veronika Kolářová, Marie Mikulová, Jiří Mírovský, Anna Nedoluzhko, Jarmila Panevová, Lucie Poláková, Magda Ševčíková, Jan Štěpánek, and Šárka Zikánová. 2013. Prague Dependency Treebank 3.0.

Emily M. Bender, Dan Flickinger, and Stephan Oepen. 2002. The Grammar Matrix: An Open-Source Starter-Kit for the Rapid Development of Cross-Linguistically Consistent Broad-Coverage Precision Grammars. In John Carroll, Nelleke Oostdijk, and Richard Sutcliffe, editors, *Proceedings of the Workshop on Grammar Engineering and Evaluation at the 19th International Conference on Computational Linguistics*, pages 8–14, Taipei, Taiwan.

Dasa Berovic, Zeljko Agic, and Marko Tadić. 2012. Croatian Dependency Treebank: Recent development and initial experiments. In Nicoletta Calzolari (Conference Chair), Khalid Choukri, Thierry Declerck, Mehmet Uğur Doğan, Bente Maegaard, Joseph Mariani, Asuncion Moreno, Jan Odijk, and Stelios Piperidis, editors, *Proceedings of the Eight International Conference on Language Resources and Evaluation (LREC'12)*, Istanbul, Turkey, May. European Language Resources Association (ELRA).

Cristina Bosco and Manuela Sanguinetti. 2014. Towards a Universal Stanford Dependencies parallel treebank. In Verena Henrich, Erhard Hinrichs, Daniël de Kok, Petya Osenova, and Adam Przepiórkowski, editors, *Proceedings of TLT-13*, pages 14–25, Tübingen, Germany. European Language Resources Association (ELRA).

Sabine Buchholz and Erwin Marsi. 2006. CoNLL-X Shared Task on Multilingual Dependency Parsing. In *Proceedings of the Tenth Conference on Computational Natural Language Learning*, CoNLL-X '06, pages 149–164, Stroudsburg, PA, USA. Association for Computational Linguistics.

Atanas Chanev, Kiril Simov, Petya Osenova, and Svetoslav Marinov. 2006. Dependency conversion and parsing of the BulTreeBank. In *Proceedings of the LREC workshop Merging and Layering Linguistic Information*, pages 16–23.

Atanas Chanev, Kiril Simov, Petya Osenova, and Svetoslav Marinov. 2007. The BulTreeBank: Parsing and Conversion. In *Proceedings of the Recent Advances in Natural Language Processing Conference*, pages 114–120.

Marie-Catherine de Marneffe and Christopher D. Manning. 2008. The Stanford Typed Dependencies Representation. In *Coling 2008: Proceedings of the Workshop on Cross-Framework and Cross-Domain Parser Evaluation*, CrossParser '08, pages 1–8, Stroudsburg, PA, USA. Association for Computational Linguistics.

Marie-Catherine de Marneffe, Timothy Dozat, Natalia Silveira, Katri Haverinen, Filip Ginter, Joakim Nivre, and Christopher D. Manning. 2014. Universal Stanford Dependencies: a cross-linguistic typology. In Nicoletta Calzolari (Conference Chair), Khalid Choukri, Thierry Declerck, Hrafn Loftsson, Bente Maegaard, Joseph Mariani, Asuncion Moreno, Jan Odijk, and Stelios Piperidis, editors, *Proceedings of the Ninth International Conference on Language Resources and Evaluation (LREC'14)*, Reykjavik, Iceland, May. European Language Resources Association (ELRA).

Sašo Džeroski, Tomaž Erjavec, Nina Ledinek, Petr Pajas, Zdenek Žabokrtsky, and Andreja Žele. 2006. Towards a Slovene dependency treebank. In *In Proc. Int. Conf. on Language Resources and Evaluation (LREC*.

Georgi Georgiev, Valentin Zhikov, Kiril Simov, Petya Osenova, and Preslav Nakov. 2012. Feature-rich part-of-speech tagging for morphologically complex languages: Application to Bulgarian. In *Proceedings of the 13th Conference of the European Chapter of the Association for Computational Linguistics*, pages 492–502. Association for Computational Linguistics.

Masood Ghayoomi, Kiril Simov, and Petya Osenova. 2014. Constituency parsing of Bulgarian: Word- vs class-based parsing. In Nicoletta Calzolari (Conference Chair), Khalid Choukri, Thierry Declerck, Hrafn Loftsson, Bente Maegaard, Joseph Mariani, Asuncion Moreno, Jan Odijk, and Stelios Piperidis, editors, *Proceedings of the Ninth International Conference on Language Resources and Evaluation (LREC'14)*, Reykjavik, Iceland, May. European Language Resources Association (ELRA).

Janna Lipenkova and Milan Souček. 2014. Converting Russian Dependency Treebank to Stanford Typed Dependencies Representation. In *Proceedings of the 14th Conference of the European Chapter of the Association for Computational Linguistics*, page 143–147, Gothenburg, Sweden.

Mohamed Maamouri, Ann Bies, and Seth Kulick. 2008. Enhanced annotation and parsing of the Arabic treebank. In *In 6th International Conference on Computers and Informatics, INFOS2008*.

Joakim Nivre, Johan Hall, Sandra Kübler, Ryan McDonald, Jens Nilsson, Sebastian Riedel, and Deniz

Yuret. 2007. The CoNLL 2007 Shared Task on Dependency Parsing. In *Proceedings of the CoNLL Shared Task Session of EMNLP-CoNLL 2007*, pages 915–932, Prague, Czech Republic, June. Association for Computational Linguistics.

Joakim Nivre, Cristina Bosco, Jinho Choi, Marie-Catherine de Marneffe, Timothy Dozat, Richárd Farkas, Jennifer Foster, Filip Ginter, Yoav Goldberg, Jan Hajič, Jenna Kanerva, Veronika Laippala, Alessandro Lenci, Teresa Lynn, Christopher Manning, Ryan McDonald, Anna Missilä, Simonetta Montemagni, Slav Petrov, Sampo Pyysalo, Natalia Silveira, Maria Simi, Aaron Smith, Reut Tsarfaty, Veronika Vincze, and Daniel Zeman. 2015. Universal Dependencies 1.0. LINDAT/CLARIN digital library at Institute of Formal and Applied Linguistics, Charles University in Prague.

Joakim Nivre. 2014. Universal dependencies for Swedish. In *SLTC Conference 2014*, Uppsala, Sweden.

Slav Petrov, Dipanjan Das, and Ryan McDonald. 2012. A universal part-of-speech tagset. In Nicoletta Calzolari (Conference Chair), Khalid Choukri, Thierry Declerck, Mehmet Uğur Doğan, Bente Maegaard, Joseph Mariani, Asuncion Moreno, Jan Odijk, and Stelios Piperidis, editors, *Proceedings of the Eight International Conference on Language Resources and Evaluation (LREC'12)*, Istanbul, Turkey, May. European Language Resources Association (ELRA).

Sampo Pyysalo, Jenna Kanerva, Anna Missilä, Veronika Laippala, and Filip Ginter. 2015. Universal Dependencies for Finnish. In *Proceedings of the 20th Nordic Conference of Computational Linguistics (NODALIDA 2015)*, page 163–172.

Loganathan Ramasamy and Zdenek Žabokrtsky. 2012. Prague Dependency Style Treebank for Tamil. In *Proceedings of the 8th International Conference on Language Resources and Evaluation (LREC 2012)*, pages 23–25, Istanbul, Turkey. European Language Resources Association.

Rudolf Rosa, Jan Mašek, David Mareček, Martin Popel, Daniel Zeman, and Zdeněk Žabokrtský. 2014. Hamledt 2.0: Thirty Dependency Treebanks Stanfordized. In Nicoletta Calzolari (Conference Chair), Khalid Choukri, Thierry Declerck, Hrafn Loftsson, Bente Maegaard, Joseph Mariani, Asuncion Moreno, Jan Odijk, and Stelios Piperidis, editors, *Proceedings of the Ninth International Conference on Language Resources and Evaluation (LREC'14)*, Reykjavik, Iceland, May. European Language Resources Association (ELRA).

Manuela Sanguinetti and Cristina Bosco. 2014. Converting the parallel treebank ParTUT in Universal Stanford Dependencies. In *Proceedings of CLiC-it 2014*, pages 316–321, Pisa, Italy.

Kiril Simov and Petya Osenova. 2003. Practical annotation scheme for an HPSG treebank of Bulgarian. In *Proceedings of the 4th International Workshop on Linguistically Interpreteted Corpora (LINC-2003)*, Budapest, Hungary.

Kiril Simov, Petya Osenova, Alexander Simov, and Milen Kouylekov. 2004. Design and implementation of the Bulgarian HPSG-based treebank. In *Journal of Research on Language and Computation, Special Issue*, pages 495–522, Kluwer Academic Publishers.

Iliana Simova, Dimitar Vasilev, Alexander Popov, Kiril Simov, and Petya Osenova. 2014. Joint ensemble model for POS tagging and dependency parsing. In *Proceedings of the First Joint Workshop on Statistical Parsing of Morphologically Rich Languages and Syntactic Analysis of Non-Canonical Languages*, pages 15–25, Dublin, Ireland, August. Dublin City University.

Naiwen Xue, Fei Xia, Fu-dong Chiou, and Marta Palmer. 2005. The Penn Chinese TreeBank: Phrase Structure Annotation of a Large Corpus. *Nat. Lang. Eng.*, 11(2):207–238, June.

Daniel Zeman. 2008. Reusable tagset conversion using tagset drivers. In Bente Maegaard Joseph Mariani Jan Odijk Stelios Piperidis Daniel Tapias Nicoletta Calzolari (Conference Chair), Khalid Choukri, editor, *Proceedings of the Sixth International Conference on Language Resources and Evaluation (LREC'08)*, Marrakech, Morocco, May. European Language Resources Association (ELRA). http://www.lrec-conf.org/proceedings/lrec2008/.

Types of Aspect Terms in Aspect-Oriented Sentiment Labeling

Natalia Loukachevitch
Lomonosov
Moscow State University
Moscow, Russia
louk_nat@mail.ru

Evgeny Kotelnikov, Pavel Blinov
Vyatka State Humanities University
Kirov, Russia
kotelnikov.ev@gmail.com
blinoff.pavel@gmail.com

Abstract

The paper studies the diversity of ways to express entity aspects in users' reviews. Besides explicit aspect terms, it is possible to distinguish implicit aspect terms and sentiment facts. These subtypes of aspect terms were annotated during SentiRuEval evaluation of Russian sentiment analysis systems organized in 2014–2015. The created annotation gives the possibility to analyze the contribution of non-explicit aspects to the overall sentiment of a review, their main patterns, and possible use.

1 Introduction

When the authors of texts express their opinions about some entities, they often indicate specific properties (or aspects) of the entity that evoke positive or negative sentiments. Revealing these aspects and related sentiment is very important for various directions of automatic sentiment analysis, including analysis of user reviews, reputation monitoring, or social mood analysis because such analysis helps to find problems or strong points of the discussed entities. Therefore, so-called Aspect-Based Sentiment Analysis (ABSA) becomes more popular (Liu and Zhang, 2012; Bagheri et al., 2013; Popescu and Etzioni, 2005; Feldman, 2013; Poria et al., 2014).

Entity aspects are expressed in texts with aspect terms and can usually be classified into categories. For example, *Service* aspect category in restaurant reviews can be expressed in such terms as *staff*, *waiter*, *waitress*, *server*, and etc. Aspect-based sentiment analysis includes several stages, such as revealing aspect terms and their categories, extraction of sentiments expressed toward found aspects, and visualization of extracted information.

It is usually supposed that an aspect of an entity is conveyed by a noun or a noun group that explicitly denotes a property of an entity and does not contain sentiment within itself, so called explicit aspects. So, in aspect-based sentiment analysis evaluations organized in the framework of SemEval conference, only explicit aspects were annotated (Pontiki et al., 2014; Pontiki et al., 2015). However, aspects can be expressed in an implicit way. For example, the phrase *ready to help* expresses positive sentiment toward restaurant service, without mentioning aspects explicitly.

In SentiRuEval evaluation of aspect-based sentiment analysis of Russian texts (Loukachevitch et al., 2015), besides explicit aspects, so-called implicit aspects (sentiment words with implied aspects) and sentiment facts (phrases with implicit sentiments and aspects such as *answered all questions*) were labeled. These annotations give a new possibility to study the contribution of various types of aspects into the overall sentiment of users' reviews and their possible use in sentiment-oriented summaries. This evaluation is the second Russian sentiment analysis evaluation event after ROMIP sentiment analysis tracks in 2011-2013 (Chetviorkin and Loukachevitch, 2013).

In this paper, we consider subtypes of aspect terms and principles of aspect labeling in the framework of SentiRuEval evaluation. Also, we present the analysis of manually labeled aspect terms expressed implicitly and show their usefulness for generating sentiment-oriented summaries.

2 Related Work

For studying aspect-oriented sentiment analysis, several datasets were created. The restaurant review dataset created by Ganu et al. (2009) uses six coarse-grained aspect categories (e.g., FOOD, PRICE, SERVICE) and four overall sentence polarity labels (positive, negative, conflict, neutral). Each sentence is assigned to one or more aspect categories together with a polarity label for each category.

Proceedings of the 5th Workshop on Balto-Slavic Natural Language Processing, pages 90–95,
Hissar, Bulgaria, 10–11 September 2015.

Hu and Liu (2004) created the product review dataset containing 100 reviews for each of five electronics products. They labeled terms naming aspects (e.g., voice dialing) together with their sentiment strength scores. They found that aspects can be expressed explicitly or implicitly, as the size aspect in the sentence *it fits in a pocket nicely*.

Zhang and Liu (2011) argue that there are many types of expressions that do not bear sentiments on their own, but they imply sentiment in specific contexts. One such type of expressions involves resources, which are important for many application domains. For example, money is a resource in probably every domain, gas is a resource in the car domain, and ink is a resource in the printer domain. An expression containing a quantifier (*some, more, large, small*, etc.) in combination with a resource term may often look like a reference to an objective fact but, in practice, it often implies a specific sentiment.

In (Gupta, 2013; Tutubalina and Ivanov, 2014; Zhang et al., 2012), extraction of so-called technical problems mentioned by users in reviews was discussed. Technical problems can also be considered as specific types of sentiment-oriented facts. Besides, some non-opinionated words can have negative or positive associations (connotations (Feng et al., 2013)) that their appearance in a text can imply relevant sentiment, e.g., word *hair* has usually the negative connotation in the restaurant domain (*hair on the plate*).

The dataset created by Ganu et al. (2009) was used as a basis for aspect-based review analysis evaluation at SemEval in 2014 (Pontiki et al., 2014). The dataset included isolated, out of context sentences in two domains: restaurants and laptops. The set of aspect categories for restaurants included: FOOD, SERVICE, PRICE, AMBIENCE, ANECDOTES/MISCELLANEOUS.

In 2015 SemEval evaluations of the aspect-based sentiment analysis of reviews was focused on entire reviews (Pontiki et al., 2015). Aspect categories of terms became more complicated and now consist of Entity-Attribute pairs (E-A), for example FOOD-PRICE, FOOD-QUALITY. In both cases, only explicit aspects (comprising named entities, common nouns, or multiword noun groups) were labeled and used for systems testing. The ultimate goal of the ABSA was formulated as generation of summaries enumerating all the aspects and their overall polarity (Figure 1).

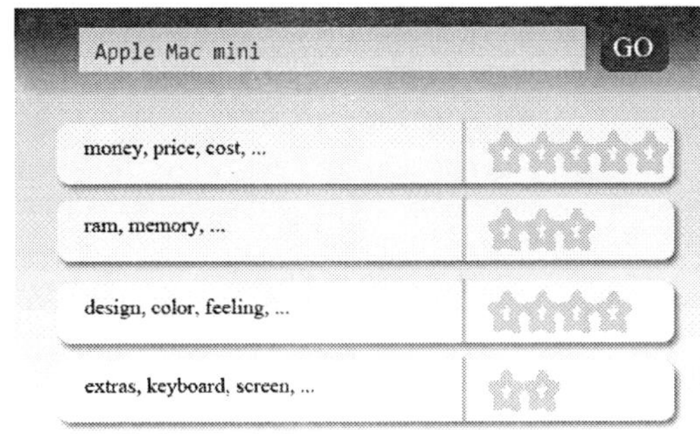

Figure 1: Sentiment-aspect summary as a goal for aspect-based sentiment analysis (Pontiki et al., 2015).

3 SentiRuEval Testing of Russian Sentiment Analysis Systems

The SentiRuEval evaluation organized in 2014–2015 was focused on entity-oriented sentiment analysis of Twitter and aspect-oriented analysis of users reviews in Russian. For evaluation of aspect-oriented sentiment analysis systems, two domains (restaurant reviews and automobile reviews) were chosen (Loukachevitch et al., 2015).

During the annotation phase, not only explicit aspects but also aspects expressed implicitly (see Section 4) were marked up. To each labeled aspect, its sentiment (positive, negative, neutral, or both) and aspect category should be assigned to. For restaurant reviews, aspect categories included: FOOD, SERVICE, INTERIOR (including ambience), PRICE, GENERAL. For automobiles, aspect categories were: DRIVEABILITY, RELIABILITY, SAFETY, APPEARANCE, COMFORT, COSTS, GENERAL.

The aspect categories with their sentiment scores (positive, negative, both, or absent) were also attached to the whole review.

The participants were to solve one or more of the following tasks in two domains: automatic extraction of explicit aspects, automatic extraction of all aspect terms, extraction of sentiments towards explicit aspects, automatic categorization of explicit aspects into aspect categories, and sentiment analysis of the whole review according to aspect categories.

The labeling of training and test data was conducted with BRAT annotating tool (Stenetorp et al., 2012). Aspects in each review were labeled by a single linguist under inspection of a supervisor. Besides, to check up the quality of aspect labeling, several specialized procedures were implemented. So, some accidental mistakes were found and corrected (Loukachevitch et al., 2015).

Altogether, about 200 reviews were prepared for each domain as a training collection and additional 200 reviews in each domain served as a test collection. Table 1 shows labeled data statistics in two domains.

Nine Russian groups and individual researchers were participants of SentiRuEval–2015. The results of the participants are described in (Loukachevitch et al., 2015). All data and results are publicly available.[1] In this paper, we analyze the aspect labeling carried out in the framework of SentiRuEval.

	Restaurants Train / Test	**Automobiles** Train / Test
Number of reviews	201 / 203	217 / 201
Number of explicit aspects	2,822 / 3,506	3,152 / 3,109
Number of implicit aspects	636 / 657	638 / 576
Number of sentiment facts	523 / 656	668 / 685

Table 1: Number of aspect terms found in reviews.

4 Labeling Types of Aspects in SentiRuEval

In contrast to SemEval ABSA labeling, the ultimate goal of aspect labeling at SentiRuEval is to generate summaries in form of informative keywords expressing both aspect and related sentiment. It was supposed that such summaries can better convey the mood of users' opinions than traditional star-oriented summaries. Keyword-based interfaces are appropriate not only for desktop computers, but also for mobile devices.

The similar approach is described in (Yatani et al., 2011). However, in that work, only sentiment-oriented adjective-noun word pairs were extracted (see Figure 2). Besides, extraction of implicit sentiment and aspects was not considered. The SentiRuEval labeling was directed to study various forms of aspect-sentiment tags that can be utilized for visualization of users' opinions. From this point of view, it was found that the labeling of several types of aspect-related expressions is useful including explicit aspects, implicit aspects, and sentiment facts.

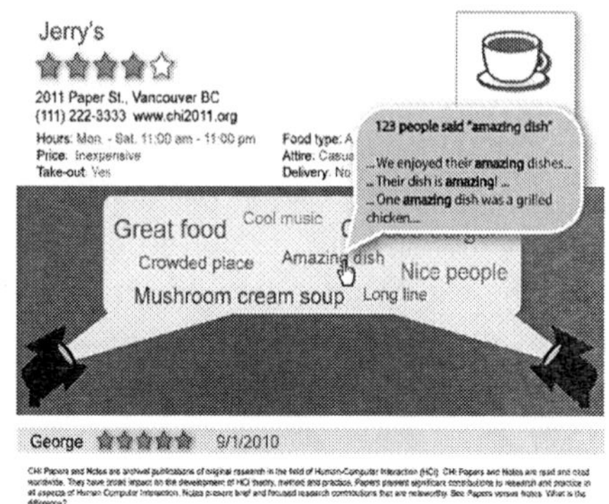

Figure 2: Example of the aspect-oriented review summary as a set of sentiment-aspect keywords (Yatani et al., 2011).

As in previous works, **explicit aspect terms** denote some parts of an entity (such as an engine, a compartment, or a trunk of a car) or its characteristics (appearance of a car). They can also denote produced products (pasta, desserts), related services (staff, personnel), or surrounding conditions (music, noise, smell, and etc.). The cost (price) related aspect is present in most domains. To form sentiment-oriented keywords, explicit aspects should be combined with sentiment words.

Explicit aspects are usually expressed by nouns or noun groups, but in some aspect categories, it is possible to encounter explicit aspects expressed as verbs or verb groups. For example, in restaurant reviews, such verbs as *eat*, *drink* (FOOD category); *greet* (SERVICE) are often used to express explicit aspects. In the car domain, frequent examples of such verbs and verb groups are *look* (APPEARANCE), *speed up*, *park*, *hold the road* (DRIVABILITY). [2]

Verbs expressing explicit aspects can be met in constructions with sentiment-oriented adverbs such as *ate very well*, *greeted well*, etc. Keywords in such forms (*greeted well*) can be presented to users in sentiment-oriented summaries.

Therefore, in the SentiRuEval data, verbs may also be labeled as explicit aspect terms. The presence of verbs in aspect categories varies.

Implicit aspect terms are evident sentiment words having appraisal as a sense component but,

[1] http://goo.gl/Wqsqit

[2] These and all further examples are translated from Russian.

in the current domain, these words also imply a specific aspect category. Frequent examples of implicit aspect terms in the restaurant domain are *tasty* (positive+FOOD), *polite* (positive+SERVICE), *comfortable* (positive+INTERIOR), *cosy* (positive+INTERIOR), *expensive* (negative+PRICE).

In the car domain, frequently mentioned implicit aspects are *beautiful* (positive+APPEARANCE), *mighty* (positive+DRIVABILITY), *spacious* (positive+COMFORT), *comfortable* (positive+COMFORT), *reliable* (positive+RELIABILITY), *safe* (positive+SAFETY), *economical* (positive+PRICE). Phrases that included an implicit aspect term and a negation or intensifier were also considered as implicit aspect terms (*not comfortable* (negative+INTERIOR)).

The importance of these words for automatic sentiment analysis is in that implicit aspects allow a sentiment system to reveal the implied opinion about entity characteristics even if an explicit aspect term is unknown, written with an error, or referred to in a complicated way. In a keyword-oriented interface, implicit aspects can be presented alone (*tasty*), or with the corresponding category (*tasty food*). In Russian, implicit aspects can be shown in an adverb form: *vkusno* (*tastily*).

Sentiment facts are single words or short, syntactically correct phrases that do not mention the user sentiment directly but inform about user's opinion via mentioning facts. In the restaurant domain, frequent sentiment facts include such expressions as: *large portions*, *large choice of dishes* (FOOD); *waited for a long time*, *forgot*, *didn't bring* (SERVICE); *dim lights*, *plenty of space* (INTERIOR); *come again*, *come back* (GENERAL). In sentiment facts, aspects are also often implicit.

Sentiment facts express the specificity of an object under review and can be directly depicted (in an appropriate form) as sentiment keywords.

In the SentiRuEval data, the amount of reviews with more than 10% of implicit sentences (containing only implicit aspects or sentiment facts without mentioning explicit aspects) ranges from 15 to 30% across training and test collections. For some reviews, the amount of such sentences constitutes up to 40%. Figure 3 shows that more than a half of the reviews in the SentiRuEval restaurant training collection (106 of 201) contains sentences with implicitly expressed aspects.

If we compare the SentiRuEval aspect annotation with labeling in the framework of SemEval ABSA-2015 then it can be seen that the ABSA dataset also contains sentences with implicit aspects and sentiment facts but such sentences are marked with the label *target=NULL* (Pontiki et al., 2014; Pontiki et al., 2015) what means an absent (null) target.

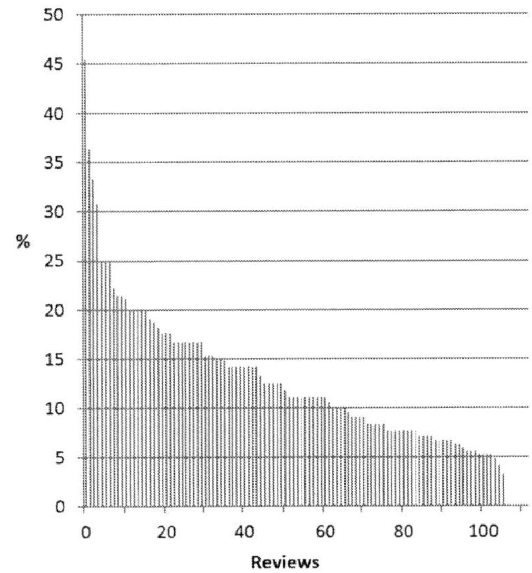

Figure 3: The distribution of sentences with only implicitly expressed aspects in the SentiRuEval restaurant training collection (201 reviews).

In the NULL-labeled ABSA examples, it is often possible to mark-up sentiment facts. For example, in the following sentence from the ABSA guidelines marked with NULL target "They never brought us complimentary noodles, ignored repeated requests for sugar, and threw our dishes on the table", three sentiment facts could be annotated: *never brought*, *ignored repeated requests*, and *threw our dishes*.

5 Syntactic Patterns and Semantic Subtypes of Sentiment Facts

Extraction of sentiment facts is not a simple task because syntactic structures of sentiment facts are quite diverse. Their most frequent syntactic patterns are different in two domains (Table 2). It is important to note that in Verb+Noun patterns, a noun can be in function of a subject or an object because of free word order in Russian.

The annotators were asked to label sentiment facts as minimal syntactically correct phrases indicating an aspect and a sentiment within them-

Pattern	Relative Frequency	Examples
Restaurants		
Adj+N	6.0%	broad windows cold kebab
V+N	4.0%	changed ashtrays confused orders
not+V	3.7%	not greet not bring
Automobiles		
V	16.8%	to rattle to decay
Adj+N	10.8%	huge trunk low rider
N	7.0%	noise, rust
V+N	5.8%	eats gasoline
not+V	5.8%	not break not regulated

Table 2: Most frequent patterns of sentiment facts in restaurant and automobile domains ordered by frequency in each domain.

selves but currently this requirement was not fully observed. Therefore, we can see that in the restaurant domain, syntactic patterns seem to be more diverse and the frequency of the most frequent patterns is lower.

From the lexico-semantic point of view, multiple cases of RESOURCE-BASED FACTS containing resource terms described in (Zhang and Liu, 2011) can be revealed among sentiment facts. In the restaurant domain, one can find the following kinds of resource terms: time of a restaurant guest; attention of waiters; three food-oriented resources including food on a plate, choice in a menu, and availability of a specific dish; space in a restaurant room and free tables; and money of visitors.

In the automobile domain, there are such resource terms as space in a compartment or trunk; fuel; and money for purchase, fuel, or maintenance of a car. In both domains, the resource terms are often mentioned in phrases together with quantifiers (*many*, *small*, *large*, and etc.).

The particle *not* in a phrase with a not-opinionated verb often denotes the deviation from a normal state of affairs (FAILURE FACTS). A similar effect appears from the usage of words *absence*, *absent*.

Gradable adjectives, which are a priori not correlated with a specific sentiment, in phrases with explicit aspects often become sentiment facts (*cold kebab*, *broad windows*)(GRADABILITY FACTS).

Words denoting sounds or noises (*loud*, *crackle*, and etc.) can express positive or negative sentiment facts in various domains (NOISE FACTS). They are met in both domains under analysis.

Thus, for automatic extraction of sentiment facts and utilizing them in sentiment-oriented interfaces, it is useful to extract at least: phrases with negation particles not containing sentiment words; phrases with gradual adjectives, and phrases with quantifiers. A vocabulary with noise- and failure-meaning words and phrases can be also useful for extraction of sentiment facts in various domains.

If extracted correctly, a keyword-based sentiment summary about a restaurant can include various types of aspect terms and look as follows: *nice dessert, broad windows, waited for a long time, politely, will come again*. Each keyword conveys information about both an aspect and related sentiment.

6 Conclusion

The paper studies the diversity of ways to express entity aspects in users' reviews and considers subtypes of aspect terms in aspect-oriented sentiment analysis. Besides explicit aspect terms, it is possible to distinguish implicit aspects and sentiment facts.

These subtypes of aspects were annotated during SentiRuEval evaluation of Russian sentiment analysis systems organized in 2014–2015. The created annotation allowed us to analyze the contribution of non-explicit aspects to the overall sentiment of a review, their frequent patterns and their possible use in sentiment-oriented interfaces.

The analysis of labeled sentiment facts in the SentiRuEval data revealed such types of frequent sentiment facts as RESOURCE-BASED FACTS, FAILURE FACTS, GRADABILITY FACTS, and NOISE FACTS.

Acknowledgments

This work is partially supported by RFBR grants No. 14-07-00682, No. 15-07-09306 and by the Russian Ministry of Education and Science, research project No. 586.

References

Ayoub Bagheri, Mohamad Saraee, and Franciska de Jong. 2013. An unsupervised aspect detection model for sentiment analysis of reviews. *Natural Language Processing and Information Systems*, Springer, Berlin, Heidelberg: 140–151.

Ilia Chetviorkin and Natalia Loukachevich. 2013. Evaluating sentiment analysis systems in Russian. *Proceedings of BSNLP Workshop*, ACL-2013: 12–16.

Ronen Feldman. 2013. Techniques and applications for sentiment analysis. *Communications of the ACM* 56.4: 82–89.

Song Feng, Jun S. Kang, Polina Kuznetsova, and Yejin Choi. 2013. Connotation lexicon: a dash of sentiment beneath the surface meaning. *Proceedings of ACL-2013*: 1774–1784.

Gayatree Ganu, Noemie Elhadad, and Amelie Marian. 2009. Beyond the stars: improving rating predictions using review text content. *Twelfth International Workshop on the Web and Databases WebDB-2009*: 1–6.

Narendra Gupta. 2013. Extracting phrases describing problems with products and services from twitter messages. *Computacion y Sistemas*. 17 (2): 197–206.

Bing Liu and Lei Zhang. 2012. A survey of opinion mining and sentiment analysis. *Mining Text Data*: Springer US. 415–463.

Minquing Hu and Bing Liu. 2004. Mining and summarizing customer reviews. *Proceedings of the 10th ACM SIGKDD International Conference on Knowledge Discovery and Data Mining KDD-2004*: 168–177.

Natalia Loukachevitch, Pavel Blinov, Evgeny Kotelnikov, Yulia Rubtsova, Vladimir Ivanov, and Elena Tutubalina. 2015. SentiRuEval: testing object-oriented sentiment analysis systems in Russian. *Proceedings of International Conference Dialog-2015*: 3–9.

Maria Pontiki, Haris Papageorgiou, Dimitrios Galanis, Ion Androutsopoulos, John Pavlopoulos, and Suresh Manandhar. 2014. Semeval-2014 task 4: aspect based sentiment analysis. *Proceedings of the 8th International Workshop on Semantic Evaluation (SemEval 2014)*: 27–35.

Maria Pontiki, Dimitrios Galanis, Haris Papageorgiou, Suresh Manandhar, and Ion Androutsopoulos. 2015. Semeval-2015 task 12: aspect based sentiment analysis. *Proceedings of the 9th International Workshop on Semantic Evaluation (SemEval 2015)*, Denver, Colorado.

Ana-Maria Popescu and Oren Etzioni. 2007. Extracting product features and opinions from reviews. *Natural Language Pprocessing and Text Mining*. Springer London: 9–28.

Soujanya Poria, Nir Ofek, Alexander Gelbukh, Amir Hussain, and Lior Rokach. 2014. Sentic Demo: A hybrid concept-level aspect-based sentiment analysis toolkit. *Proceedings of ESWC-2014*.

Pontus Stenetorp, Sampo Pyysalo, Goran Topi, Tomoko Ohta, Sophia Ananiadou, Junichi Tsujii J. 2012. BRAT: a Web-based tool for NLP-assisted text annotation. *Demonstrations at the 13th Conference of the European Chapter of the Association for Computational Linguistics*, Avignon: 102–107.

Elena Tutubalina and Vladimir Ivanov. 2014. Unsupervised approach to extracting problem phrases from user reviews of products. *Proceedings of the Aha! Workshop on Information Discovery in Texts*, Coling-2014: 48–53.

Koji Yatani, Michael Novati, Andrew Trusty, and Khai N. Truong. 2011. Analysis of adjective-noun word pair extraction methods for online review summarization. *Proceedings of International Joint Conference on Artificial Intelligence (IJCAI-2011)*.

Lei Zhang and Bing Liu. 2011. Extracting resource terms for sentiment analysis. *Proceedings of IJCNLP-2011*.

Wenhao Zhang, Xu Hua, and Wan Wei. 2012. Weakness Finder: find product weakness from Chinese reviews by using aspects based sentiment analysis. *Expert Systems with Applications* 39 (11): 10283–10291.

Authorship Attribution and Author Profiling of Lithuanian Literary Texts

Jurgita Kapočiūtė-Dzikienė
Vytautas Magnus University
K. Donelaičio 58, LT-44248,
Kaunas, Lithuania
jurgita.k.dz@gmail.com

Andrius Utka
Vytautas Magnus University
K. Donelaičio 58, LT-44248,
Kaunas, Lithuania
a.utka@hmf.vdu.lt

Ligita Šarkutė
Kaunas Univ. of Technology
K. Donelaičio 73, LT-44029,
Kaunas, Lithuania
ligita.sarkute@ktu.lt

Abstract

In this work we are solving authorship attribution and author profiling tasks (by focusing on the age and gender dimensions) for the Lithuanian language. This paper reports the first results on literary texts, which we compared to the results, previously obtained with different functional styles and language types (i.e., parliamentary transcripts and forum posts).

Using the Naïve Bayes Multinomial and Support Vector Machine methods we investigated an impact of various stylistic, character, lexical, morpho-syntactic features, and their combinations; the different author set sizes of 3, 5, 10, 20, 50, and 100 candidate authors; and the dataset sizes of 100, 300, 500, 1,000, 2,000, and 5,000 instances in each class. The highest 89.2% accuracy in the authorship attribution task using a maximum number of candidate authors was achieved with the Naïve Bayes Multinomial method and document-level character tri-grams. The highest 78.3% accuracy in the author profiling task focusing on the age dimension was achieved with the Support Vector Machine method and token lemmas. An accuracy reached 100% in the author profiling task focusing on the gender dimension with the Naïve Bayes Multinomial method and rather small datasets, where various lexical, morpho-syntactic, and character feature types demonstrated a very similar performance.

1 Introduction

With the constant influx of anonymous or pseudonymous electronic text documents (forum posts, Internet comments, tweets, etc.) the authorship analysis is becoming more and more topical. In this respect it is important to consider the anonymity factor, as it allows everyone to express their opinions freely, but on the other hand, opens a gate for different cyber-crimes. Therefore the authorship research –which for a long time in the past was mainly focused on literary questions of unknown or disputed authorship– drifts towards more practical applications in such domains as forensics, security, user targeted services, etc. Available text corpora, linguistic tools, and sophisticated methods even more accelerate the development of the authorship research field, which is no longer limited to authorship attribution (when identifying who, from a closed-set of candidate authors, is the actual author of a given anonymous text document) only. Other research directions involve the author verification task (when deciding if a given text is written by a certain author or not); the plagiarism detection task (when searching for similarities between two different texts or parts within a single text); the author profiling task (when extracting information about author's characteristics, typically covering the basic demographic dimensions as the age, gender, native language or psychometric traits); etc. In this paper we focus on authorship attribution (AA) and author profiling (AP) problems covering the age and gender dimensions.

Some researchers claim that in the scenario when an author makes no efforts to modify his/her writing style, authorship identification problems can be tackled due to an existing "stylometric fingerprint" notion –an individual and uncontrolled habit to express thoughts in certain unique ways, which is kept constant in all writings by the same author. Van Halteren (2005) even named this phenomenon a "human stylome" in analogy to a DNA "genome". However, Juola (2007) argues that strict implications are not absolutely correct, be-

Proceedings of the 5th Workshop on Balto-Slavic Natural Language Processing, pages 96–105,
Hissar, Bulgaria, 10–11 September 2015.

cause the "genome" is stable, but the writing style tends to evolve over time. More stable (e.g., gender) and changing (e.g., age, social status, education, etc.) demographic characteristics affect the writing style, thus making AP a solvable task for these dimensions.

With the breakthrough of the Internet era literary texts in the authorship research were gradually replaced with e-mails (Abbasi and Chen, 2008), (de Vel et al., 2001), web forum messages (Solorio et al., 2011), online chats (Cristani et al., 2012), (Inches et al., 2013), Internet blogs (Koppel et al., 2011) or tweets (Sousa-Silva et al., 2011; Schwartz et al., 2013), which, in turn, contributed to a development of Computational Linguistic methods able to cope effectively with the following problems: short texts, non-normative language texts, many candidate authors, etc. The discovered advanced techniques helped to achieve even higher accuracy in AA and AP tasks on literary texts (under so-called "ideal conditions"). Although the research on literary texts have lost popularity due to the decrease in demand of their practical applications, the results obtained on literary texts can still be interesting from the scientific point of view, as it may perform some kind of a baseline function in the comparative research. In this respect we believe that our present paper, which focuses on literary texts, will deliver valuable results. Besides, the obtained AA and AP results will be compared with the results previously reported on the Lithuanian language covering other functional styles and language types.

2 Related Works

Despite archaic rule-based approaches (attributing texts to authors/characteristics depending on a set of manually constructed rules) and some rare attempts to deal with unlabeled data (Nasir et al., 2014; Qian et al., 2014) automatic AA and AP tasks are tackled with Supervised Machine Learning (SML) or Similarity-Based (SB) techniques (for review see (Stamatatos, 2009)). In the SML paradigm, texts of known authorship/characteristic (training data) are used to construct a classifier which afterwards attributes anonymous documents. In the SB paradigm, an anonymous text is attributed to the particular author/characteristic whose text is the most similar according to some calculated similarity measure. The comparative experiments prove superiority of the SB methods over the SML techniques, e.g., Memory-Based Learning produced better results compared to Naïve Bayes and Decision Trees (Zhao and Zobel, 2005); the Delta method surpassed performance levels achieved by the popular Support Vector Machine method (Jockers and Witten, 2010). However, the SB approaches are considered to be more suitable for the problems with a big number of classes and limited training data, e.g., the Memory-Based Learning method applied on 145 authors outperformed Support Vector Machines (Luyckx and Daelemans, 2008), applied on 100,000 candidate authors outperformed Naïve Bayes, Support Vector Machine and Regularized Least Squares Classification (Narayanan et al., 2012). In our research we have at most 100 candidate authors, 6 age and 2 gender groups, therefore the SML approaches seem to be the most suitable choice. Besides, many AA and AP tasks are solved using the popular Support Vector Machine method, which in the contemporary computational research is considered as the most accurate, thus the most suitable technique for different text classification problems (e.g., superiority of Support Vector Machine is proved in (Zheng et al., 2006)). However, a selection of classification method itself is not as important as a proper selection of an appropriate feature type.

Starting from Mendenhall (1887) the first stylometric techniques were based on the quantitative features (so-called "style markers") such as a sentence or word length, number of syllables per word, type-token ratio, vocabulary richness function, lexical repetition, etc. (for review see (Holmes, 1998)). However, these feature types are considered to be suitable only for homogeneous and long texts (e.g., entire books) and for the datasets having only a few candidate authors. The first modern pioneering work of Mosteller and Wallace (1963) –who obtained promising AA results on The Federalist papers with the Bayesian method applied on frequencies of a few dozens function words– triggered many posterior experiments with various feature types. In the contemporary research the most widespread approach is to represent text documents as vectors of frequencies, which elements cover specific layers of linguistic information (lexical, morpho-syntactic, semantic, character, etc.). The best feature types are determined only after an experimental investigation.

Since most AA and AP research works deal with Germanic languages, providing no recommendations that could work with the morphologically rich, highly inflective, derivationally complex languages (such as Lithuanian), having relatively free word order in sentences, our focus is on the research done for the Baltic and Slavic languages, which by their nature and characteristics are the most similar to Lithuanian.

The AA experiments for the Polish language were performed with the literary texts of 2 authors using the feed-forward multilayer Perceptron method (with one or two hidden layers) and the sigmoid activation function trained by the back-propagation algorithm (Stańczyk and Cyran, 2007). The experiments with lexical (function words), syntactic (punctuation marks), and combination of both feature types revealed superiority of syntactic features. Eder (2011) applied the Delta method on the Polish, English, Latin, German datasets each containing 20 prose writers and then compared obtained AA results. A bootstrap-like procedure –testing a large number of randomly chosen permutations of original data with the k-Nearest Neighbor method in each trial and calculating an average accuracy score– helped to avoid fuzziness with unconvincing results. The best results for the Polish language texts were achieved with a mix of word unigrams and bigrams, with word unigrams for English, with a combination of words and character penta-grams for Latin, with character tri-grams for German.

Kukushkina et al. (2001) applied first-order Markov chains on the Russian literary texts written by 82 authors. All matrices –containing transition frequency pairs of text elements– composed during the training process for each candidate author were later used to compute probabilities of anonymous texts. The researchers investigated word-level (an original word form or it's lemma) character bigrams, pairs of coarse-grained or fine-grained part-of-speech tags and obtained the best results with word-level (in the original form) character bigrams. Kanishcheva (2014) presented the implemented software able to solve AA tasks for the Russian language. The offered linguistic model is based on statistical characteristics and can fill the lexical database of the author's vocabulary. Any attribution decision is taken after calculations of a proximity value between texts.

For the Croatian language the AA task was solved using the Support Vector Machine method with the radial basis (Reicher et al., 2010). The researchers used 4 datasets (newspaper texts of 25 authors, on-line blogs of 22 authors, Croatian literature classics of 20 authors, Internet forum posts of 19 authors). They tested a big variety of features and their combinations: function words, idf weighted function words, frequencies of coarse-grained part-of-speech tags, fine-grained part-of-speech tags with normalized frequencies, part-of-speech tri-grams, part-of-speech tri-grams with function words, other features (including punctuation, frequencies of word lengths, sentence-length frequency values, etc.). The best results were achieved with a combination of function words, punctuation marks, word and sentence length frequency values.

Zečević (2011) investigated byte-level character n-grams on the Serbian newspaper dataset of 3 authors. The researcher explored an influence of the author profile size (varying from 20 up to 5,000 most frequent n-grams) and the n-gram length (up to 7). All n-grams were stored in a structure called a prefix tree; an author attribution decision was taken by the 1-Nearest Neighbor algorithm based on the distance metric combining the dissimilarity measure and the simplified profile intersection. The best results were achieved with the n-grams of $n > 2$ and the profile size larger than 500. In the posterior work (Zečević and Utvić, 2012) researchers added 3 more candidate authors to the dataset and investigated an impact of syllables using the simplified profile intersection similarity measure. However, syllables were not robust enough to outperform byte-level character n-grams.

Other research works (as for the Slovene language in (Zwitter Vitez, 2012)) demonstrate potentials to solve AA or AP tasks. They represent available text corpora, linguistic tools and discuss possible methods, feature types, an importance of AA and AP tasks, etc.

For the Lithuanian language the AA research was done with 100 candidate authors and two datasets of parliamentary transcripts and forum posts (Kapočiūtė-Dzikienė et al., 2015). The researchers explored the Naïve Bayes Multinomial and Support Vector Machine methods with a big variety of feature types: lexical, morpho-syntactic, character, and stylistic. The best results on the parliamentary transcripts dataset were achieved with the Support Vector Machine method and morpho-syntactic features; on the forum posts dataset – with the Support Vector Machine method and character features. The previous AP research on the Lithuanian language was done with parliamentary transcripts focusing on the age, gender, and political attitude dimensions (Kapočiūtė-Dzikienė et al., 2014). The best results on the age dimension were achieved with the Support Vector Machine method and a mix of lemma unigrams, bi-grams, and tri-grams; on the gender and political attitude dimensions – with the Support Vector Machine method and a mix of lemma unigrams and bi-grams.

Hence, AA and AP research using classification methods is done on parliamentary transcripts (representing normative language) and forum posts (representing non-normative language) for the Lithuanian language, but there are no reported results on literary texts so far. Since a purpose of this paper is to perform the comparative analysis with the previous research done on parliamentary transcripts and forum posts, AA and AP tasks with literary texts will be solved by keeping all experimental conditions (concerning methods and their parameters, feature types, author set sizes, dataset sizes, etc.) as similar as possible.

3 Methodology

In a straightforward form, both AA and AP problems fit a standard paradigm of a text classification problem (Sebastiani, 2002).

Thus, text documents d_i belonging to the dataset D are presented as numerical vectors capturing statistics (absolute counts in our case) of potentially relevant features. Each d_i can be attributed to one element from a closed-set of candidate authors/characteristics, defined as classes $C = \{c_j\}$.

A function φ determines a mapping how each d_i is attributed to c_j in a training dataset D^T.

Our goal is to find a method (by combining classification techniques, feature types, and feature sets) which could discover as close approximation of φ as possible.

3.1 Datasets

186 literary works (in particular, novels, novellas, essays, publicistic novels, drama) taken from the Contemporary Corpus of the Lithuanian Language (Marcinkevičienė, 2000) cover the period of 37 years from 1972 to 2012. These literary works were split into text snippets containing 2,000 symbols (including white-spaces), thus an average text document length varies from ~283 to ~290 tokens. Although the average text length does not fit the recommendations given by Eder (2010) (2,500 tokens for Latin and 5,000 for English, German, Polish or Hungarian) or Koppel et al. (2007) (500 tokens), these texts are not as extremely short as used in, e.g., in Luyckx (2011) or Micros and Perifanos (2011) AA research works, where reasonable results were achieved with only ~60 tokens per text.

After previously described pre-processing, we composed 3 datasets:

- *LIndividual*, which was used in our AA task (see Table 1). The experiments with this dataset involved balanced/full versions and the increasing number of candidate authors (3, 5, 10, 20, 50, and 100).
- *LAge* used in our AP task by focusing on the age dimension (see Table 2) contains 6 age groups (*≤29*, *30-39*, *40-49*, *50-59*, *60-69*, and *≥70*).[1] The age group of any author was determined by calculating a difference between the author's birth date an the publishing date of his/her literary work. An opposite to the related research works (e.g., (Schler et al., 2006) or (Koppel et al., 2009)) we did not eliminate intermediate age groups, thus we did not simplify our task. The experiments performed with the balanced dataset versions (unless there was not enough text samples in the "main pool") of 100, 300, 500, 1,000, 2,000, 5,000 text documents in each class.
- *LGender* used in our AP task focusing on the gender dimension (see Table 2) contains 2 gender groups (*male* and *female*). The experiments performed with the balanced dataset versions of 100, 300, 500, 1,000, 2,000, 5,000 text documents in each class.

A distribution of 100 authors by their age and gender is given in Table 3. The *LAge* and *LGender* datasets contain randomly selected texts, providing no meta information about their authors.

[1]The chosen grouping is commonly used in the social studies, e.g., in the largest data archive in Europe (http://www.gesis.org), as well as in the Lithuanian Data Archive for Social Science and Humanities (http://www.lidata.eu).

Numb. of classes	Numb. of text documents	Numb. of tokens	Numb. of distinct tokens (types)	Numb. of distinct lemmas	Avg. numb of tokens in a doc.
3	450	128,622	39,306	20,099	285.83
	2,156	612,030	105,200	42,347	283.87
5	750	214,117	58,282	26,846	285.49
	3,099	877,788	136,798	51,638	283.25
10	1,500	430,849	84,838	35,424	287.23
	5,102	1,456,039	176,146	64,001	285.39
20	3,000	867,657	133,163	52,005	289.22
	8,661	2,492,637	236,505	84,566	287.80
50	7,500	217,6019	229,726	84,952	290.14
	16,317	4,721,452	343,827	124,117	289.36
100	15,000	4,347,165	332,251	120,676	289.81
	25,564	7,395,147	436,686	159,175	289.28

Table 1: Statistics about *LIndividual*: an upper value in each cell represents the balanced dataset of 150 texts in each class, a lower value– imbalanced (full). The set of authors is the same in both dataset versions.

Dataset	Numb. of text documents	Numb. of tokens	Numb. of distinct tokens (types)	Numb. of distinct lemmas	Avg. numb of tokens in a doc.
LAge	27,264	7,912,886	454,165	165,432	290.23
LGender	10,000	2,899,837	271,189	99,242	289.98

Table 2: Statistics about the balanced *LAge* and *LGender* datasets containing 5,000 text documents in each class. The *LGender* dataset is not completely balanced due to the lack of texts in the age groups of $\leq$*29* and $\geq$*70.*

	$\leq$29	30-39	40-49	50-59	60-69	$\geq$70
Male	5	13	13	13	13	12
Female	7	8	6	4	3	3
Total	12	21	19	17	16	15

Table 3: Distribution of authors by their age and gender.

3.2 Machine Learning Methods

In order to compare obtained AA and AP results with the previously reported, experimental conditions have to be as similar as possible. Thus, the choice of classification method was restricted to Naïve Bayes Multinomial (NBM) (introduced by Lewis and Gale (1994)) and Support Vector Machine (SVM) (introduced by Cortes and Vapnik (1995)). Both SML techniques are used in the recent AA and AP tasks due to their advantages.

3.3 Features

The choice of features (by which documents are represented) is as important as the choice of classification method. To find out what could work with the Lithuanian literary texts, we tested a big variety of different feature types, covering stylistic, character, lexical and morpho-syntactic levels:

- *sm* – style markers: an average sentence and word length; a standardized type/token ratio.
- *fwd* – function words (topic-neutral): prepositions, pronouns, conjunctions, particles, interjections, and onomatopoeias, which were automatically recognized in texts with the Lithuanian morphological analyzer-lemmatizer "Lemuoklis" (Zinkevičius, 2000).
- *chr* – (language-independent) document-level character n-grams with $n \in [2, 7]$.
- *lex* – tokens and a mix of their n-grams up to $n \in [2, 3]$ (e.g., in $n = 3$ case not only tri-grams, but bi-grams and unigrams would be used as well).
- *lem* – lemmas and a mix of their n-grams up to $n \in [2, 3]$. The lemmatization was done with "Lemuoklis" which replaced recognized words with their lemmas, transformed generic words into appropriate lower-case letters and all numbers into a special tag.
- *pos* – coarse-grained part-of-speech tags (such as noun, verb, adjective, etc., determined with "Lemuoklis") and a mix of their n-grams up to $n \in [2, 3]$.
- *lexpos*, *lempos*, *lexmorf*, *lemmorf* – the compound features of *lex+pos*, *lem+pos*,

lex+morf, *lem+morf*, respectively, and a mix of their n-grams up to $n \in [2, 3]$. Here *morf* indicates a fine-grained part-of-speech tag composed of coarse-grained tag with the additional morphological information as case, gender, tense, etc.

4 Experimental Setup and Results

All experiments were carried out with the stratified 10-fold cross-validation and evaluated using the accuracy and f-score metrics.[2]

For each dataset version (described in Section 3.1) the random $\sum P^2(c_j)$ and majority $\max P(c_j)$ baselines were calculated (where $P(c_j)$ is the probability of class c_j) and the higher one of these values is presented in the following figures. The statistical significance between different results was evaluated using McNemar's (1947) test with one degree of freedom.

In all experiments we used WEKA 3.7 machine learning toolkit (Hall et al., 2009); 1,000 the most relevant features (using the types described in Section 3.3), ranked by the calculated χ^2 values; the SVM method with the SMO polynomial kernel (Platt, 1998) (because it gave the highest accuracy in the comparative experiments, done with parliamentary transcripts and forum data (Kapočiūtė-Dzikienė et al., 2015)) and the NBM method (described in Section 3.2). Remaining parameters were set to their default values.

The highest achieved accuracies (in terms of all explored feature types) with both classification techniques for AA and AP tasks are presented in Figure 1 and Figure 2, respectively. For the accuracies obtained with different feature types using the most accurate classification method and the datasets presented in Table 1, Table 2 see Table 4.

5 Discussion

All obtained results are reasonable, as they exceed the random and majority baselines.

If we compare the results in Figure 1 with the previously reported results on parliamentary transcripts and forum posts (Kapočiūtė-Dzikienė et al., 2015), SVM is not the best technique in all cases here. Despite it slightly outperforms NBM on the smaller datasets (with $<$20 candidate authors), but under-performs on the larger ones. We suppose that the simple NBM technique coped effectively with our AA task due to the following reasons: used literary texts are more homogeneous (a literary work/author rate is 1.86), longer ($\sim$1.34 and $\sim$6.88 times longer compared to parliamentary transcripts and forum posts, respectively), have more stable vocabulary, and clearer synonymy compared to parliamentary transcripts (covering a period of 23 years) or forum posts (covering a bunch of different topics). Moreover, the writing style of each author in literary works is expressed more clearly, therefore the drop in the accuracy when adding new authors to the dataset was not as steep as with parliamentary transcripts or forum posts. Even with 100 candidate authors the accuracy on literary texts almost reaches the threshold of 90% (see Figure 1) exceeding the results of parliamentary transcripts and forum posts by $\sim$18.6% and $\sim$54.6%, respectively. Besides, the dataset balancing boosted the accuracy on parliamentary transcripts and reduced on forum posts, but gave no noticeable impact on literary texts. Since literary texts written by the same author are very similar in style, new texts added to the dataset could not make any significant impact.

Zooming into the feature types in Table 4 allows us to state that lexical information dominates character on the smaller datasets (having $\leq$50 candidate authors). However, when the number of candidates is small ($\leq$20) many different features (based on character, lexical, lemma or compound lexical and morpho-syntactic information) perform equally well; with 50 – only unigrams of lemmas (sometimes complemented with part-of-speech tags) are significantly better compared to the rest types; with 100 – only character tri-grams are the best. The most surprising is the fact that the character feature type gave the best results on the largest dataset. Typically when dealing with morphologically rich languages and normative texts, morphological features are the most accurate (e.g., on Greek (Stamatatos et al., 2001) or on Hebrew (Koppel et al., 2006) texts). The Lithuanian language is not an exception, i.e., the experiments with parliamentary transcripts showed that token lemmas (or their n-grams) is the best feature type, whereas on forum posts (where the morphological tools could not be maximally helpful due to the text specifics) character features gave the highest accuracy. On the other hand, a robustness of character n-grams is not very surprising: i.e.,

[2]F-scores show the same trend as accuracy values in all our experiments, therefore we do not present them in the following figures and tables.

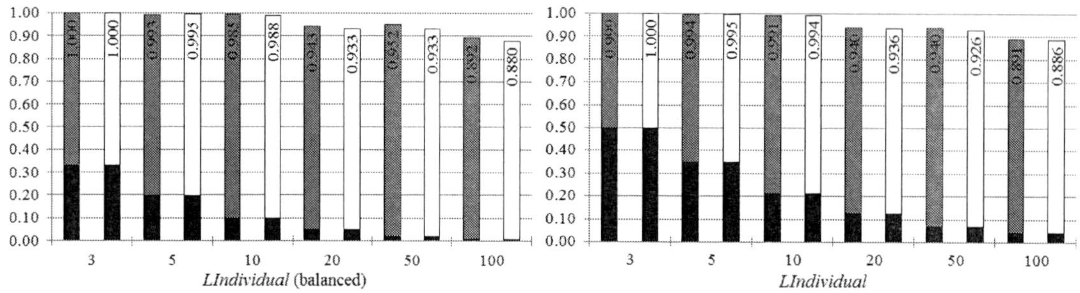

Figure 1: The accuracy (y axis) dependence on a number of candidate authors (x axis). Each column shows the maximum achieved accuracy over all explored feature types. Grey columns represent the NBM method, white – SVM, black parts represent the higher value of random/majority baselines.

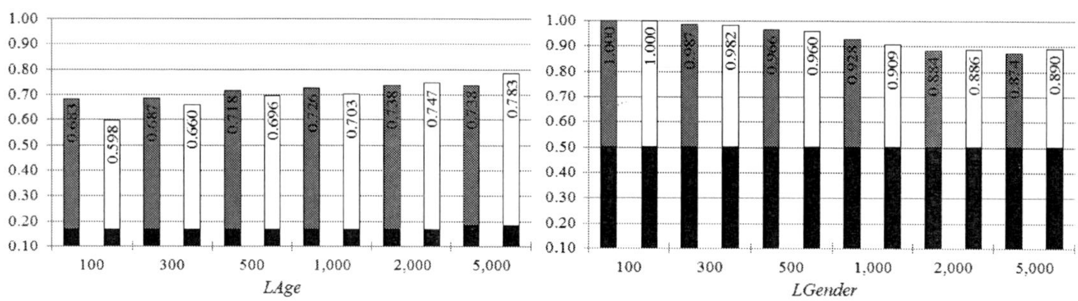

Figure 2: The accuracy (y axis) dependence on a number of instances in each class (x axis). For the other notations see the caption of Figure 1.

character n-grams can capture lexical preferences without any need of linguistic background knowledge; moreover, we used document-level character n-grams which incorporate information about contiguous words. Besides, literary texts are not too complicated for AA tasks, therefore shorter character n-grams (tri-grams in our case) are enough to capture author's style differences without mapping too obviously to specific words.

The SVM method outperformed the NBM method on the larger datasets (having more instances in each class) in all AP tasks (see the results on *LAge* and *LGender* presented in Figure 2 and on parliamentary transcripts reported by Kapočiūtė et al. (2014)). The results obtained with literary texts focusing on the age dimension do not contradict the results achieved with parliamentary transcripts: the highest boost in the accuracy is reached on the largest datasets (containing 5,000 instances in each class). The results obtained with literary texts focusing on the gender dimension are absolutely opposite, i.e., the best performance on literary texts was demonstrated with the smaller datasets, on the parliamentary transcripts – with the largest. We suppose that this unexpected situation (when the smaller datasets seem more optimal for capturing the gender characteristics) happened when instances were randomly selected from the "main pool", i.e., if the first selected instances were the most typical for the writing style of males and females, less characteristic instances added afterwards could only degrade AP performance. However, the precise answer to this question is possible only after a detailed error analysis which is planned in our future research. Nevertheless the dataset of 100, 300 or 500 instances in each class is too small to be recommended for any AP tasks.

Zooming into Table 4 allows us to state that token lemmas is the best feature type on *LAge*. Besides, lemma information (in particular, a mix of lemma tri-grams, bi-grams, and unigrams) gave the best results on parliamentary transcripts as well. Marginally the best feature type dealing with the largest *LGender* dataset is token lemmas complemented with the part-of-speech information; with the smaller *LGender* datasets various lexical, morpho-syntactic, and character feature types demonstrated high and very similar per-

Feature type	*LIndividual* (balanced)						*LIndividual*						*LAge*	*LGender*
	3	5	10	20	50	100	3	5	10	20	50	100		
sm	0.616	0.380	0.249	0.163	0.089	0.045	0.635	0.441	0.312	0.195	0.114	0.072	0.245	0.560
fwd	0.942	0.825	0.823	0.701	0.575	0.442	0.966	0.874	0.862	0.751	0.634	0.480	0.445	0.710
chr2	0.989	0.965	0.973	0.896	0.874	0.782	0.990	0.978	0.979	0.911	0.895	0.836	0.649	0.811
chr3	0.998	0.992	0.986	0.932	0.934	**0.892**	0.998	0.991	0.989	0.920	0.921	**0.891**	0.722	0.859
chr4	0.998	0.991	0.985	0.922	0.896	0.756	0.997	0.988	0.986	0.914	0.896	0.791	0.726	0.858
chr5	0.993	0.983	0.973	0.915	0.833	0.662	0.995	0.987	0.979	0.906	0.854	0.703	0.698	0.849
chr6	0.987	0.980	0.962	0.897	0.787	0.633	0.993	0.984	0.968	0.894	0.824	0.672	0.678	0.843
chr7	0.987	0.977	0.958	0.884	0.761	0.611	0.992	0.985	0.961	0.884	0.795	0.639	0.656	0.834
lex1	**1.000**	**0.993**	0.993	0.937	0.928	0.841	0.998	**0.994**	**0.991**	0.933	0.909	0.820	0.753	0.884
lex2	**1.000**	0.991	0.991	0.933	0.916	0.840	0.998	**0.994**	0.989	0.929	0.895	0.777	0.745	0.885
lex3	**1.000**	0.992	0.991	0.934	0.916	0.841	0.998	**0.994**	0.989	0.929	0.895	0.775	0.745	0.884
lem1	0.998	0.989	0.993	**0.943**	**0.952**	0.889	**0.999**	0.990	**0.991**	**0.940**	**0.940**	0.882	**0.783**	0.889
lem2	0.998	0.991	0.992	0.936	0.941	0.886	**0.999**	0.991	0.990	0.936	0.925	0.837	0.771	0.884
lem3	0.998	0.988	0.991	0.938	0.941	0.885	**0.999**	0.989	0.990	0.937	0.925	0.834	0.769	0.884
pos1	0.702	0.632	0.549	0.356	0.218	0.143	0.890	0.641	0.553	0.368	0.209	0.142	0.340	0.616
pos2	0.882	0.768	0.784	0.612	0.516	0.408	0.891	0.780	0.789	0.641	0.529	0.430	0.437	0.649
pos3	0.909	0.797	0.817	0.691	0.615	0.516	0.909	0.801	0.818	0.689	0.618	0.533	0.441	0.648
lexpos1	**1.000**	0.992	0.993	0.940	0.925	0.838	0.998	**0.994**	0.990	0.933	0.908	0.814	0.750	0.883
lexpos2	**1.000**	0.991	0.991	0.934	0.910	0.839	0.998	0.993	0.990	0.927	0.892	0.776	0.741	0.880
lexpos3	**1.000**	0.991	0.990	0.936	0.911	0.837	0.998	0.993	0.989	0.927	0.892	0.774	0.741	0.878
lempos1	0.998	0.989	0.993	0.943	0.951	0.888	**0.999**	0.990	**0.991**	**0.940**	0.938	0.880	0.741	**0.890**
lempos2	**1.000**	0.992	0.991	0.938	0.939	0.887	0.998	0.992	0.989	0.935	0.924	0.840	0.770	0.885
lempos3	**1.000**	0.989	0.991	0.937	0.939	0.886	0.998	0.992	0.990	0.934	0.923	0.835	0.771	0.882
lexmorf1	**1.000**	0.991	**0.995**	0.939	0.926	0.838	0.998	**0.994**	0.990	0.933	0.907	0.814	0.749	0.882
lexmorf2	**1.000**	0.992	0.989	0.935	0.912	0.835	0.997	0.993	0.989	0.927	0.890	0.772	0.740	0.880
lexmorf3	**1.000**	0.991	0.990	0.935	0.911	0.835	0.997	0.992	0.989	0.927	0.890	0.771	0.739	0.879
lemmorf1	**1.000**	0.992	0.991	0.937	0.932	0.850	0.998	**0.994**	**0.991**	0.932	0.913	0.828	0.754	0.886
lemmorf2	**1.000**	0.988	0.989	0.930	0.916	0.850	0.998	0.993	0.988	0.927	0.894	0.783	0.745	0.875
lemmorf3	**1.000**	0.988	0.990	0.930	0.916	0.849	0.998	**0.994**	0.988	0.926	0.895	0.782	0.746	0.876

Table 4: The accuracy values achieved on *LIndividual* with NBM; on *LAge* and *Gender* with SVM and 5,000 instances in each class. In each column the best results are presented in bold, the results that do not significantly differ from the best one are underlined.

formance. Besides, the best feature type on parliamentary transcripts is a mix of lemma bi-grams and unigrams. However, a robustness of lemmata is not surprising having in mind that we were dealing with the morphologically complex language and normative texts.

6 Conclusions

In this paper we report the first authorship attribution and author profiling results obtained on the Lithuanian literary texts. The results are compared with previously reported on parliamentary transcripts and forum posts.

When solving the authorship attribution task we experimentally investigated the effect of the author set size by gradually increasing the number of candidate authors up to 100. The best results dealing with the maximum author set were achieved with the Naïve Bayes Multinomial method and character tri-grams. The results exceeded the baselines by ~88.2% and reached 89.2% of the accuracy.

When solving the author profiling task we experimentally investigated the effect of balanced dataset size by gradually increasing the number of instances in each class up to 5,000. The best results for the age dimension were achieved with the maximum dataset, token lemmas, and the Support Vector Machine method; for the gender dimension very good performance was demonstrated already with the small datasets, using lemma unigrams and the Support Vector Machine method. The results focusing on the age and gender dimensions exceeded baselines by ~60% and ~50% reaching 78.3% and 100% of the accuracy, respectively.

The comparative analysis show that it is much easier to capture age, gender and individual author differences with literary texts than with parliamentary transcripts or forum posts.

In the future research we are planning to make the detailed error analysis, which could help us to improve the accuracy; to expand the number of authors and profiling dimensions.

Acknowledgments

This research was funded by a grant (No. LIT-8-69) from the Research Council of Lithuania.

References

Ahmed Abbasi and Hsinchun Chen. 2008. Writerprints: a stylometric approach to identity-level identification and similarity detection in cyberspace. *ACM Transactions on Information Systems*, 26(2):1–29.

Corina Cortes and Vladimir Vapnik. 1995. Support-vector networks. *Machine Learning*, 20(3):273–297.

Marco Cristani, Giorgio Roffo, Cristina Segalin, Loris Bazzani, Alessandro Vinciarelli, and Vittorio Murino. 2012. Conversationally-inspired stylometric features for authorship attribution in instant messaging. In *Proceedings of the 20th ACM International Conference on Multimedia*, pages 1121–1124.

Olivier de Vel, Alison M. Anderson, Malcolm W. Corney, and George M. Mohay. 2001. Mining e-mail content for author identification forensics. *SIGMOD Record*, 30(4):55–64.

Maciej Eder. 2010. Does size matter? Authorship attribution, small samples, big problem. In *Digital Humanities 2010: Conference Abstracts*, pages 132–135.

Maciej Eder. 2011. Style-markers in authorship attribution a cross-language study of the authorial fingerprint. *Studies in Polish Linguistics*, 6(1):99–114.

Mark Hall, Eibe Frank, Holmes Geoffrey, Bernhard Pfahringer, Peter Reutemann, and Ian H. Witten. 2009. The WEKA data mining software: an update. *SIGKDD Explorations*, 11(1):10–18.

David I. Holmes. 1998. The evolution of stylometry in humanities scholarship. *Literary and Linguistic Computing*, 13(3):111–117.

Giacomo Inches, Morgan Harvey, and Fabio Crestani. 2013. Finding participants in a chat: authorship attribution for conversational documents. In *International Conference on Social Computing*, pages 272–279.

Matthew L. Jockers and Daniela M. Witten. 2010. A comparative study of machine learning methods for authorship attribution. *Literary and Linguistic Computing*, 25(2):215–223.

Patrick Juola. 2007. Future trends in authorship attribution. In *Advances in Digital Forensics III - IFIP International Conference on Digital Forensics*, volume 242, pages 119–132.

Olga Kanishcheva. 2014. Using of the statistical method for authorship attribution of the text. In *Proceedings of the 1st International Electronic Conference on Entropy and Its Applications*, volume 1.

Jurgita Kapočiūtė-Dzikienė, Ligita Šarkutė, and Andrius Utka. 2014. Automatic author profiling of Lithuanian parliamentary speeches: exploring the influence of features and dataset sizes. In *Human Language Technologies – The Baltic Perspective*, pages 99–106.

Jurgita Kapočiūtė-Dzikienė, Ligita Šarkutė, and Andrius Utka. 2015. The effect of author set size in authorship attribution for Lithuanian. In *NODALIDA 2015: 20th Nordic Conference of Computational Linguistics*, pages 87–96.

Moshe Koppel, Dror Mughaz, and Navot Akiva. 2006. New methods for attribution of rabbinic literature. *A Journal for Hebrew Descriptive, Computational and Applied Linguistics*, 57:5–18.

Moshe Koppel, Jonathan Schler, and Elisheva Bonchek-Dokow. 2007. Measuring differentiability: unmasking pseudonymous authors. *Journal of Machine Learning Research*, 8:1261–1276.

Moshe Koppel, Jonathan Schler, and Shlomo Argamon. 2009. Computational methods in authorship attribution. *Journal of the Association for Information Science and Technology*, 60(1):9–26.

Moshe Koppel, Jonathan Schler, and Shlomo Argamon. 2011. Authorship attribution in the wild. *Language Resources and Evaluation*, 45(1):83–94.

Olga Vladimirovna Kukushkina, Anatoly Anatol'evich Polikarpov, and Dmitrij Viktorovich Khmelev. 2001. Using literal and grammatical statistics for authorship attribution. *Problems of Information Transmission*, 37(2):172–184.

David D. Lewis and William A. Gale. 1994. A sequential algorithm for training text classifiers. In *17th Annual International ACM-SIGIR Conference on Research and Development in Information Retrieval*, pages 3–12.

Kim Luyckx and Walter Daelemans. 2008. Authorship attribution and verification with many authors and limited data. In *Proceedings of the 22Nd International Conference on Computational Linguistics*, volume 1, pages 513–520.

Kim Luyckx. 2011. Authorship attribution of e-mail as a multi-class task. In *Notebook for PAN at CLEF 2011. Cross-Language Evaluation Forum (Notebook Papers/Labs/Workshop)*.

Rūta Marcinkevičienė. 2000. Tekstynų lingvistika (teorija ir paktika) [Corpus linguistics (theory and practice)]. *Darbai ir dienos*, 24:7–63. In Lithuanian.

Quinn Michael McNemar. 1947. Note on the sampling error of the difference between correlated proportions or percentages. *Psychometrika*, 12(2):153–157.

Thomas Corwin Mendenhall. 1887. The characteristic curves of composition. *Science*, 9(214):237–246.

George K. Mikros and Kostas Perifanos. 2011. Authorship identification in large email collections: experiments using features that belong to different linguistic levels. In *Notebook for PAN at CLEF 2011. Cross-Language Evaluation Forum (Notebook Papers/Labs/Workshop)*.

Frederik Mosteller and David L. Wallace. 1963. Inference in an authorship problem. *Journal Of The American Statistical Association*, 58(302):275–309.

Arvind Narayanan, Hristo Paskov, Neil Zhenqiang Gong, John Bethencourt, Emil Stefanov, Eui Chul Richard Shin, and Dawn Song. 2012. On the feasibility of internet-scale author identification. In *Proceedings of the 2012 IEEE Symposium on Security and Privacy*, pages 300–314.

Jamal Abdul Nasir, Nico Görnitz, and Ulf Brefeld. 2014. An off-the-shelf approach to authorship attribution. *The 25th International Conference on Computational Linguistics*, pages 895–904.

John C. Platt. 1998. Fast training of support vector machines using sequential minimal optimization. In *Advances in Kernel Methods – Support Vector Learning*, pages 185–208.

Tieyun Qian, Bing Liu, Li Chen, and Zhiyong Peng. 2014. Tri-training for authorship attribution with limited training data. In *Proceedings of the 52nd Annual Meeting of the Association for Computational Linguistics*, volume 2, pages 345–351.

Tomislav Reicher, Ivan Krišto, Igor Belša, and Artur Šilić. 2010. Automatic authorship attribution for texts in Croatian language using combinations of features. In *Knowledge-Based and Intelligent Information and Engineering Systems*, volume 6277, pages 21–30.

Jonathan Schler, Moshe Koppel, Shlomo Argamon, and James W. Pennebaker. 2006. Effects of age and gender on blogging. In *Proceedings of AAAI Spring Symposium on Computational Approaches for Analyzing Weblogs*, pages 199–205.

Roy Schwartz, Oren Tsur, Ari Rappoport, and Moshe Koppel. 2013. Authorship attribution of micro-messages. In *Empirical Methods in Natural Langauge Processing*, pages 1880–1891.

Fabrizio Sebastiani. 2002. Machine learning in automated text categorization. *ACM Computing Surveys*, 34:1–47.

Thamar Solorio, Sangita Pillay, Sindhu Raghavan, and Manuel Montes-y Gómez. 2011. Modality specific meta features for authorship attribution in web forum posts. In *The 5th International Joint Conference on Natural Language Processing*, pages 156–164.

Rui Sousa-Silva, Gustavo Laboreiro, Luís Sarmento, Tim Grant, Eugénio C. Oliveira, and Belinda Maia. 2011. 'twazn me!!! ;(' Automatic authorship analysis of micro-blogging messages. In *Proceedings of the 16th International Conference on Natural Language Processing and Information Systems*, pages 161–168.

Efstathios Stamatatos, Nikos Fakotakis, and Georgios Kokkinakis. 2001. Computer-based authorship attribution without lexical measures. *Computers and the Humanities*, 35(2):193–214.

Efstathios Stamatatos. 2009. A survey of modern authorship attribution methods. *Journal of the Association for Information Science and Technology*, 60(3):538–556.

Urszula Stańczyk and Krzysztof A. Cyran. 2007. Machine learning approach to authorship attribution of literary texts. *International Journal of Applied Mathematics and Informatics*, 1(4):151–158.

Hans Van Halteren, R. Harald Baayen, Fiona Tweedie, Marco Haverkort, and Anneke Neijt. 2005. New machine learning methods demonstrate the existence of a human stylome. *Journal of Quantitative Linguistics*, 12:65–77.

Andelka Zečević and Miloš Utvić. 2012. An authorship attribution for Serbian. In *Local Proceedings of the Fifth Balkan Conference in Informatics*, pages 109–112.

Andelka Zečević. 2011. N-gram based text classification according to authorship. In *Proceedings of the Student Research Workshop associated with Recent Advances in Natural Language Processing*, pages 145–149.

Ying Zhao and Justin Zobel. 2005. Effective and scalable authorship attribution using function words. In *Proceedings of the Second AIRS Asian Information Retrieval Symposium*, pages 174–189.

Rong Zheng, Jiexun Li, Hsinchun Chen, and Zan Huang. 2006. A framework for authorship identification of online messages: writing-style features and classification techniques. *Journal of the American Society for Information Science and Technology*, 57(3):378–393.

Vytautas Zinkevičius. 2000. Lemuoklis – morfologinei analizei [Morphological analysis with Lemuoklis]. *Darbai ir dienos*, 24:246–273. In Lithuanian.

Ana Zwitter Vitez. 2012. Authorship attribution: specifics for Slovene. *Slavia Centralis*, 1(14):75–85.

Classification of Short Legal Lithuanian Texts

Vytautas Mickevičius[1,2] **Tomas Krilavičius[1,2]**
Vaidas Morkevičius[3]
[1]Vytautas Magnus University, [2]Baltic Institute of Advanced Technologies,
[3]Kaunas University of Technology, Institute of Public Policy and Administration
vytautas.mickevicius@bpti.lt, t.krilavicius@bpti.lt,
vaidas.morkevicius@ktu.lt

Abstract

Statistical analysis of parliamentary roll call votes is an important topic in political science because it reveals ideological positions of members of parliament (MP) and factions. However, it depends on the issues debated and voted upon. Therefore, analysis of carefully selected sets of roll call votes provides a deeper knowledge about MPs. However, in order to classify roll call votes according to their topic automatic text classifiers have to be employed, as these votes are counted in thousands. It can be formulated as a problem of classification of short legal texts in Lithuanian (classification is performed using only headings of roll call vote).

We present results of an ongoing research on thematic classification of roll call votes of the Lithuanian Parliament. The problem differs significantly from the classification of long texts, because feature spaces are small and sparse, due to the short and formulaic texts. In this paper we investigate performance of 3 feature representation techniques (*bag-of-words*, *n-gram* and *tf-idf*) in combination with Support Vector Machines (with different kernels) and Multinomial Logistic Regression. The best results were achieved using *tf-idf* with SVM with linear and polynomial kernels.

1 Introduction

Increasing availability of data on activities of governments and politicians as well as tools suitable for analysis of large data sets allows political scientists to study previously under-researched topics. As parliament is one the major foci of attention of the public, the media and political scientists, statistical analysis of parliamentary activity is becoming more and more popular. In this field, parliamentary voting analysis might be discerned as getting increasing attention (Jackman, 2001; Poole, 2005; Hix et al., 2006; Bailey, 2007).

Analysis of the activity of the Lithuanian parliament (the Seimas) is also becoming more popular (Krilavičius and Žilinskas, 2008; Krilavičius and Morkevičius, 2011; Mickevičius et al., 2014; Užupytė and Morkevičius, 2013). However, overall statistical analysis of the MP voting on all the questions (bills etc.) during the whole term of the Seimas (four years) might blur the ideological divisions that arise from the differences in the positions taken by MPs depending on their attitudes towards the governmental policy or topics of the votes (Roberts et al., 2009; Krilavičius and Morkevičius, 2013). Therefore, one of the important tasks is creating tools to compare the voting behavior of MPs with regard to the topics of the votes and changes in the governmental coalitions.

One of the options to assign a thematic category to each topic is manual annotation. However, due to a large amount of voting data and constantly increasing database (there are up to 10000 roll call votes in each term of the Seimas) it becomes complicated. Better solution may be introduced by using automatic classification with machine learning and natural language processing methods.

Some attempts to classify Lithuanian documents were already made (Kapočiūtė-Dzikienė et al., 2012; Kapočiūtė-Dzikienė and Krupavičius, 2014; Mickevičius et al., 2015), but they pursue different problems, i.e., the first one works with full text documents, the second tries to predict faction from the record and the last one is quite sparse (only the basic text classifiers are examined). This paper presents a broader research which aims to find an optimal automatic text classifier for short political texts (topics of parliamentary votes) in Lithuanian. The methods used are rather well known and standard with other languages than

Proceedings of the 5th Workshop on Balto-Slavic Natural Language Processing, pages 106–111,
Hissar, Bulgaria, 10–11 September 2015.

Lithuanian. However, due to specific type of analyzed short legal texts and high inflatability of Lithuanian language (Kapočiūtė-Dzikienė et al., 2012) these methods must be tested under different conditions.

New tasks tackled in this paper include experiments with: (1) different features, namely bag-of-words, *n-gram* and *tf-idf*; (2) different classifiers: Support Vector Machines (Harish et al., 2010; Vapnik and Cortes, 1995; Joachims, 1998), including different kernels (Shawe-Taylor and Cristianini, 2004), and Multinomial Logistic Regression (Aggarwal and Zhai, 2012); (3) identifying the most efficient combinations of text classifiers and feature representation techniques.

Automatic classification of Seimas' voting titles is a part of an ongoing research dedicated to creating an infrastructure that would allow its user to monitor and analyze the data of roll call voting in the Seimas. The main idea of the infrastructure is to enable its users to compare behaviors of the MPs based on their voting results.

2 Data

2.1 Data Extraction

All data used in the research is available on the Lithuanian Parliament website[1]. In order to convert data into suitable format for storage and analysis, a custom web crawler was developed and used. The corpus used in the research was generated applying the following steps: (1) The object of analysis are the titles of debates in Lithuanian Parliament; (2) Following a unique ID (which is assigned to every debate in Seimas) every debate title was examined (no titles were skipped); (3) The analyzed time span goes from 2007-09-10 to 2015-04-14; (4) Only titles of debates that included at least one roll call voting were selected for the analysis. Using such approach 11521 text documents were retrieved.

2.2 Preprocessing and Descriptive Statistics

In order to eliminate the influence of functional words and characters (as well as spelling errors), the documents were normalized in the following way: (1) Punctuation marks and digits removed; (2) Uppercase letters converted to lowercase; (3) 185 stop words (out of 3299 unique words) were removed.

Descriptive statistics of the preprocessed text documents are provided in Table 1.

Length	Words	Characters
Minimum	2	19
Average	33	264
Maximum	775	6412

Table 1: Descriptive statistics of the corpus.

2.3 Classes

In order to achieve proper results of automatic text classification, clearly defined classes must be used. To fulfill this requirement classification scheme of Danish Policy Agendas project[2] was followed. Regarding the size of the analyzed corpus, 21 initial thematic categories were aggregated into 7 broader classes.

A set of 750 text documents were selected (see below) and manually classified to build a gold standard. To avoid bias in automatic classification towards populated classes, the amounts of documents belonging to classes should not be significantly different, therefore the text documents were not selected randomly. Instead approximately 100 of objects for each class (aggregate topic) were picked from the debates of the last term of the Seimas (from 2012-11-16). See Table 2 for the number of text documents in each class.

Class	No. of docs
Economics	126
Culture and civil rights	121
Legal affairs	106
Social policy	107
Defense and foreign affairs	82
Government operations	104
Environment and technology	103
Total	**750**

Table 2: Corpora.

3 Tools and Methods

3.1 Feature Representation Techniques

Bag-of-words. When using this method, the terms are made of single and whole words. Therefore,

[1]URL: http://www.lrs.lt

[2]URL: http://www.agendasetting.dk

the dictionary of all unique words in the corpus needs to be produced. Then a feature vector of length m is generated for each text document in the data, where m is a total number of unique words in the dictionary. Feature vectors contain the frequencies of terms in the text documents.

N-grams. Using this method text documents are divided into character sets (substrings) of length n insomuch as the first substring contains all the characters of the documents from the 1st to n-th inclusive. Second substring contains all characters of the document from 2nd to $(n+1)$-th inclusive. This principle is used throughout the whole text document, the last substring containing characters from $(k-n+1)$-th to k-th, where k is the number of characters in the text document. This process is applied to each text document and a dictionary of unique substrings (considered as terms) of length n (n-grams) is generated. Character sets is one of several ways to use n-grams. However, character n-grams tend to show significantly better results in this case (Mickevičius et al., 2015) than word n-grams, therefore it was decided to discard word n-grams in the study.

tf-idf. The idea of *tf-idf* (term frequency - inverse document frequency) method is to estimate the importance of each term according to its frequency in both the text document and the corpus). Suppose t is a certain term used in a document d, which belongs to corpus D. Then each element in the feature vector of d is calculated using (1), (2) and (3) formulas:

$$tf(t,d) = 0.5 + \frac{0.5 \cdot f(t,d)}{\max\{f(w,d) : w \in d\}} \quad (1)$$

$$idf(t,d,D) = \log \frac{N}{1 + |\{d \in D : t \in d\}|} \quad (2)$$

$$tfidf(t,d,D) = tf(t,d) \cdot idf(t,d,D), \quad (3)$$

where $f(t,d)$ is a *raw term frequency* (count of term appearances in the text document), $\max\{f(w,d) : w \in d\}$ is a *maximum raw frequency* of any term in the document, N is a *total number of documents* in the corpus, and $|\{d \in D : t \in d\}|$ is a *number of documents* where the term t appears. The base of the logarithmic function does not matter, therefore natural logarithm was used. The term itself was defined as a single separate word (identically to *bag-of-words* method).

3.2 Text Classifiers

Support Vector Machines (SVM) (Harish et al., 2010; Vapnik and Cortes, 1995; Joachims, 1998). A document d is represented by a vector $x = (w_1, w_2, \ldots, w_k)$ of the counts of its words (or *n-grams*). A single SVM can only separate 2 classes: a positive class $L1$ (indicated by $y = +1$) and a negative class $L2$ (indicated by $y = -1$). In the space of input vectors x a hyperplane may be defined by setting $y = 0$ in the linear equation $y = f_\theta(x) = b_0 + \sum_{j=1}^{k} b_j w_j$. The parameter vector is given by $\theta = (b_0, b_1, ..., b_k)$. The SVM algorithm determines a hyperplane which is located between the positive and negative examples of the training set. The parameters b_j are estimated in such a way that the distance ξ, called margin, between the hyperplane and the closest positive and negative example documents is maximized. The documents having distance ξ from the hyperplane are called support vectors and determine the actual location of the hyperplane.

SVMs can be extended to a non-linear predictor by transforming the usual input features in a non-linear way using a feature map. Subsequently a hyperplane may be defined in the expanded (latent) feature space. Such non-linear transformations define extensions of scalar products between input vectors, which are called kernels (Shawe-Taylor and Cristianini, 2004).

Multinomial Logistic Regression (Aggarwal and Zhai, 2012). An early application of regression to text classification is the Linear Least Squares Fit (LLSF) method, which works as follows. Let the predicted class label be $p_i = \overline{A} \cdot \overline{X_i} + b$, and y_i is known to be the true class label, then our aim is to learn the values of A and b, such that the LLSF $\sum_{i=1}^{n} (p_i - y_i)^2$ is minimized.

A more natural way of modeling the classification problem with regression is the logistic regression classifier, which differs from the LLSF method by optimizing the likelihood function. Specifically, we assume that the probability of observing label y_i is:

$$p(C = y_i | X_i) = \frac{exp(\bar{A} \cdot \bar{X_i} + b)}{1 + exp(\bar{A} \cdot \bar{X_i} + b)}. \quad (4)$$

In the case of binary classification, $p(C = y_i|X_i)$ can be used to determine the class label. In the case of multi-class classification, we have $p(C = y_i|X_i) \propto exp(\bar{A} \cdot \bar{X_i} + b)$, and the class label with the highest value according to $p(C = y_i|X_i)$ would be assigned to X_i.

3.3 Testing and Quality Evaluation

Training and testing of the classifiers was performed using 750 selected text documents with training:testing data ratio being 2:1. All selected documents were ordered randomly and a non-exhaustive 6-fold cross validation was applied.

Standard evaluation measures of *precision* $\left(P_n = \frac{\text{TP}_n}{\text{TP}_n+\text{FP}_n}\right)$, *recall* $\left(R_n = \frac{\text{TP}_n}{\text{TP}_n+\text{FN}_n}\right)$ and *F-score* $\left(F_n = \frac{2 \cdot P_n \cdot R_n}{P_n+R_n}\right)$ were used for each class and overall, and where

- *True positive (TP)*: number of documents correctly assigned class C_n;
- *False positive (FP)*: number of documents incorrectly assigned to class C_n;
- *False negative (FN)*: number of documents that belong, but were not assigned to C_n;
- *True negative (TN)*: number of documents correctly assigned to class, different than C_n.

Baseline accuracy was calculated using the following equation $ACC_B = \frac{1}{N^2}\sum_{i=1}^{m} N_i^2$, where N is the total number of documents in the training dataset, N_i is the number of documents in the training dataset that belong to class C_i, and m is the number of classes. In this case: $ACC_B = 0,151$.

4 Experimental Evaluation

4.1 Method Selection

3 variations of the most popular feature selection methods were used, see statistics in Table 3.

Feature set	Unique terms	
	Overall	Per doc
bag-of-words	3130	0,27
3-gram	3995	0,35
tf-idf	3130	0,27

Table 3: Descriptive statistics of the feature sets.

Due to good performance (Mickevičius et al., 2015) SVM classifier was examined more in depth. Multinomial Logistic Regression was selected as a second classifier in order to test its suitability to Lithuanian political texts.

Logistic Regression is a powerful method with no parameters that would be crucial to adjust. SVM is quite the opposite with the following changeable parameters: *kernel* function, *degree* (for polynomial kernel only), *cost* and *gamma* (for all kernels except linear).

Parameters were tuned using cross-validation to find the best performance thus determining the most suitable values for each parameter. *Cost* and *gamma* parameters were picked of a range from 0.1 to 3 by a step of 0.1, and 6 different kernel functions were tested: linear, 2 to 4 degree polynomial, Gaussian radial basis and sigmoid function.

4.2 Classification Results

After the parameter tuning phase the most suitable parameter values were found and maximal classification quality (*F-score*) was achieved with each tested classifier and feature representation method, see Table 4.

Classifier	b-o-w	3-gram	tf-idf
SVM linear	0.716	0.683	**0.825**
SVM pol. 2 deg.	0.701	0.613	**0.815**
SVM pol. 3 deg.	0.646	0.593	**0.815**
SVM pol. 4 deg.	0.589	0.567	**0.815**
SVM radial	0.610	0.169	0.728
SVM sigmoid	0.325	0.091	0.057
LogReg	0.696	0.667	**0.793**

Table 4: Best performing classifiers, F-score.

Five classifier and feature representation method combinations produced exceptionally good results in comparison to other combinations. It is easy to see that *tf-idf* features are superior to *bag-of-words* and *n-gram* regardless of the classifier.

The aforementioned classifiers were subjected to deeper analysis where *precision*, *recall* and *F-score* measures were estimated for each class. The results are shown in Tables 5, 6, 7, 8 and 9 while averaged *F-score* for each of the 5 best classifiers are depicted in Table 4.

Best performing classifier for each class is depicted in Figure 1. Further analysis did not yield information about certain classifier being unsuitable due to neglect of one or more classes. Considering a narrow margin that separates the quality of tested classifiers (the highest *F-score* is 0.825, the lowest is 0.793) it would be fair to consider all 5 of them being equally suitable for classifying roll call votes headings of the Lithuanian Parliament.

Class	Prec.	Rec.	F-score
1	**0.978**	0.913	**0.944**
2	0.936	0.835	0.883
3	0.649	0.710	0.678
4	0.846	**0.846**	**0.846**
5	0.863	**0.824**	**0.843**
6	**0.777**	0.732	**0.754**
7	0.591	0.898	0.713

Table 5: SVM, linear kernel, tf-idf.

Class	Prec.	Rec.	F-score
1	0.973	0.892	0.931
2	0.936	**0.839**	0.885
3	0.699	**0.757**	0.727
4	0.810	0.813	0.811
5	**0.893**	0.765	0.824
6	0.698	**0.750**	0.723
7	**0.612**	0.867	**0.718**

Table 6: SVM, 2 degree polynomial kernel, tf-idf.

Class	Prec.	Rec.	F-score
1	0.973	0.895	0.932
2	**0.940**	**0.839**	**0.887**
3	0.703	**0.757**	0.729
4	0.805	0.813	0.809
5	0.886	0.765	0.821
6	0.701	**0.750**	0.725
7	0.609	0.857	0.712

Table 7: SVM, 3 degree polynomial kernel, tf-idf.

Class	Prec.	Rec.	F-score
1	0.973	0.895	0.932
2	**0.940**	**0.839**	**0.887**
3	0.703	**0.757**	0.729
4	0.805	0.813	0.809
5	0.880	0.765	0.818
6	0.700	0.746	0.722
7	0.609	0.857	0.712

Table 8: SVM, 4 degree polynomial kernel, tf-idf.

5 Results, Conclusions and Future Plans

1. *Tf-idf* feature matrix produced significantly better results than any other feature matrix.

Class	Prec.	Rec.	F-score
1	0.911	**0.934**	0.922
2	0.905	**0.839**	0.871
3	**0.837**	0.698	**0.761**
4	**0.874**	0.774	0.821
5	0.826	0.654	0.730
6	0.725	0.693	0.709
7	0.428	**0.939**	0.588

Table 9: Multinomial Logistic Regression, tf-idf.

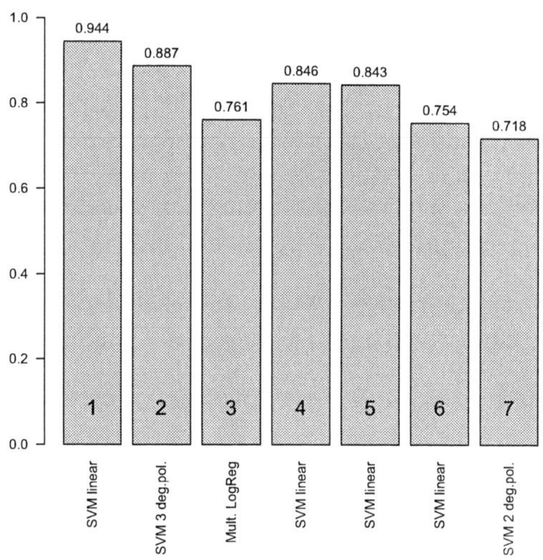

Figure 1: Best classifier for each class, F-score.

2. Linear and polynomial kernels produced the best results when using SVM classifier.

3. Support Vector Machines and Multinomial Logistic Regression are suitable for classification of titles of votes in the Seimas.

These results are part of a work-in-progress of creating an infrastructure for monitoring activities of the Lithuanian Parliament (Seimas). Future plans include investigation of other text classifiers, feature preprocessing and selection techniques.

Certain titles of the Seimas debates present a challenge even for human coders due to ambiguity. For that reason multi-class classification and analysis of larger datasets (additional documents attached to the debates and votes) are planned in the future. A critical review and stricter definitions of classes, as well as qualitative error analysis are also included in the future plans.

References

Charu C. Aggarwal and ChengXiang Zhai. 2012. *A Survey of Text Classification Algorithms*. Springer US.

Michael A. Bailey. 2007. Comparable preference estimates across time and institutions for the court, Congress, and presidency. *American Jrnl. of Political Science*, 51(3):433–448.

Bhat S. Harish, Devanur S. Guru, and Shantharamu Manjunath. 2010. Representation and classification of text documents: a brief review. *IJCA,Special Issue on RTIPPR*, (2):110–119.

Simon Hix, Abdul Noury, and Gérard Roland. 2006. Dimensions of politics in the European Parliament. *American Jrnl. of Political Science*, 50(2):494–520.

Simon Jackman. 2001. Multidimensional analysis of roll call. *Political Analysis*, 9(3):227–241.

Thorsten Joachims. 1998. Text categorization with support vector machines: learning with many relevant features. In *Proc. of ECML-98, 10th European Conf. on Machine Learning*, pages 137–142, DE.

Jurgita Kapočiūtė-Dzikienė and Algis Krupavičius. 2014. Predicting party group from the Lithuanian parliamentary speeches. *ITC*, 43(3):321–332.

Jurgita Kapočiūtė-Dzikienė, Frederik Vaasen, Algis Krupavičius, and Walter Daelemans. 2012. Improving topic classification for highly inflective languages. In *Proc. of COLING 2012*, pages 1393–1410.

Tomas Krilavičius and Vaidas Morkevičius. 2011. Mining social science data: a study of voting of members of the Seimas of Lithuania using multidimensional scaling and homogeneity analysis. *Intelektinė ekonomika*, 5(2):224–243.

Tomas Krilavičius and Vaidas Morkevičius. 2013. Voting in Lithuanian Parliament: is there anything more than position vs. opposition? In *Proc. of 7th General Conf. of the ECPR Sciences Po Bordeaux*.

Tomas Krilavičius and Antanas Žilinskas. 2008. On structural analysis of parlamentarian voting data. *Informatica*, 19(3):377–390.

Vytautas Mickevičius, Tomas Krilavičius, and Vaidas Morkevičius. 2014. Analysing voting behavior of the Lithuanian Parliament using cluster analysis and multidimensional scaling: technical aspects. In *Proc. of the 9th Int. Conf. on Electrical and Control Technologies (ECT)*, pages 84–89.

Vytautas Mickevičius, Tomas Krilavičius, Vaidas Morkevičius, and Aušra Mackutė-Varoneckienė. 2015. Automatic thematic classification of the titles of the Seimas votes. In *Proc. of the 20th Nordic Conference of Computational Linguistics (NoDaLiDa 2015)*, pages 225–232.

Keith T. Poole. 2005. *Spatial Models of Parliamentary Voting*. Cambridge Univ. Press.

Jason M. Roberts, Steven S. Smith, and Steve R. Haptonstahl. 2009. The dimensionality of congressional voting reconsidered.

John Shawe-Taylor and Nello Cristianini. 2004. *Kernel Methods for Pattern Analysis*. Cambridge University Press.

Rūta Užupytė and Vaidas Morkevičius. 2013. Lietuvos Respublikos Seimo narių balsavimų tyrimas pasitelkiant socialinių tinklų analizę: tinklo konstravimo metodologiniai aspektai. In *Proc. of the 18th Int. Conf. Information Society and University Studies*, pages 170–175.

Vladimir N. Vapnik and Corinna Cortes. 1995. Support-vector networks. *Machine Learning*, 2:273–297.

Author Index

Association for Computational Linguistics
209 N. Eighth Street
Stroudsburg, Pennsylvania 18360

ISBN 978-1-5108-1785-2